Published by New Art Press

The publisher and authors have attempted to be as accurate as possible in the creation of this book. The content, including but not limited to: statistics, screenshots, availability of products, etc., are as accurate as possible, as of publication date. Due to the rapidly changing nature of the Internet, some statistics, terms of service, etc., may have changed. While all attempts have been made to verify the information provided in this publication, neither the authors nor the publisher assume any responsibility for errors, omissions, or contrary interpretations of the subject matter herein. The views expressed are those of the authors alone and should not be taken as expert instruction or commands. The reader is responsible for his or her own actions.

Some of the links (excluding any and all links to Amazon.com) in this eBook may be 'affiliate links'. This means if you click on the link and purchase the item, we may receive an affiliate commission. Please understand that we only recommend products or services we use personally and believe will add value to our readers. We are disclosing this in accordance with the Federal Trade Commission's 16 CFR, Part 255: 'Guides Concerning the Use of Endorsements and Testimonials'.

Typeset in Cambria with permission from Microsoft.

ISBN-13: 978-0-9730710-6-1
ISBN-10: 0-9730710-6-0

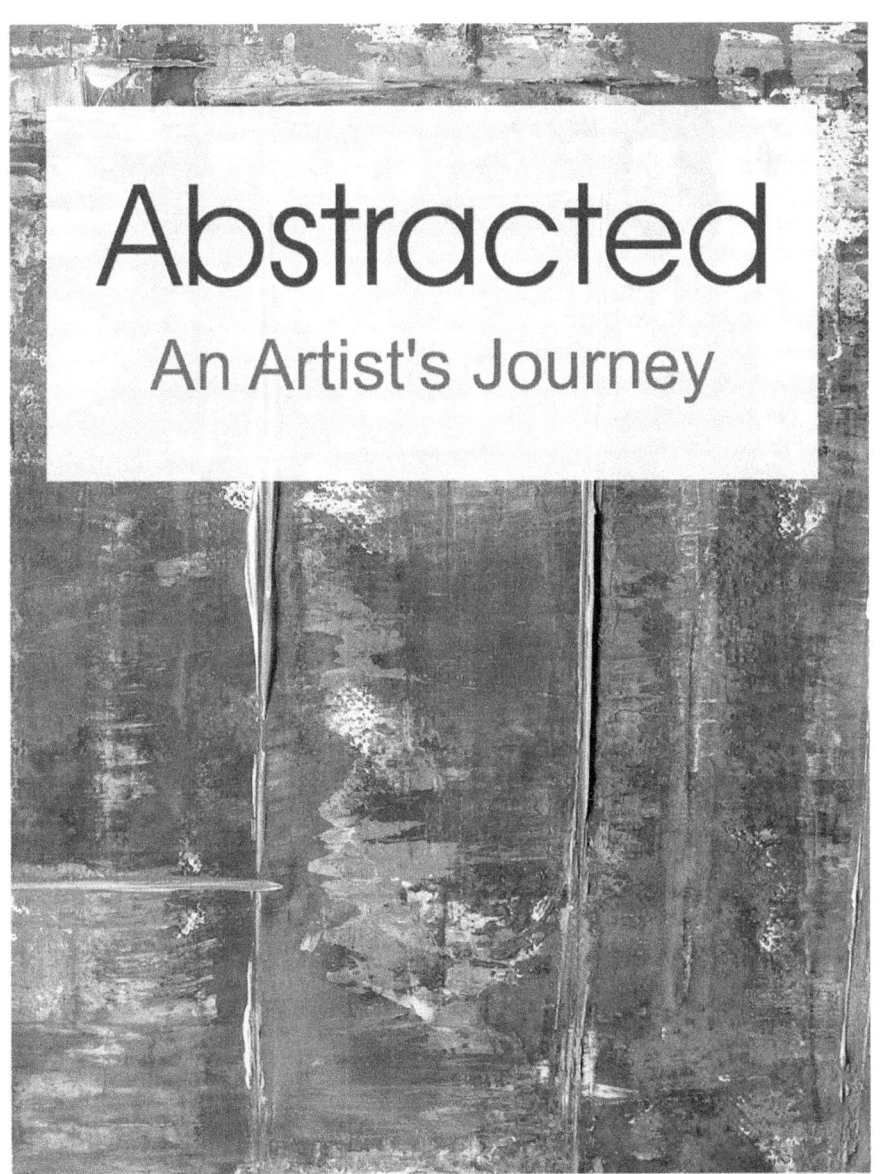

Abstracted

An Artist's Journey

Norman Pirollo

Abstracted

An Artist's Journey

Norman Pirollo

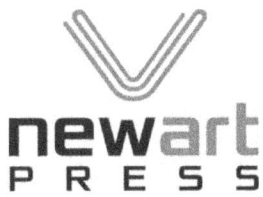

CONTENTS

❧❦

INTRODUCTION

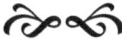

"All our dreams can come true, if we have the courage to pursue them"

Walt Disney

I WROTE THIS BOOK to share the creative journey of my development as a visual artist. The journey begins with an introduction to my background in the computer industry, shifts to my interest in working with wood and ultimately ends with abstract painting. At face value, these pursuits could not be more different from one another. One might ask how you can get from computers to woodworking to creating fine art. The answer lies in the intermediate steps of the journey. A computer career led to woodworking, progressed to sculpture, and subsequently to wall-mounted wood art. Having arrived at this point in my quest to become a visual artist, it was a straight line to painting and consequently abstract painting.

The journey was not an easy one, having been primarily self-taught and without a background in the visual arts. I quickly understood the need to associate with fellow artists and establish a dialogue with them. This helped considerably in my understanding of the art world and the process of creating art. There were periods of doubt where my decision to pursue the arts came across as eccentric. Friends and acquaintances, although supportive, were often left in amazement at my decision to pursue a career in the visual arts. Through determination and perseverance, my knowledge of the arts increased as I slowly envisioned myself as an artist.

The radical shift from creating tangible, functional objects to painting abstracts was something I had never foreseen doing. After all, paintings are purely decorative and fulfill no function aside from enriching one's life. This was the most difficult obstacle to overcome. Realizing that knowledge of art history was critical to my success, I immersed myself into the visual arts by reading and studying art movements, art periods and well-known artists of these periods. Art history is a discipline in itself and can be overwhelming through the sheer volume of available information. Copious amounts of reading helped considerably in putting the pieces together and understanding the art movements and art styles of each period.

Since the visual arts would ultimately become the third career in the continuum of my life, I had little time to spare in the learning process. The bulk of my formative years had already past; it was now time to act quickly and ramp up my knowledge of the arts. Although the daunting task of learning a completely new discipline was at times discouraging, I viewed it as a welcome experience. After all, had I not been successful, I could always return to my previous occupation. Knowing and understanding this helped considerably in maintaining my inner peace. Throughout my life, I have sought to challenge myself in acquiring new knowledge and skills, and so this would become part of the continuum.

There were many false starts in transitioning from the computer field to woodworking to becoming a self-employed visual artist. The opportunity to work at something I truly enjoy has ultimately brought solace and independence to my life. I never look back at missed opportunities. I also owe gratitude to a supportive spouse, friends and colleagues who had an influence in my journey. It is important to have a spouse or partner that supports your journey. It is also important to view any setbacks as valuable experience in your own journey. The time and effort invested in following your own dream will be well worth it. Hopefully this book will inspire you to pursue your dream. Life is short and if we aren't doing what we enjoy, what is the point. Throughout this book, every effort has been made to keep art jargon down to a minimum to keep you captivated and to maintain your interest.

Norman Pirollo

LOVE OF ALL THINGS WOOD

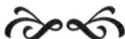

"An essential aspect of creativity is not being afraid to fail"

Edwin Land

MY COLLEGE AND UNIVERSITY education led me to a career in the computer industry. When I began in this industry, it was an exciting period. Computers had not yet become mainstream and were rapidly shrinking in size as computer chip technology increased in density. Computers in the home were many years away and still in the realm of science fiction. Existing technologies began to appear antiquated and computers would soon relieve us of monotonous day-to-day tasks. The sheer number of students entering the Computer Science academic path was overwhelming as this was to be wave of the future. I soon became one of these students and was eager to learn as much as possible about computer technology.

Over the next years and decades I held various roles in the computer industry. My career began as a hardware technician and ended as a software support engineer. The evolution of computers over this thirty-year period was astounding. Computers began as curiosities and eventually evolved into mass consumer items. The software that ran computers had also evolved from handcrafted code to widely available, common software packages. This evolution ultimately eroded my fascination with computers.

Computers had now become black boxes. It had become more interesting to use the vast selection of available software packages than to fiddle and program the actual computers.

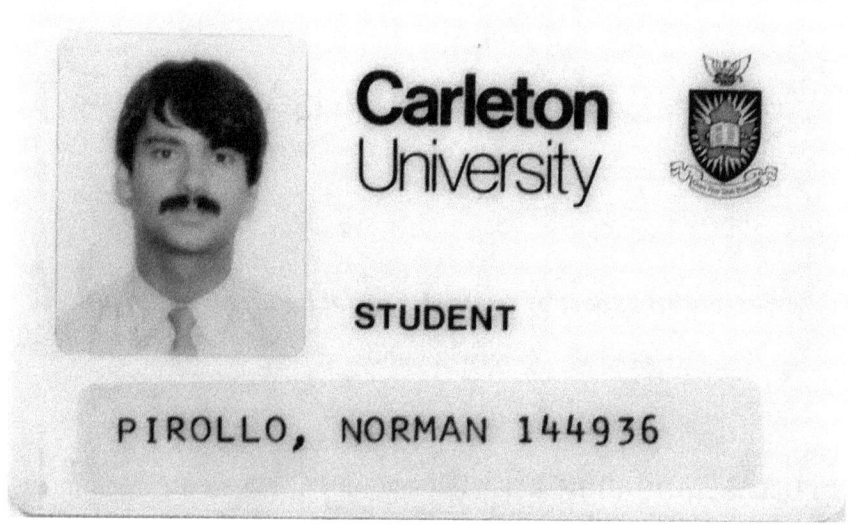

Carleton University, Computer Science Program 1984-1988

I began to seek other outlets for my creativity. In the latter years of my computer industry career, I developed an affinity for creating tangible objects. The satisfaction derived from my computer employment was diminishing year over year. Having witnessed multiple computer product cycles come and go, computer complexity increasing, and an ever-increasing volume of computer hardware and software, left me disillusioned. In light of this, I began to develop a second career as a woodworker and furniture maker.

Working at my day job and moonlighting as a woodworker overcame the dilemma of diminishing job satisfaction. I soon began to realize my creative side was suffering while working at my career. Developing computer software programs would only go so far in addressing any repressed creativity. To satisfy this creative urge, a need to make tangible objects became more appealing. Through woodworking, I suddenly gained a new, positive energy and outlook on life.

Woodworking and the wood medium greatly appealed to me and I slowly began to create objects such as small boxes. Within a year or two of pursuing college level woodworking and cabinetmaking courses, I began to slowly outfit a woodworking shop. Soon, my job was merely viewed as financial support for my growing hobby.

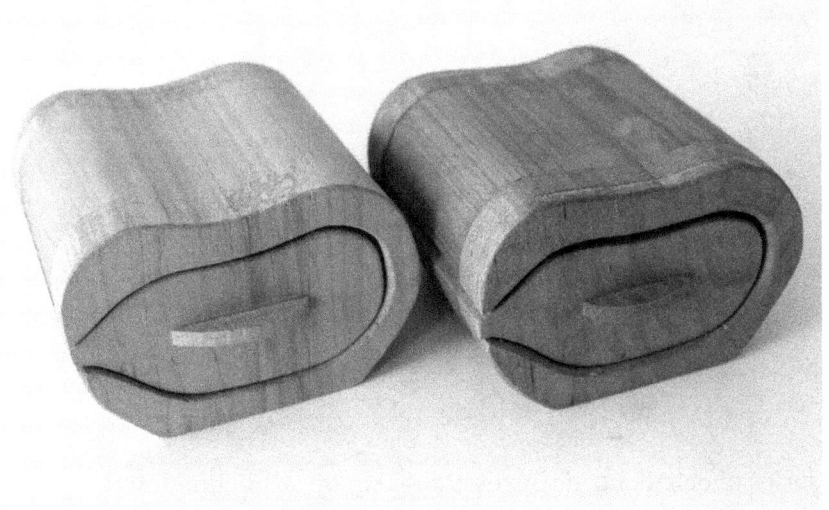

First band sawn boxes created in 1993 with shaped, organic styling.

The transition to woodworking was sporadic. Beginning with a few woodworking courses, I returned to focus on my computer career and later pursued more woodworking studies. My financial state was precarious during this time as it was vital to support my lifestyle, my home and myself. Opting out of a computer career was out of the question for several more years, although the idea did cross my mind on multiple occasions.

Convincing myself that I would slowly develop my woodworking skills became a hedge against losing my computer career position. In the worse case scenario, I could always resort to woodworking as a means of supporting myself, even if only temporarily. Pay scales for woodworkers were dismal, however, and many were in it for the love of wood and woodworking. All this combined to keep me firmly entrenched in my computer career for many more years to come.

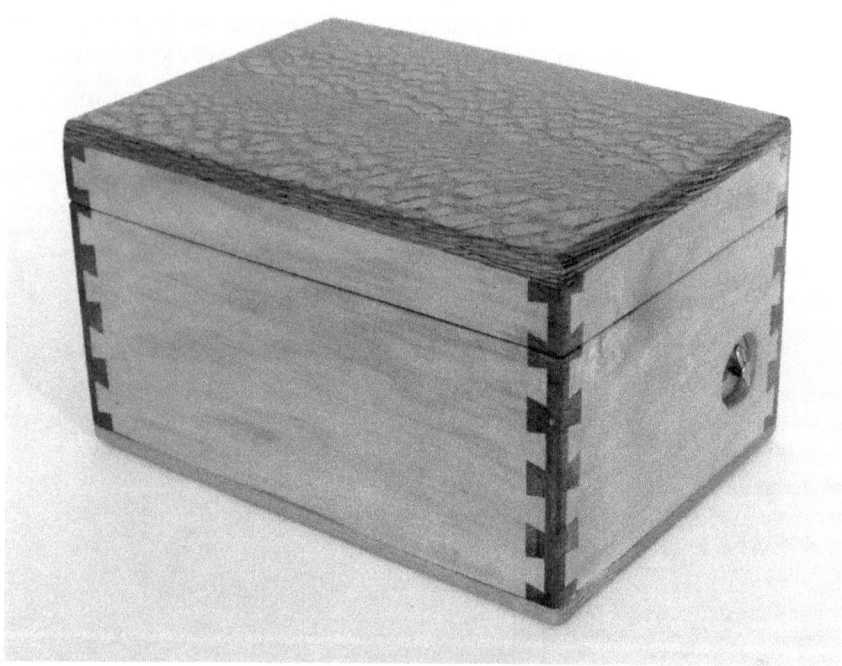

A series of ornate music boxes created in the 1995 timeframe.

As my career advanced, greater challenges were sought with computers, even to the extent of returning to school for a one year period to pursue a different, more rewarding aspect of computer technology. After the one year period, I graduated as a software developer and had the knowledge to write complex computer code. This would hopefully introduce a creative component into my computer career. I began to seek positions involving computer programming.

During this period, my pursuit of woodworking continued. The immense learning curve of developing woodworking skills was a welcome challenge as it introduced a new direction in my life. I began to appreciate wood and how it applied to so many aspects of our lives. From home construction to furniture, wood is ubiquitous in our surroundings. Less so than in previous generations but it continues to be a stable, reliable medium from which to build upon.

Over the following years, I grappled with a dual personality, sustaining a computer industry persona and the woodworker who blossomed whenever discussion revolved around woodworking. Discussing computers was increasingly becoming a chore. My interest in computers was waning and I found myself relying on many years of experience to push me through. Often, I would research the unique properties of different woods and how best to use them.

Designing wood objects in my mind and putting the designs to paper as sketches became a pastime. The pure joy of being able to create objects from raw wood was incredibly enticing. The woodworking hobby fulfilled me in many ways in the period from 1992-1999.

Towards the latter part of the 1990s, confidence in my woodworking skills had grown to where a new woodworking business was launched. A niche was discovered in creating jewelry boxes and I successfully pursued this. The business **White Mountain Design** was part-time where I would work at my computer job during the day and at the business in the evenings and weekends. Knowing that I could fall back on my own business provided me with a strong sense of financial independence. The reliance on my computer career was slowly diminishing.

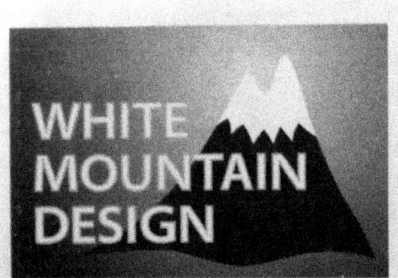

A first business card of my new woodworking business, 1996.

A small woodworking studio was set up where a newly designed series of elegant jewelry boxes could be methodically crafted. The jewelry box designs were contemporary and included a few elements to distinguish the designs from the competition. The boxes were individually handcrafted and the interior components hand-fitted. My clientele was far and wide.

A few of the boxes were shipped to Europe but my main market was North America, primarily the US. I vividly recall these years and the lengths I went to ensure that each jewelry box would be flawless. The desire of ensuring that my clients were completely satisfied was a priority. They would hopefully not consider returning their order for any reason. This criterion raised the quality of my work and continually ensured the use of the best quality woods and hardware in the designs.

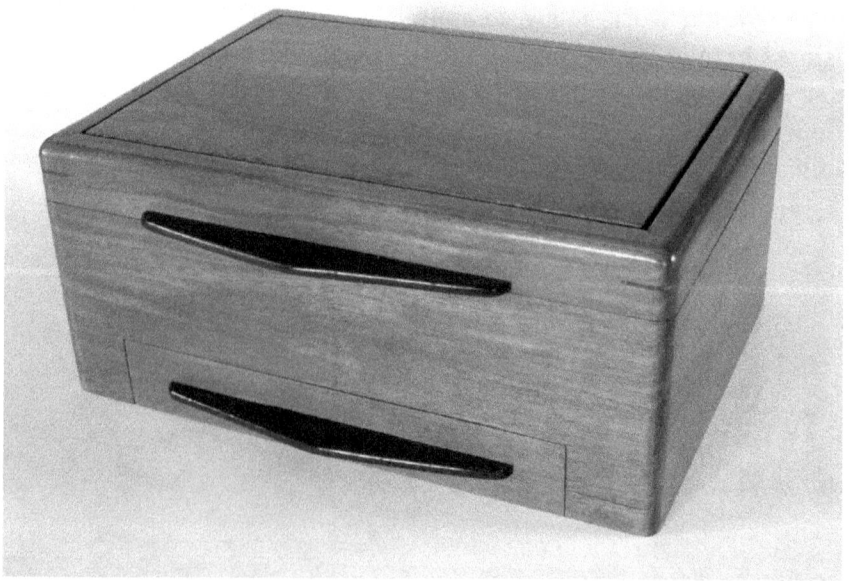

New series of elaborate, contemporary styled jewelry boxes, 1997.

The jewelry boxes were soon offered in a selection of high quality handpicked woods. It was necessary for the woods to have matching grain throughout the exterior of the box.

The matching grain element created a harmonious aesthetic in each of the jewelry boxes. With this in mind, I would research different domestic and exotic woods. Different characteristics of the woods used in my designs included color, grain pattern, durability, stability and surface texture. The jewelry box designs were offered in an increasing variety of woods to appeal to a larger clientele. I also began to experiment and mix woods within each box. Highly figured woods would be used in the top of the box where conventional woods used for the sides.

This particular combination had great appeal, as the highly figured top became a focal point of the box. The research and experiments with exotic woods led me to develop an appreciation of these highly figured woods. Each of the wood surfaces exhibited a unique set of graphics or grain pattern in an abstract context. Woods such as Australian lacewood, tiger maple, flame birch, Bird's Eye maple, all had very unique graphics where figured wood was the common characteristic.

The fascination with figured woods continued as I eventually progressed from creating jewelry boxes to making furniture. Continuing in my computer career, further time and money was invested into an advanced furniture making education. In the late 1990s, it became clear that a computer career was not in my cards for much longer.

Downsizing at major corporations had become commonplace and even the computer industry was not immune to this. Large computer firms began to shed workers in droves. Computers had become increasingly reliable and software was now turnkey with little customization necessary. Promises of increasingly longer computer uptime became a competitive edge for many computer manufacturers, greatly decreasing the need for regular computer repair and service. The writing was on the wall as computer technology marched into the mainstream. Computers had now become a commodity.

With all this in mind, I soon realized the need to develop a second career for my future. My career choice revolved around designing and creating furniture, specifically contemporary styled furniture.

To be distinguished from mainstream furniture makers, new and innovative designs incorporating a selection of high-quality figured woods would be offered.

In the period from 2000-2008, I re-entered the computer world with an interesting and unique job position that only involved a three-day workweek. This arrangement allowed me to devote many days per week to my woodworking business. My wife and I also had a new home built with an adjoining woodworking studio. The furniture making studio was designed with large windows to draw in ambient light and featured a spacious interior where I could immerse myself at furniture making. In this period, the new woodworking studio was sufficiently large to be able to create furniture.

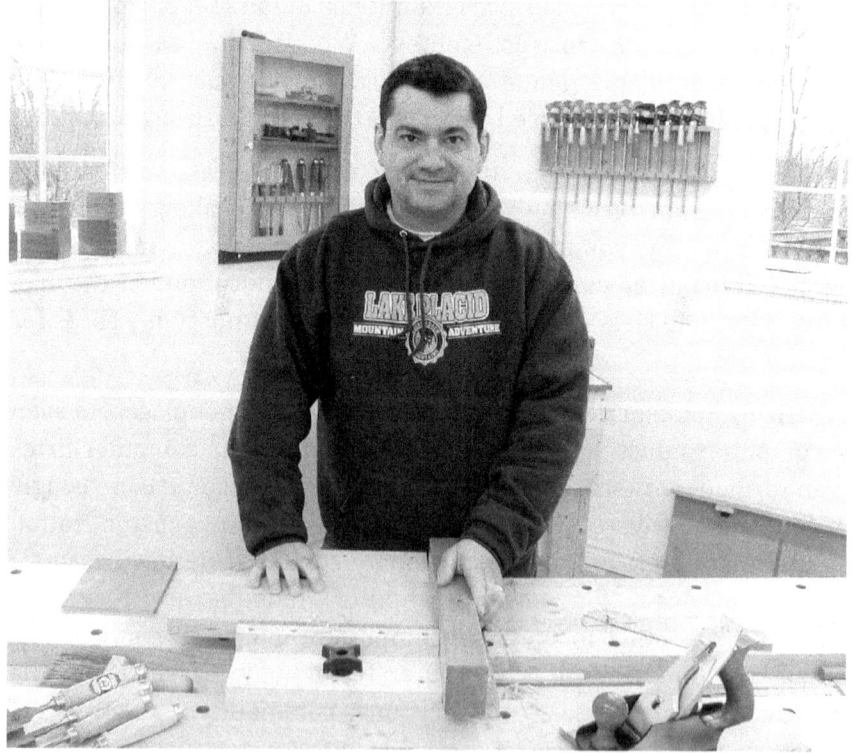

At one of my workbenches in my new furniture making studio.

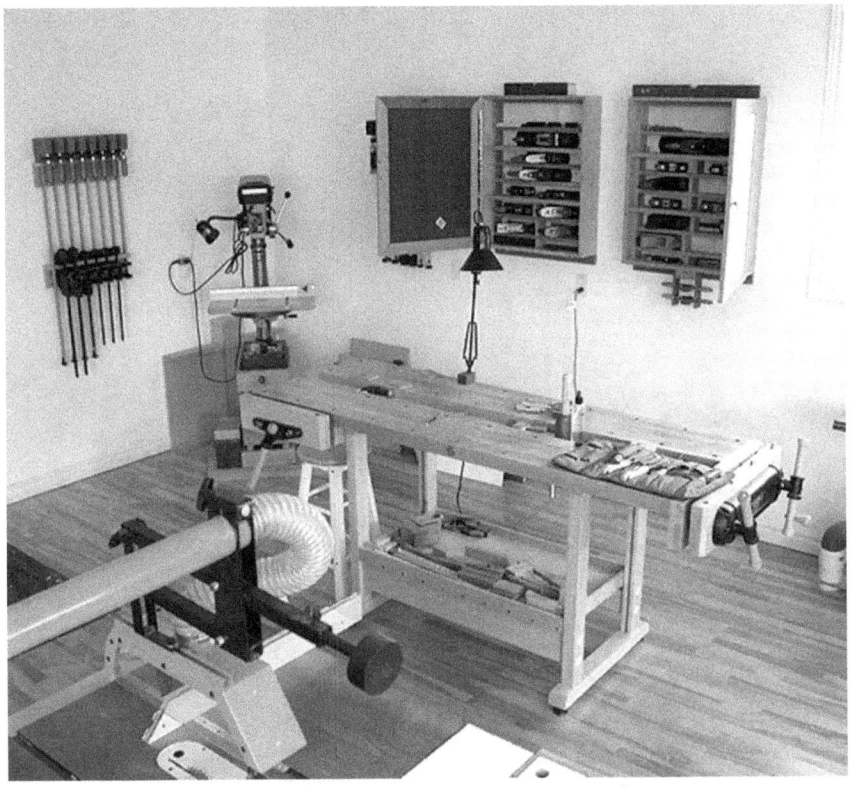

An overhead view of a section of the new furniture making studio.

My initial pieces were derived from a James Krenov design, the basic standalone display cabinet. James Krenov, an American of Scandinavian descent, was a renowned furniture maker who revered wood. He had written a series of books documenting his furniture making techniques and philosophy. His approach would be to design a piece of furniture around the characteristics of a particular selection of woods. This was contrary to the mainstream process of designing and then making furniture simply using wood as a medium. My earliest cabinet of this genre was created in 2004. The cabinet was large and rested on a custom, integral wood stand. I used this particular cabinet to experiment with combining solid woods with figured woods. The appeal of this combination carried over from my jewelry box designs.

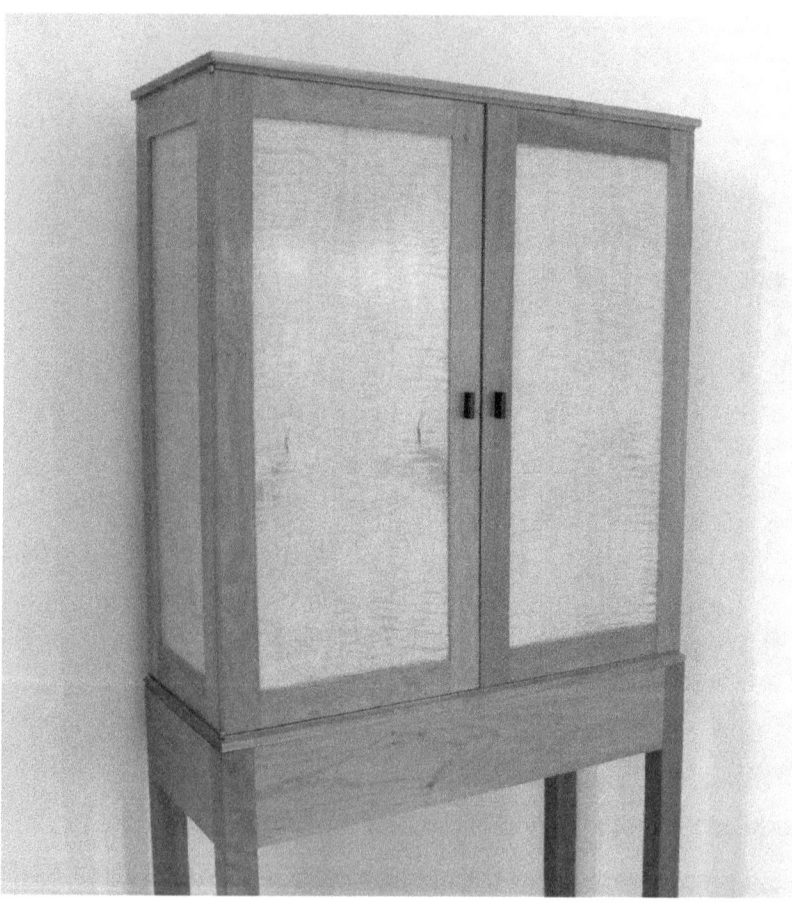

A first piece of furniture, a large standalone display cabinet, 2004.

The design for this initial cabinet adopted many of the elements of James Krenov standalone cabinets including frame and panel backs, use of knife hinges and dowel joinery for the bottom, sides, and top. The interior layout was sparse with minimal shelving. Since the cabinet was designed as a display cabinet and meant to hold art objects, the interior was designed with spacious compartments. Being so drawn to the James Krenov philosophy and style of furniture convinced me to pursue a formal education in furniture making. In this period, an upstart furniture making school had been established in my area. The **Rosewood Studio** distinguished itself as a predominantly hand tool oriented school. I attended this fine furniture making school over a period of three years.

The school was based upon the philosophy of the renowned furniture maker, James Krenov. Woodworking machines were used in the initial processing of wood, but the later stages involved the strict use of hand tools. So much so, that the use of sandpaper was frowned upon. It was instead preferred to hand plane and scrape wood to achieve a lustrous surface and smooth texture. Sanding was seen as dulling wood since the wood fibers on the surface are torn instead of cleanly cut with sharp tools. I successfully completed a selection of courses at this furniture making school in the 2004-2008 period. Each course introduced me to a new set of techniques that continually improved my skills and processes. Renowned, established furniture makers, who had been published, taught many of the courses. These makers excelled at teaching and explaining techniques they had adopted over years of experience at furniture making.

It was during this period that I also began to experiment with the use of veneers in furniture making. Through my embrace of highly figured exotic and domestic woods, I soon realized that using these woods in solid form could be considered a form of sacrilege. Instead of using a solid figured board, it could instead be resawn into thin veneer sheets and the veneers then applied to a substrate. The substrate would be a dimensionally stable wood or man-made material exhibiting next to no wood movement. This process greatly increased the yield I could derive from a single, highly figured board. Highly figured wood can be very expensive and acquiring a selection of boards with alluring graphics can be a challenge.

Sawing the boards into sheets or slices also allowed me to book match the slices to create a wider veneer sheet which exhibited a mirror effect, alternatively called book-matching. The process of attaching the veneer slices to a substrate was originally performed using a mechanical press until I invested in a vacuum veneer press. The vacuum press allowed me to perform veneering at a more rapid rate and with improved results. The veneers were now uniformly pressed onto a substrate virtually eliminating any air pockets or bubbles. By resawing my own veneers, I was also able to control the thickness of the veneer slices.

Commercial veneers sheets are typically very thin whereas resawn veneers are thicker. The extra thickness allowed me to work the surface of the wood with hand tools, much like solid wood. The use of veneers enabled me to create a more interesting aesthetic and dramatically increase the appeal of my contemporary styled furniture.

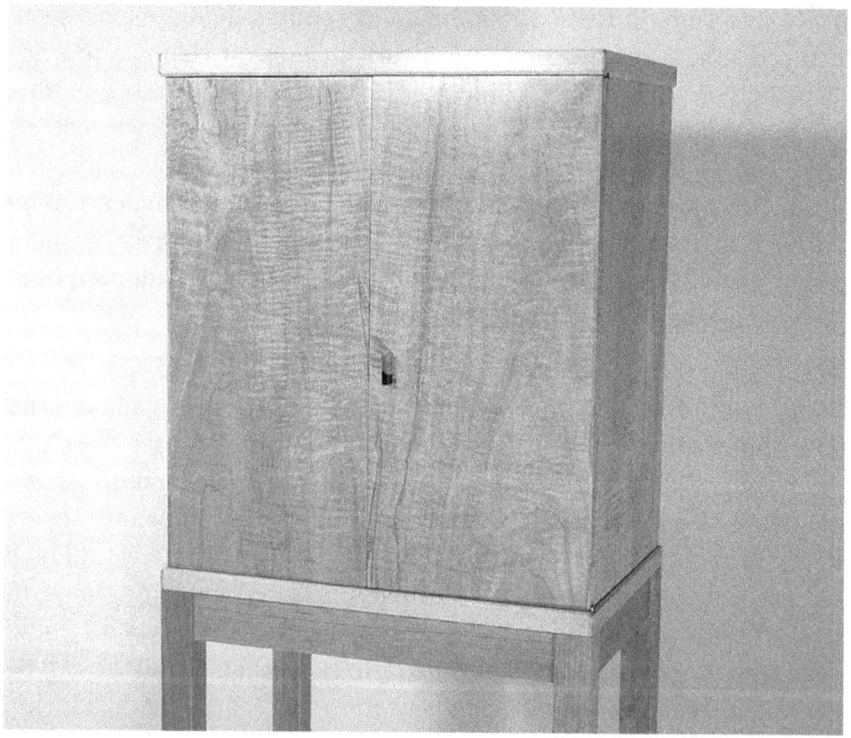

"*Chaotic Cabinet*" veneered display cabinet with veneered sides and doors using highly figured veneers.

In the two years following my education at the fine furniture making school, a series of display cabinets was completed using the veneer process. My style followed that of James Krenov, the furniture maker I much admired. Each cabinet on stand was increasingly complex and involved a greater use of highly figured veneer slices. A few of the cabinets were created speculatively while others were commission based from clients.

This was my entry into furniture making, progressing from being a box maker to creating dramatic furniture in a few short years. Although the learning curve was steep, pursuing a curriculum of courses at a fine furniture making school expedited the process.

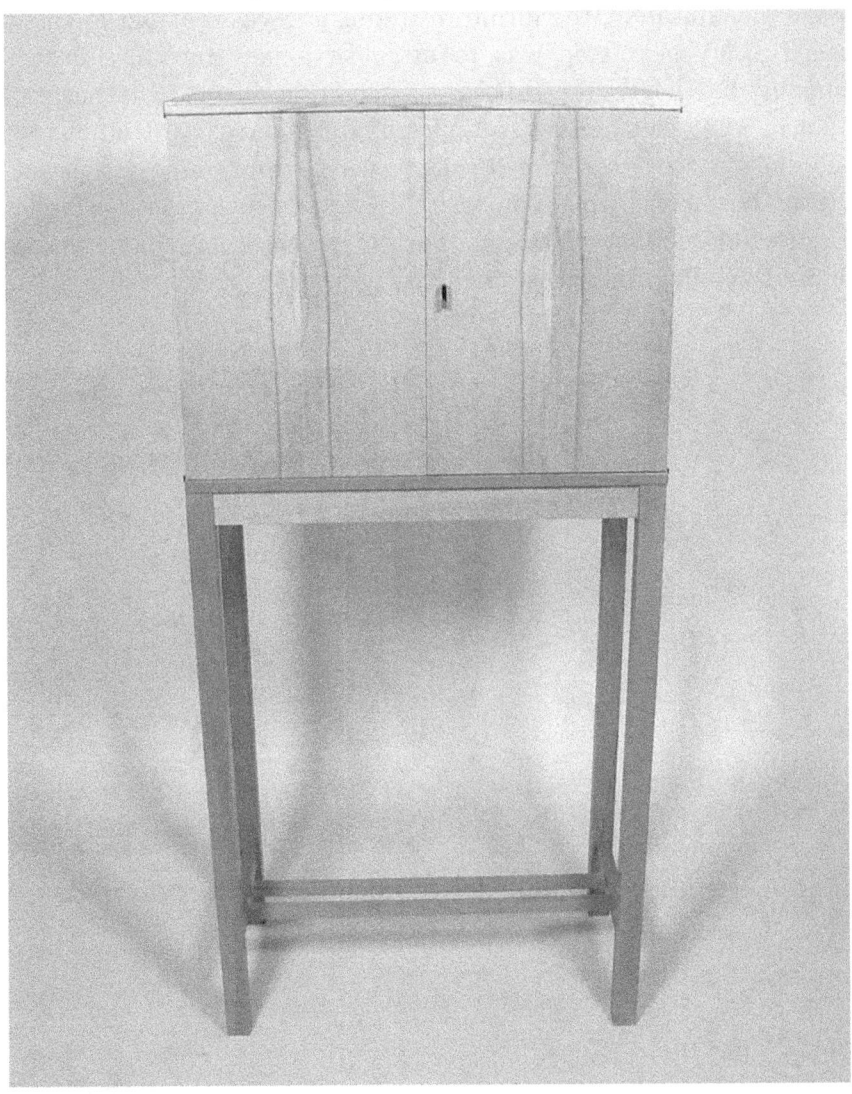

"*Twin Plumes*" cabinet, featured in forward for "**500 Cabinets**" book.

Late in 2008, I was once again downsized in my job. This third and last layoff in my computer career was to be a seminal moment in my life. This layoff directly influenced my decision to leave the computer industry for good. I felt confident at succeeding as a furniture maker; having the education, the furniture studio, and years of accumulated expertise. My next step was to establish a new furniture design company and began the process of acquiring clients. The nagging doubt of whether to return to the computer industry was ultimately shed and my focus could now shift to my new furniture design and creation business. Through my years of experience at woodworking, I reassured myself that this was the correct choice. A new chapter in my life was unfolding, one where creativity was at the forefront.

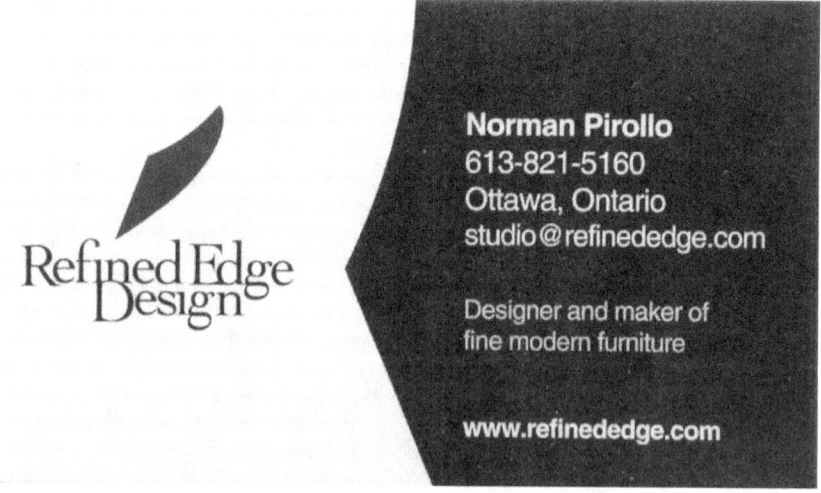

Refined Edge Design, furniture design + build, established in 2008.

The Maquette

"Creativity requires the courage to let go of certainties"
Erich Fromm

A FEW MONTHS INTO my new furniture making business and I came to a new awareness. My original focus on display cabinets created on a speculative basis would be risky. The time and materials invested in each of these cabinets was considerable and making these without a guaranteed sale was not in my best interest. My woodworking business would need to diversify into other types of furniture with an increased reliance on commissioned work. The furniture style I would focus on would be a series of contemporary styled tables.

The tables would need to be based on unique and innovative designs that had not been done before. Since I was a neophyte in the furniture making world, it was necessary that the table designs draw attention to my furniture design skills and business. The decision was made to incorporate metal into the table designs. The bright metal would contrast well with the natural tones of wood. It would be a **metal meets wood** aesthetic. The challenge of using metal in the design also intrigued me. A few weeks later, a few designs were drawn on paper as well as being rendered in **CAD** or Computer Aided Design. The logical next step would have been to create full size drawings and begin making components for each of the table designs. The problem with this approach however, was the appeal and engineering of the tables.

Although the table could be rendered on a computer screen in a 3-D format, having a real life example would be the ultimate test of its aesthetic appeal. The real life version would also help me to determine any structural flaws and weak points in the design and to test the table for stability. With so many table designs rendered, the question then became which table to actually build. With time and materials invested, determining later that the design was lacking in a vital criterion would be an inefficient and expensive process.

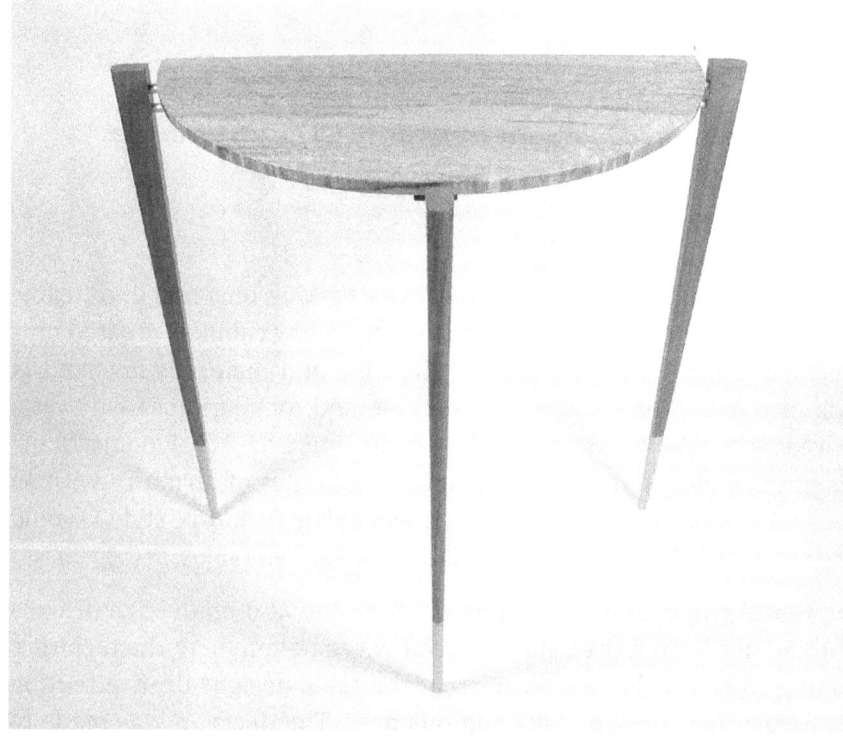

Newly designed demi-lune table incorporating wood and metal, 2009.

Recalling one of the courses I pursued while at the fine furniture making school, the subject was scale models. A renowned contemporary furniture designer was instructing the course. We had a complete segment of the course devoted to the creation of scale models of furniture. The idea was to create a small, scale model of a furniture design to determine the feasibility of the design.

A small-scale model would provide vital characteristics such as stability, aesthetic appeal and structural strength. The time and materials expended in creating scale models would be minimal in comparison to creating a full-scale version of the furniture design. Bolder, more avant-garde designs could be created using this process.

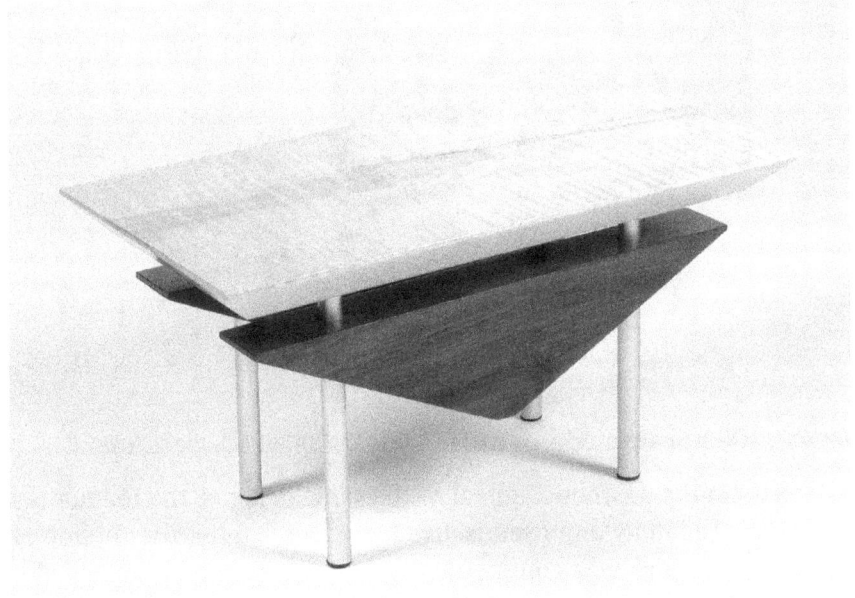

*"**Uplifting**"*, 2009. Scale model of contemporary table, wood, metal.

The small-scale furniture models were called **maquettes** and I have been following this design process ever since. Maquettes for a few of the table designs were created to determine their appeal. Since this process allowed me to quickly create a scale model with minimal use of materials, I decided to invest more time into the quality of each maquette. The maquettes or scale models were quarter scale versions of the full size furniture. The process was both rapid and efficient since the time to produce a design was dramatically reduced. Within weeks, I soon began to amass a fair number of these quirky, scaled down furniture pieces.

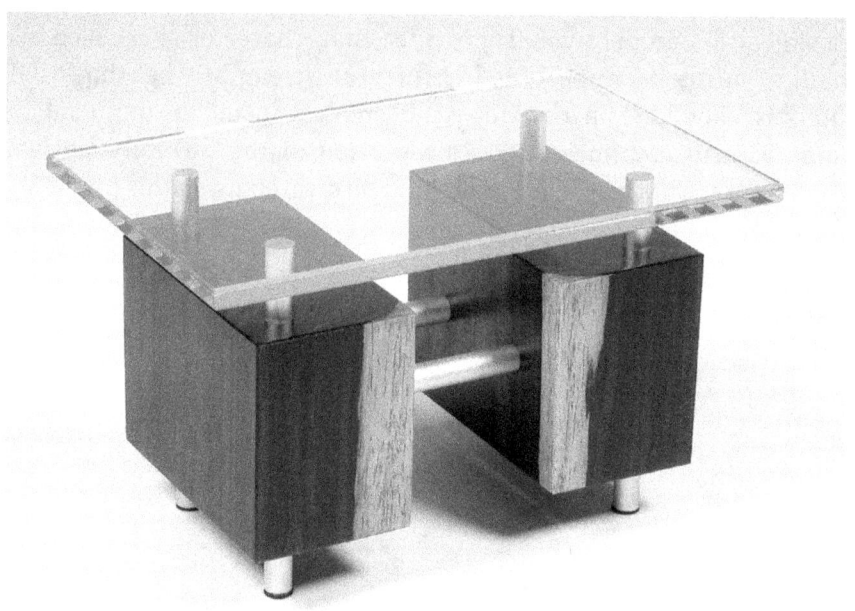

"**Nexus**", 2009. Scale model of coffee table using wood, glass, metal.

To determine the aesthetic appeal of the table designs, the maquettes were shown to family and friends. In a few cases, a full-scale version of the scaled furniture was completed. Early in 2009, the organizer of a prestigious art show to be held in Toronto a few months later contacted me. Although it was primarily a visual art show, it was open to other forms of art. After seeing sample images of my work, the organizer mentioned that my contemporary furniture designs would be a good fit for the show. Upon registering, I was to be the sole furniture maker displaying work at the show.

A few of the table designs previously mentioned were created for this show. Along with two small display cabinets and a few side and console tables, I exhibited at a booth at **art09** in Toronto, Ontario. My furniture designs were innovative and finely crafted and drew many people to my booth. Most visitors to the art show were expecting to view art and were pleasantly surprised to stumble on to my booth.

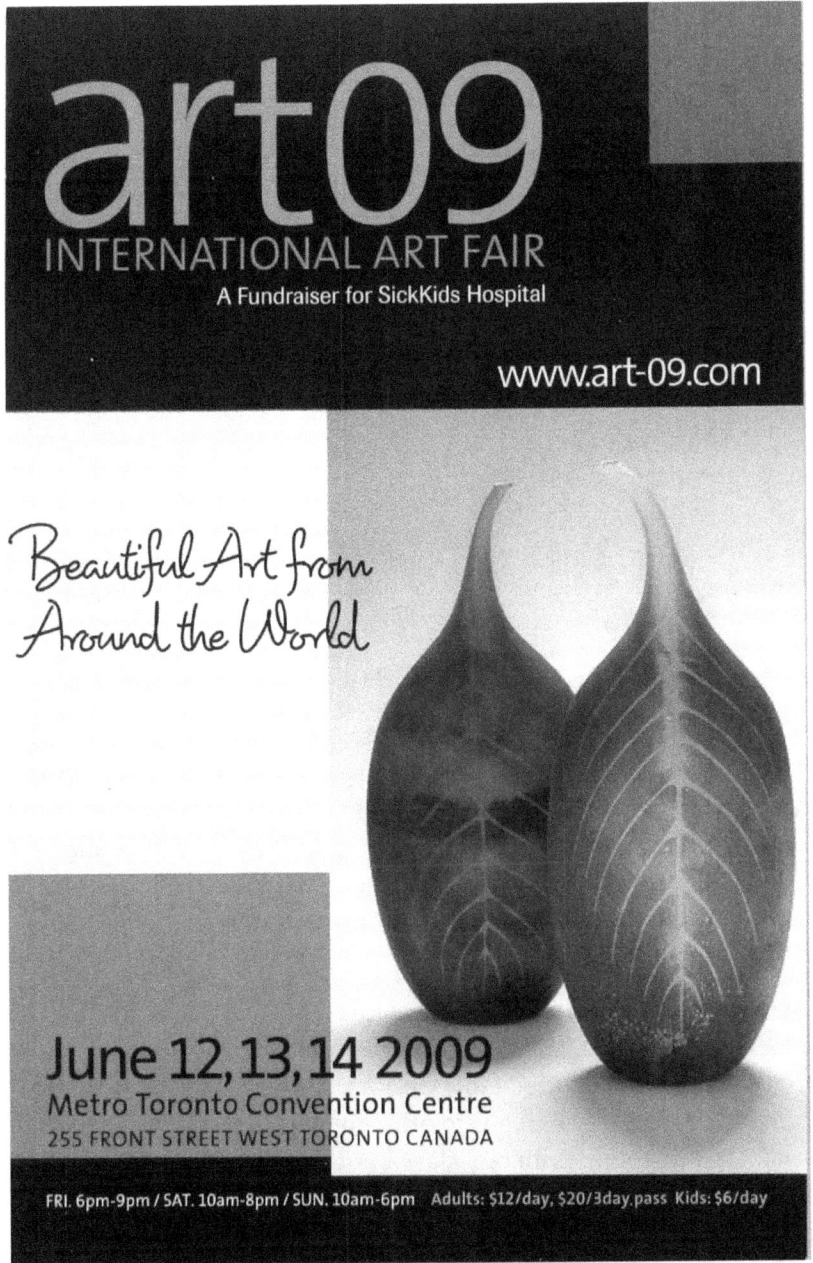

First art show entered, June 2009, Metro Toronto Convention Center

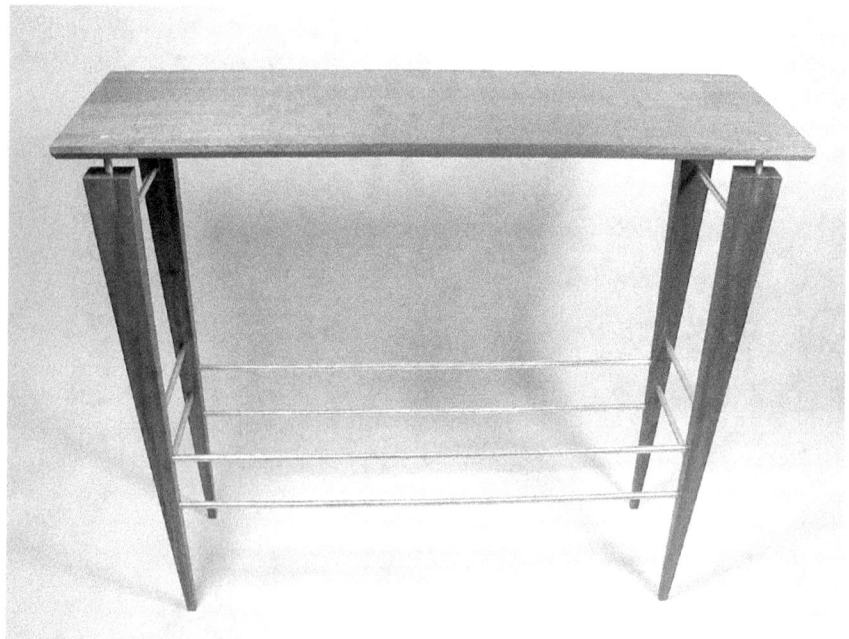

Contemporary styled hall table incorporating metal and wood, 2009

A few contacts were established through this show and two commissions were received. A local decorative art gallery also agreed to have two of my table designs in their showroom. The exposure gained was critical to me in this early stage of my furniture making business. The experience of applying, registering and successfully setting up a booth at an art show would prove valuable to me later in my art career.

The media used to create my scale maquettes was wood and metal. Glass was later introduced to the designs. The glass would serve as a table top specifically in coffee table designs. To accomplish this, it was necessary to perform research into attaching glass to metal. The glass itself was also custom, tempered glass cut to specific sizes. Tempered glass was almost mandatory since it would not shatter as easily as conventional plate glass. The advantage of creating maquettes shone when I introduced glass tabletops to my designs. It was very expensive to have tempered glass tabletops created in large, full-scale sizes. If the design was not appealing, I would be left with a large slab of glass which could probably not be used elsewhere.

The scaled down furniture pieces were fascinating to look at and received considerable attention wherever they were displayed. It was not immediately obvious to people that these were scale models of full-scale furniture.

Around this time, I received information of an upcoming touring exhibition of furniture and fine craft. The exhibition **Masterworks East** was the first of its kind where a juried selection of pieces would be displayed at different art or craft venues throughout Eastern Ontario. The exhibition would occur over a period of a few months. Information of the exhibition was sent to me through a newsletter of a provincial craft organization I was a member of. With all these scale maquettes of furniture in my possession, one of the more interesting pieces was submitted as a fine craft entry.

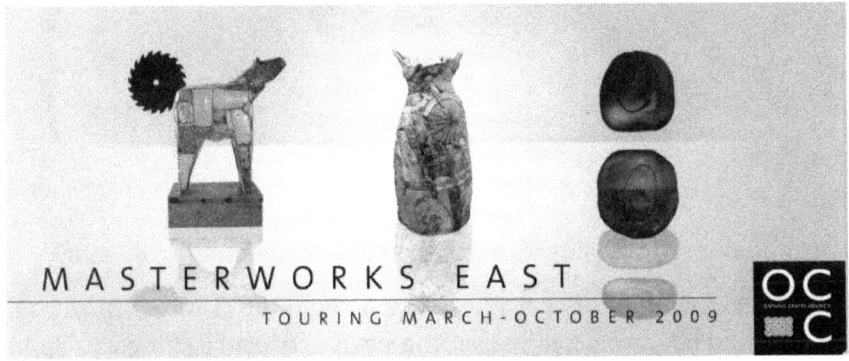

Recall that an extra effort was placed in creating many of these scale models of furniture to both raise the quality and bring out fine details. As a fine craft entry, a scale model or maquette of an appealing side table design was chosen. The table top was ovoid or egg-shaped with three corners. The top was created from highly figured wood. Each corner had a metal component attached to a shaped two-toned leg. This was a design that eventually evolved into a full-scale table.

The maquette of a table was aesthetically pleasing and at the same time very unique. It garnered a lot of attention when displayed. After photographing the scale table, my entry was submitted along with a bio and a small entry fee. I then continued with my furniture making. The jurying process occurred over a few weeks, enough time for me to completely forget about the submission.

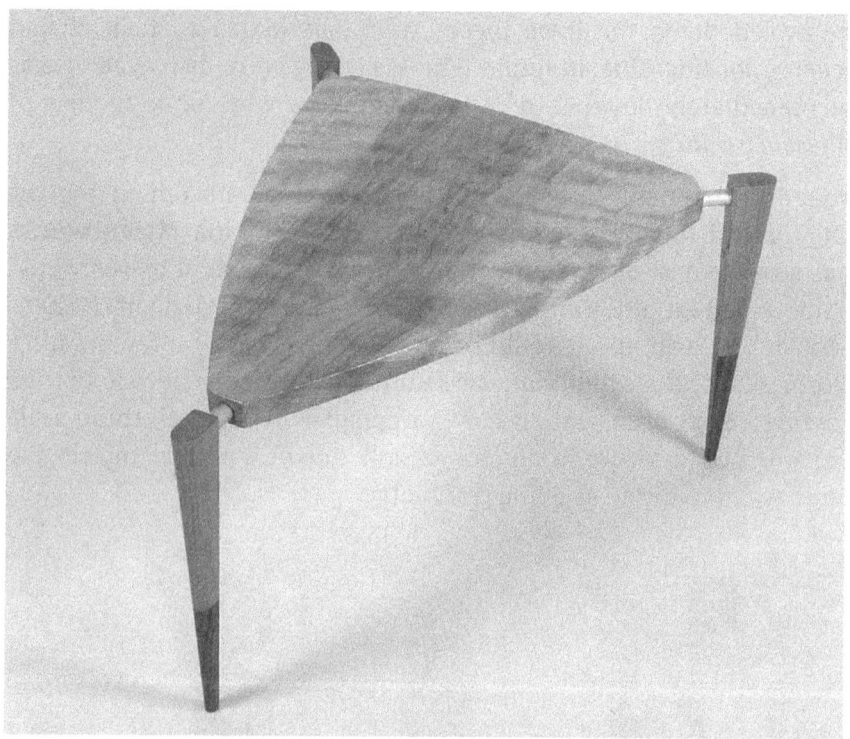

Scale model of Trinity Side Table with ovoid shaped table top, 2009.

It was a few weeks later that I heard back from the craft organization. My entry had been selected in the **fine craft sculpture** category. Upon reading the letter, I was ecstatic. This was the very first time I had entered an exhibition with something other than furniture. In previous exhibitions I participated in, the entry was typically a table or display cabinet. Entering a maquette of furniture in the fine craft category never crossed my mind had it not been for this specific call for entry.

The piece was delivered to the first of the many venues in the touring exhibition and displayed for a period of two weeks at each of the venues. The organization also asked if I was willing to give a talk at the opening of the exhibition. The talk would center on my wood craft, techniques, methods and my inspiration as a maker. The request was gladly accepted. This would also be my very first speaking engagement.

It would be an opportunity for me to talk about my furniture making journey and designs as well as the craft of working with wood. After the talk, my entry was part of the touring exhibition for the remainder of the summer of 2009. It was later revealed that the touring exhibition was a success and well received at the different venues in cities and towns of Eastern Ontario. Following this experience, I concluded that my small maquettes could be entered in the sculpture category of other craft exhibitions.

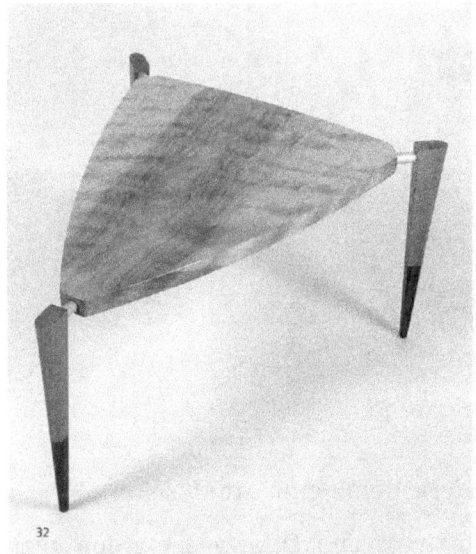

Masterworks East, 2009. Catalog entry for Trinity sculpture

A few months later, news was out that an International Juried Art Exhibition in upper New York State, the **Frederic Remington Art Museum,** put out a call for entry of fine art and craft.

A sculpture with art deco styled elements was designed and entered into this exhibition. This particular sculpture was mixed media incorporating metal and wood. An element of inlay was also included into the piece. My entry was accepted in the sculpture category and it was on exhibit for a few weeks in the fall of 2009. The principal juror for this exhibition approached me while at the opening of the exhibition and suggested that I should join an Ottawa based art organization with my sculptural work.

The juror, **Terry Sametz,** was a longstanding member of this art organization. He invited me to attend one of the monthly meetings and decide from there. I attended, was introduced to a few members as well as the executive, and decided to join.

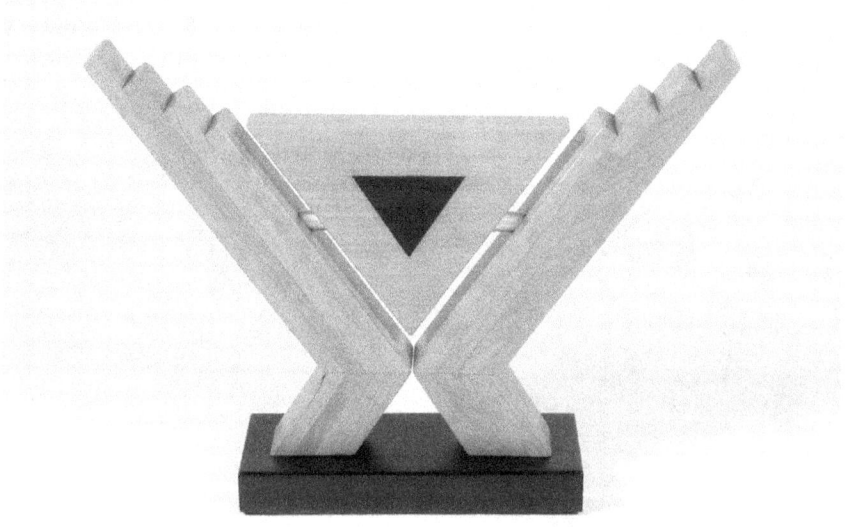

"***Reverence***", 2009. Shown at Frederic Remington Art Museum.

The organization, **OWAA,** was a west end Ottawa art group that included many artist members. The organization also held rotating exhibitions of member's artwork on a monthly basis. This appealed to me as I would be able to exhibit any new work created. Exhibiting my work on a regular basis would motivate me to create new and exciting sculptural work.

A regular venue for my sculptural work would also increase awareness and exposure of my work. After joining, sculptures were created and submitted on a monthly basis. The sculptures were displayed in glass display cabinets along with the work of other sculptors in the organization. My membership in OWAA was over a period of three years. During this period, my sculptural work evolved from fairly linear work to more organic work.

The early sculptures were primarily maquettes or scale models of furniture, whereas later sculptures were purely non-objective and not based on functional furniture designs. The opportunity to exhibit my work inspired me to become more creative with sculptural work. I would soon add stone as a medium. Combining alternate media with wood was appealing to me as well as providing a challenge. Attaching stone, glass and metal to wood is typically performed with special glues and this involved research and experimentation. In some cases, the alternate medium was captured tightly in a pocket of the wood sculpture.

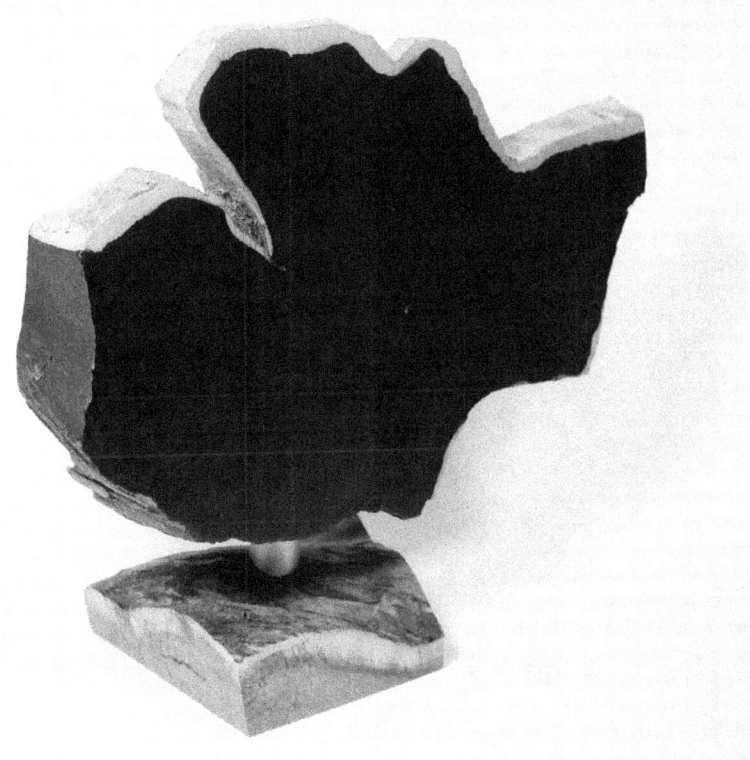

"*Genesis*", 2010. Sculpture combining wood and metal.

Over a three-year period, my recognition as a local sculptor increased. With wood as my primary medium both for my furniture designs and sculptural work, the sculptures and furniture dovetailed well together.

I also entered other exhibitions during this period, always seeking opportunities for exposure and to show my work. In conversations with other sculptors, they would often mention the importance of getting the work out there. Exposure was key to becoming a successful sculptor. Of course, the quality and appeal of the sculptures was equally as important. With this understanding, I sought other opportunities to show my sculptures. To introduce an element of color, a variety of woods were combined in a few of the sculptures. The contrasting woods would hopefully draw people to the work.

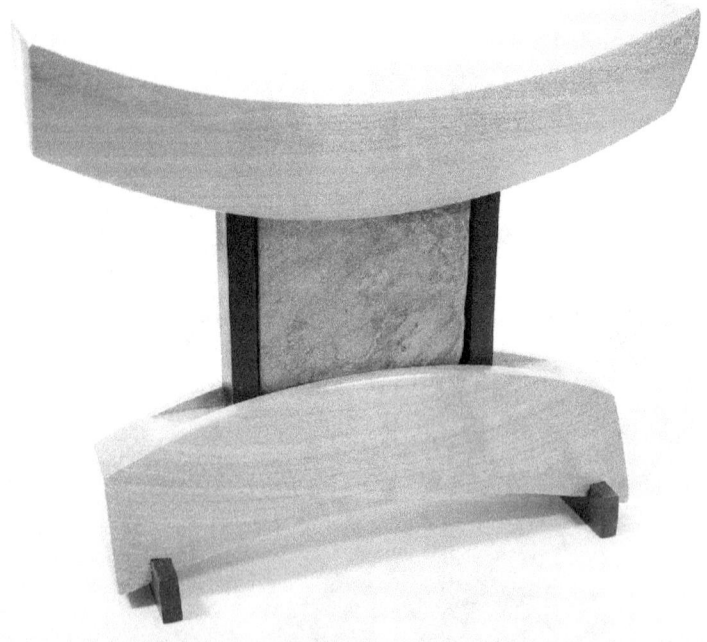

"*Shrine*", 2011. Organic sculpture combining wood and stone.

Since the OWAA group was primarily a visual arts organization, most of the art was 2-D and hung on walls. The few sculptors in the group were confined to showing their work in well-lit glass display cases. I often wondered what it would be like to have my own artwork hanging on walls. Observing and assisting other artists in exhibition setups or **hangings** brought me closer to conventional paintings and glass-mounted photography as forms of art.

The OWAA group consisted of many fine artists. Having virtually no expertise or education in the arts, I learned a considerable amount in conversations with these artists. The mystique of the artist began to intrigue me and I often considered painting as a new direction in my developing art career. During the hanging of an exhibition, the visual artwork was closely analyzed to determine what style of art appealed to me. Styles and genres of fine art could be examined at these hangings. It was comparable to attending a new art exhibition every month.

The exposure to period art and contemporary art styles launched my education into the visual arts. Participating in the monthly group exhibition "hangings" allowed me to view new art and to discuss art with the curator along with other artists. Without a formal education in fine art, I would often ask many questions ranging from the subject of the painting, the composition of the painting, to the actual techniques of applying the paint medium to the canvas. In turn, many of the visual artists would inquire and ask about my sculptural work. This gave me the opportunity to establish a dialogue about my own work.

A few of the members of the group were professional artists and I had the opportunity to ask about their lifestyle as artists. My curiosity was piqued on how I would adapt to such a lifestyle. How to cope with the irregular income? Would I enjoy marketing my own work? What pressures and challenges did artists typically experience over their careers? Would a career in the visual arts be rewarding? Was I up to this radical change in lifestyle?

FORM OVER FUNCTION

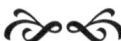

"I am always doing that which I cannot do, in order that I may learn how to do it"

Pablo Picasso

IN THE SUMMER OF 2009, I began to delve into art history. As an inherently curious individual, the evolution of art over the centuries intrigued me. A similar investigative process had already been performed where different furniture styles predominant over periods in history were researched. I was now increasingly aware of how styles evolved and how people's tastes changed over time. A furniture style would be in vogue for a number of years until it became fairly ubiquitous, then it would begin to be rejected. Human nature was that there was greater cachet in owning an object not owned by a large number of people. Style changes formed a never-ending cycle. Once a style became popular, it was time to establish a new style.

Interestingly, I found that this cycle also applied to art. It was both the style of the art and subject matter that evolved over different periods of time. Earlier art depicted portraiture whereas later art would include images of landscapes and inanimate objects. This greatly simplifies the evolution of art however. Painting in itself evolved over centuries with better quality media, brushes and canvases. The method by which paintings were composed also evolved with the advent of perspective. Perspective made paintings appear more realistic in scale.

Therefore, it was in 2009 that my art history education began. I purchased a few books on art history and began to delve into them. Art history is typically broken down into art periods which make the learning more palatable. I decided to begin my education at the pre-Renaissance period of art and continue through to Post-modernist art. Following this process would help me to understand the evolution of art and the many styles of art that had been spawned over several centuries. A few of the books selected to read were specific to art periods, whereas others were more general in their art coverage.

Delving into art history was a large departure from my furniture making. Art is non-functional whereas furniture is functional. In light of my twenty years of woodworking expertise in creating functional objects and furniture, it was somewhat challenging to understand the visual art movement. In my furniture making, the practical application of a piece of furniture was always a consideration in its design. The functionality of furniture usually took precedence, whereas aesthetics were secondary. All this theory could be discarded when it came to visual art. The merits of art lay not in its practical application but instead in emotion, composition, subject matter, colors and depth.

It was a confusing time for me, but also exciting. In this period, having mastered woodworking and furniture making, research into the visual arts would likely not affect my wood craft. Perhaps an exploratory phase was necessary to determine if I should pursue alternative interests in life? A few years earlier I would not even contemplate this as my woodworking was progressing along in the knowledge acquisition phase. After all, I would only be reading and studying art history and not acting on it. Some doubt did cross my mind that perhaps my time would be better spent at developing my skills in creating sculptural work. It was during a four-week vacation in the summer of 2009 that I applied myself to learning about art history. During this period, I immersed myself into understanding art history and its evolution. Perhaps I could apply some of this new knowledge to my sculptural work? Opening my eyes and becoming aware of the visual art world and its history could only benefit my sculptural work.

I began with general information on art history, with an overview of the periods of art. Acquiring a thorough understanding of art history would provide the basis necessary to learn about visual art. Through my technical background, it was fascinating at how the process of painting evolved over the centuries. The largest and boldest advancements occurred in the Renaissance period when both perspective and color realism were introduced to painting. This intrigued me and I also read how geometry and mathematics became a component of art. Successive art periods were fascinating to me; how art was originally created on commission to the church and royalty. In later periods art had become more mainstream where the subject matter and compositions had changed considerably. Over time, there was more art available in the public domain and a market for art had developed, featuring large-scale art exhibitions.

The Renaissance period evolved into the Romanticism period into the Modern Art period. The most recent Contemporary art period would be most interesting to me as my sculptural work has its roots in contemporary design. Without pursuing formal art studies at anytime in my life, I felt it necessary to at least understand the different art periods. After all, I had accomplished a similar education in furniture design. There were a series of successive furniture design periods that influenced the style and elements of furniture. Interestingly, I also embraced contemporary furniture design after reading about the furniture design periods.

The educational phase of understanding the visual arts also influenced me in other ways. The local art association **OWAA** went to great lengths to acquire glass display cabinets for sculptural work. This raised concern that displaying my art elsewhere would increasingly present a challenge. Most other arts organizations were set up for hanging art and their exhibitions emphasized this type of art. The calls for entry typically specified wall-mounted or hanging art in oils, acrylics, watercolor and even photography. Entering sculptural work into a few, difficult to find exhibitions would become a challenge. In light of this, it was necessary to make extra efforts in seeking and applying to art exhibitions that accepted sculptural work.

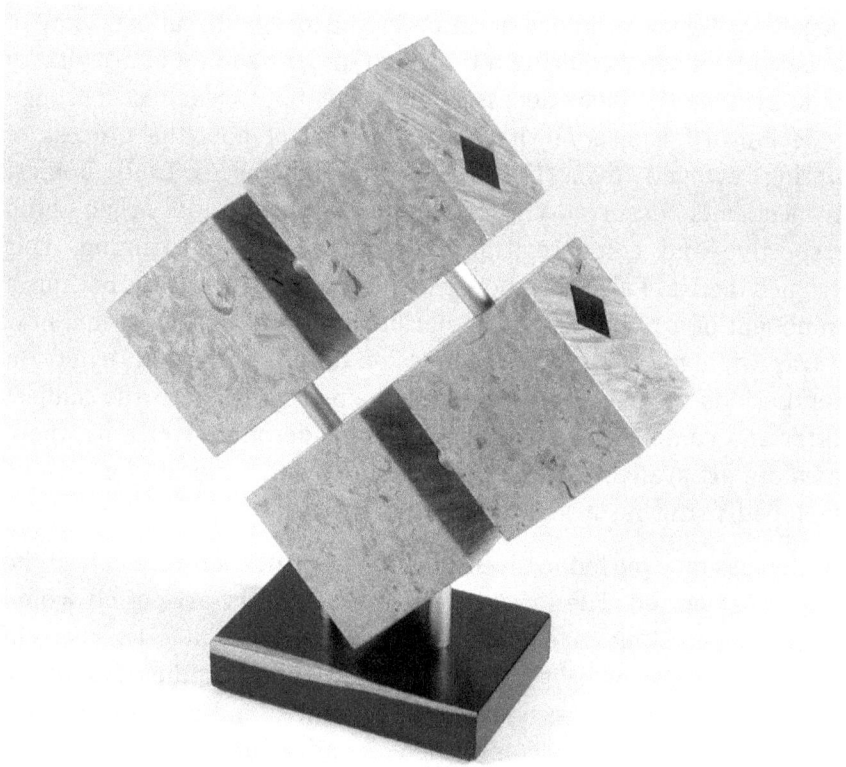

"***Cube***", 2010. Sculpture incorporating burl wood, blackwood, metal

Due to the nature of sculptures and the need for freestanding plinths and stands to display them, sculptures would need to be protected from visitors. Glass cabinets would only suffice for smaller work. These obstacles and the diminished opportunities for exposure of my sculptural work caused me to seek other avenues of art creation. During this reflective period, many thoughts raced through my mind. A return to art school was an intriguing option; however my furniture making would need to be abandoned to be able to accomplish this. As a firm believer in a formal education in subjects, I nonetheless looked into this option. This option included college or university level arts programs. A third option would be to pursue an evening program at a local art school that included a basic selection of courses in art history. It was the art history component that was most appealing to me since I had already established myself as a wood sculptor.

In my mind, painting was not even considered nor was it in my future. I thought it to be a considerable challenge to learn how to paint so late in my life. After all, I would be considered an emerging artist whereas my peers had already amassed decades of art experience.

While on vacation in the summer of 2009, my wife and I had a chance encounter with a well-known artist visiting Canada from Italy. A book had been forgotten on a restaurant table. Noticing this, I was determined to return it to its owner. It was only then that I noticed the image on the cover of the art book was a patron in the restaurant. As I was handing the book over to him, we introduced ourselves and instantly connected. This artist was originally from Canada but had moved to the Tuscany region of Italy to pursue his dream of creating art and opening an art gallery. In a short time he had become successful and the quality and breadth of his work was impressive. Over a period of a few days, we had several interesting conversations about art. While initially feeling somewhat intimidated in his presence, this feeling was overcome as the days passed. After all, he was a true artist, whereas I was a furniture maker who ventured into sculptural work. The following days we spent discussing art had me pondering a career in the arts. Most importantly, he had become an accomplished artist. The success rate of someone like me to make such a radical change late in life would be an obstacle, but not an insurmountable one.

Upon return from the vacation, my focus returned to furniture making. As my business and livelihood, it was necessary for this to work in order to sustain myself. I worked on a few new table designs and then made the actual tables. Two of the designs were entered into local furniture exhibitions. Since leaving my former career, furniture design and creation became my new career. The tables were designed to be statement pieces, where all my skills were utilized in creating designs that were unique and aesthetically pleasing. The shift from studying art history back to creating furniture was difficult. The introspection continued, and occasionally my wish was not to have been exposed to the art world. It was too late to turn back the clock however; art would soon become part of my life. Perhaps I was growing tired of furniture making and needed a new outlet for my creativity?

Ideally, my woodworking skills could be channeled into either the visual art or the decorative art spectrum. This was already accomplished to a small degree through the small, sculptural pieces I was making. As referred to earlier, the limitations of sculptural work in the art world would be a challenge. Through the creation of hanging art, I could enter almost any art exhibition, except perhaps those that requested a theme be followed. Another dilemma facing me was that of functional versus non-functional objects. Until now, my primary focus had been furniture, which is by definition designed to be practical unless it was **art furniture**. Art furniture focused more on the aesthetics and less so on the functionality of a furniture piece. Images of dressers with wild, curved sides came to mind. It is well known that these furniture pieces are not designed with longevity or durability in mind. Instead, art furniture pieces focus on a styling trend or are considered statement pieces. The shift from finely crafted contemporary furniture designs to art furniture was not appealing, as it would dramatically reduce the quality and detail placed into my work.

The creation of decorative arts was another option, but this classification is alternatively known as **fine craft** or **applied art**. Fine arts and applied arts are distinguished from each other in the art world. Applied art, also knows as decorative art or fine craft would present a similar limitation to that of sculptural work. The available venues to exhibit such work were very few and far between. The touring exhibition of fine craft referred to in an earlier chapter was one such exhibition. I titled this chapter **Form over Function** as a play on words. The expression **form follows function** is commonly used in architecture and design. It states that the shape of an object should be primarily based on its function. This principle does not apply to the fine arts but more so to furniture design, architecture and objects. My dilemma would be the dramatic shift to the form or appearance of an object versus the function of an object. Art by definition is non-functional and designed to be decorative. This was completely in contrast to the work currently performed in my furniture making.

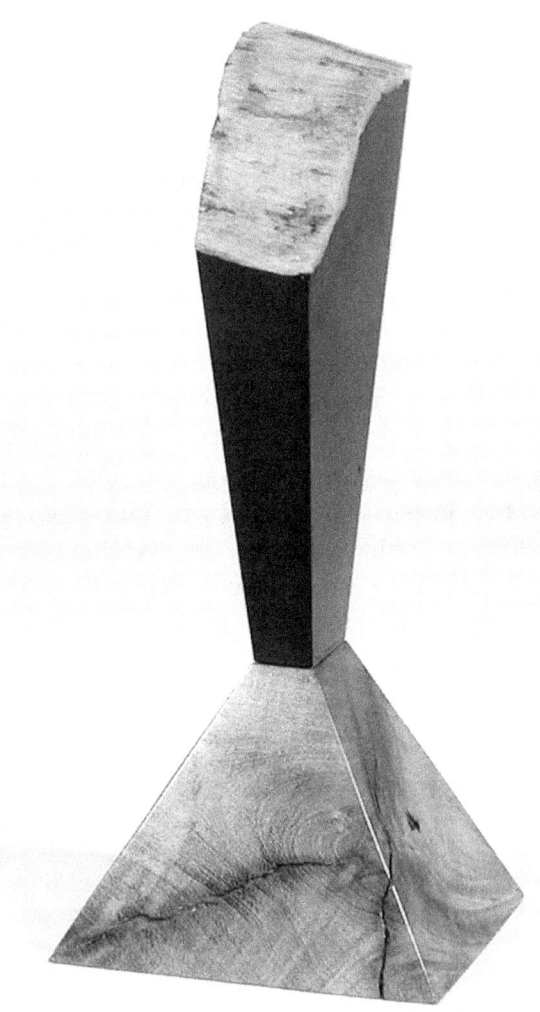

*"**Slice of Nature**"*, 2011. Organic sculpture, mesquite and blackwood.

Adding to the dilemma was the acknowledgement of creating objects whose sole purpose was to provide beauty to the beholder. Should I pursue the creation of functional, decorative art objects or pursue the creation of non-functional visual art. After some trepidation, I continued at my furniture making in order to support myself and the large investment made in my furniture making studio.

During this period, as a source of revenue, I also developed tutorials and woodworking related courses. Maintaining my woodworking skills along with a presence in the woodworking community was critical to the success of my effort at reinventing myself as an artist.

With this in mind, I continued at furniture making. The occasional sculptures created would maintain my presence in the art world. I was also made aware that sculptural work was more difficult to market than conventional forms of fine art, specifically paintings. Sculptures involve a display stand or plinth and an area of the home dedicated to the sculpture. A painting could be conveniently hung anywhere without danger of it being damaged. The sculptural work I was creating was small in dimensions where a stand was not necessary. This attribute helped considerably in marketing the small sculptures but limited expansion into larger sculptural work. Until discovering a form of hanging art that dovetailed with my woodworking, furniture making would be my creative outlet. Curved elements were also incorporated into my furniture designs in this period.

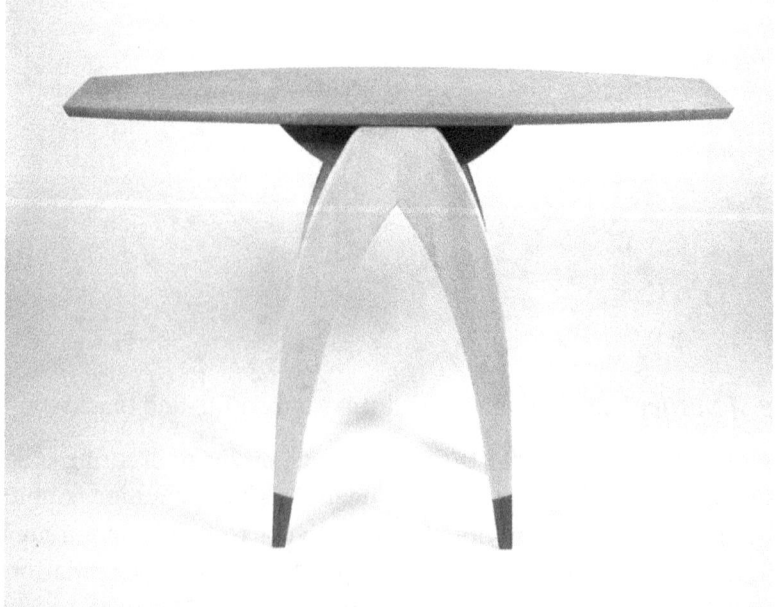

"*Wishbone Table*", 2009. Curved elements, bloodwood and maple. Entered in the **Wood Objects 2009** exhibition.

Wood As Art

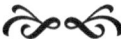

"Art just doesn't happen by accident. It is about pulling new tricks and trying new things"

Nicholas Meyer

IT WAS IN THIS PERIOD of furniture making that I began to incorporate highly figured veneers into many of my display cabinet furniture designs. The veneering process allowed me to extract greater yields from highly figured boards. Sawing a board into several thin slices was an efficient use of the wood in the board. Veneered surfaces are primarily decorative and it made little sense to use the complete thickness of a board for door or side panels. I was drawn to figured wood veneers through early experiments with veneering. Each highly figured board provided an abstract pattern of grain and slicing the board would reveal even more interesting patterns. In furniture making, these patterns are alternatively referred to graphics.

While assembling a book-matched selection of veneer slices to create a mirror effect, I was curious to how the veneers would look on a wall. By hanging the veneered panel on a wall, I could determine if the idea had aesthetic appeal. The panel of figured wood could become a form of art. My next step was to temporarily create and hang a veneered panel. The panel was prepared with several coats of clear shellac to bring out the depth, clarity and figure of the wood. If the aesthetic of the panel was not captivating when hung on a wall, the shellac could always be removed and the panel re-used in another application.

Once hung on a wall and with indirect lighting, I was pleasantly surprised at how the figure of the wood came through. The decision was made to pursue this idea further. Since the panel was fairly thin, it would be subject to changes in moisture levels in the air. This could cause the panel to distort or warp. The panel would, therefore, need to be uniformly attached to a box–like structure. The box would provide depth to the panel and also keep it from warping in high moisture conditions. This was the woodworker in me working on a solution to a possible problem.

Deciding to use this particular panel as a sacrificial panel, I created a temporary box the thickness of a conventionally framed piece of art. The figured veneer panel was then attached to this box structure and more coats of shellac applied to the complete unit, specifically the showy parts. Once again, the boxed panel was hung on the wall. The result was more interesting than before since the wood selected for the box was darker, providing a contrasting frame for the veneered panel. The idea began to have merit. Next, two more boxed panels would be designed and created with more interesting veneers or possibly a combination of veneers.

The veneered panel would need to accurately mate with the box frame to provide a coherent aesthetic, where the front panel would appear to be integral with the box frame. I began to design the next version of wood art panel using a combination of veneers, some darker, some lighter. This would allow me to create a secondary pattern or graphic on the panel, an example would be a serpentine line where the two veneers slices meet. Using this technique, organic patterns, linear patterns, and geometric patterns could be created on the panel. This design element along with the figure and color of the veneer slices would evolve into a wood art piece. Soon after, two more versions of the wood art pieces were completed. Due to a limitation in the width of veneer slices, the wood art pieces were narrow in width and longer in length. The length or height could be varied, but the width would be limited to approximately 12 inches. After initial positive feedback, I coined the term **wood art** for this new, innovative form of art.

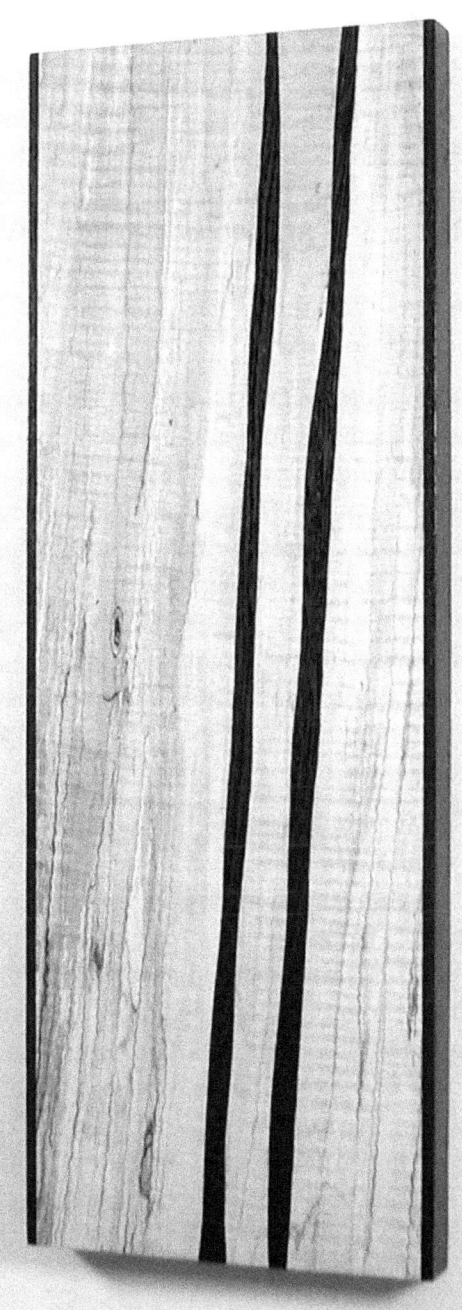

"***Striations***", 2010. Spalted elm with blackwood inlay and edging

After completing these new wood art pieces and applying a clear, translucent shellac finish, the decision was made to enter one in the very next monthly exhibition at the art association I was a member of. This would be the very first hanging art I ever created. Since a glass display case was available to me for my small sculptural work, a sculpture could also be entered into the exhibition. I was curious to the reaction this first wall-mounted wood art piece would receive. There were questions raised when a few of the group members noticed my new work. Was this a new direction for me? Was I abandoning wood sculptures?

The feedback from the other artists and the general public was overwhelmingly positive throughout the exhibition. Some comments referred to the uniqueness of the art. A few visitors appreciated how wood was being used as an art form. This feedback inspired me to pursue this direction and to create more wood art. I soon designed the next series of wood art. These new pieces would contain elements of inlay as well as contrasting colors. The technique developed to create the wood art panels was fairly revolutionary. The panels, once assembled and finished, could also be used as components of high-end furniture. Creating this new form of wood art opened up many new possibilities for me and I was once again invigorated.

Within a period of a few weeks in late 2009, several more pieces of this wood art were available and I was now actively seeking exhibition opportunities. I recall submitting a few of the pieces into conventional art exhibitions, with or without a theme. Over the next weeks and months, the new wood art slowly gained acceptance as a form of art. This had been a concern of mine since the medium was wood and the element of painting was missing. It was wall-mounted art however, possibly in the realm of mixed media but not exactly as it only involved a single medium. I was pleasantly surprised at the acceptance of the wood art pieces into a few initial exhibitions. This encouraged me to work further on creating interesting compositions.

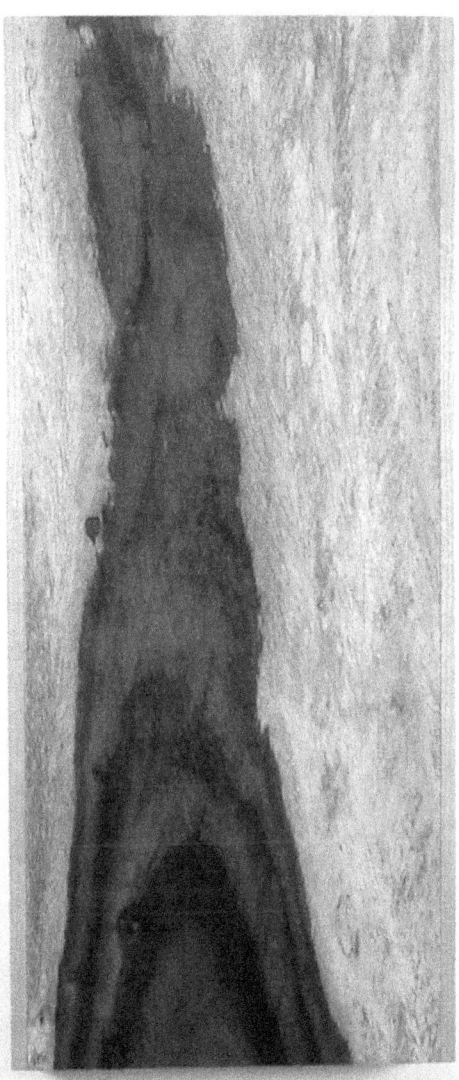

*"**Rising Flame**"*, 2010. Padauk (heartwood, sapwood combination)

In light of this temporary departure from sculptural work, I began to join other visual art groups. In many cases, an artist needs to be a member of an art group or association to be able to hang their work at the group exhibitions. There were several local arts groups available to join.

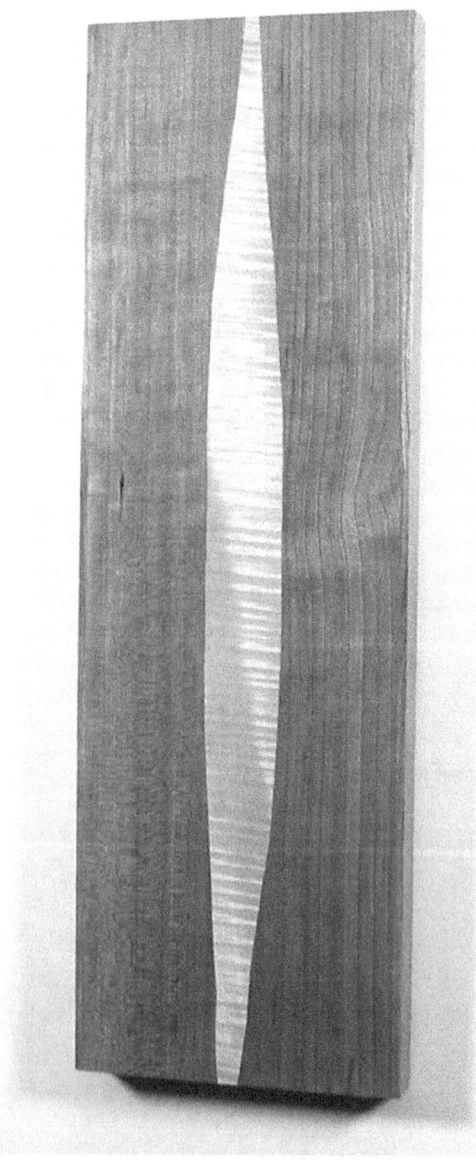

*"**Converging**"*, 2010. Black cherry with curly maple inlay, cherry edge

I now had visual art available to enter art exhibitions with. A few of the arts groups also held annual shows where members could display their work in a booth and have it available for sale.

Accomplishing this would necessitate a larger body of work to fill the three walls of a booth. Never shying away from opportunities and challenges, work was begun on a large body of work of this new wood art genre. A few of the new designs involved mixed wood species to introduce colors into the composition. There are different woods available with unique, natural colors. Padauk, a red wood, would be combined with a lighter wood to provide a stark contrast. The composition of the art piece was created through organically styled joinery combining the two different types of wood. The joinery was often curved and non-linear.

In the year 2010, three exhibitions occurred where I had been invited to display my wood art. The exhibitions were either group exhibitions or sharing wall space with another artist. The opportunity to display my work locally and acquiring exposure was rewarding. Only a year earlier, my work was limited to small sculptures. I had now progressed into the realm of fine art. Exhibition opportunities such as the ones mentioned were many and this would drive my art career forward in a relatively short time. With the renewed confidence developed in my work, the decision was made to label myself a **wood artist**. Soon, new business cards were designed and my web site was updated to indicate that I was a wood artist. The web site would consist of two categories, sculptural work and wall-mounted wood art. This allowed me to pursue both forms of art.

A few of the wood art pieces incorporated elements of inlay to create abstract compositions. Small squares and lines of contrasting woods came together in different configurations. Inlay work was my forte and incorporating it into art would provide me the opportunity to improve my skills further. In many cases, there would be an inclusion or defect in the veneered panel and this would create an interesting composition. Inclusions ranged from small contrasting color slivers to shaded areas depicting unusual shapes. Veneered panels with unusual graphics or inclusions creating an interesting composition were sought. The inclusion would become the focal point of the art piece.

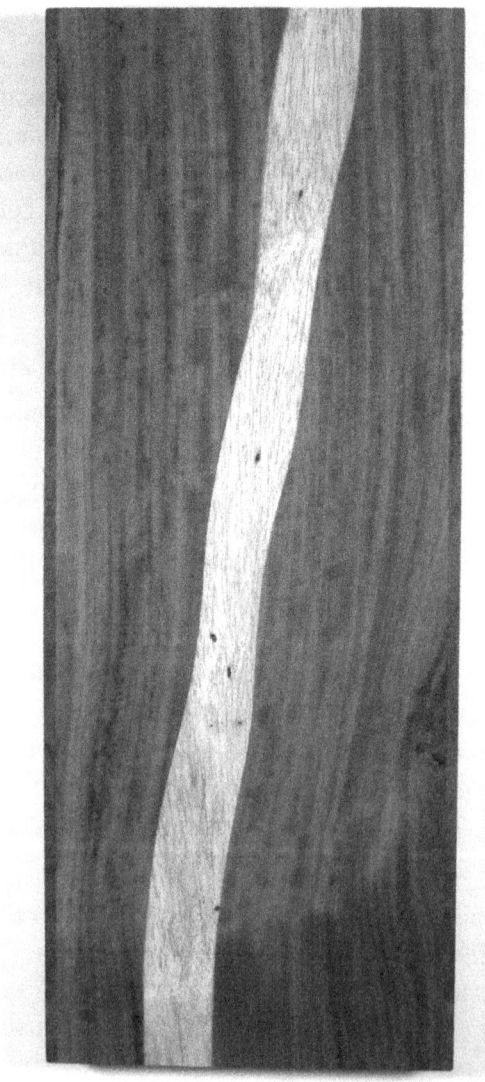

"***Desert Stream***", 2010. Padauk (heartwood, softwood combination)

In the early summer of 2010, I was invited to participate in a group exhibition at a fairly well known art gallery in Glen Nevis, Ontario. The **Abbey for the Arts** held rotating exhibitions of small groups of artists where the exhibitions typically following a theme.

The theme for this particular exhibition was **Summer Moods** and my entry consisted of a selection of wood art pieces to address this theme. This was to be my very first art exhibition at a gallery where my new wood art pieces could be shown. Typically, a gallery will have an opening night or **vernissage** for the exhibition. The gallery had arranged entertainment for the opening and also provided some food and drink. Many people attended, providing me the opportunity to discuss art with both artists and visitors. I thoroughly enjoyed the experience and decided to pursue the visual arts further.

Towards the final months of 2010, I was invited by gallery curator **Terry Sametz** to be part of a group exhibition at the upscale **Santé Gallery** in downtown Ottawa, Ontario. Three visual artists were selected to be part of the group exhibition. This particular art gallery held rotating art exhibitions every few weeks.

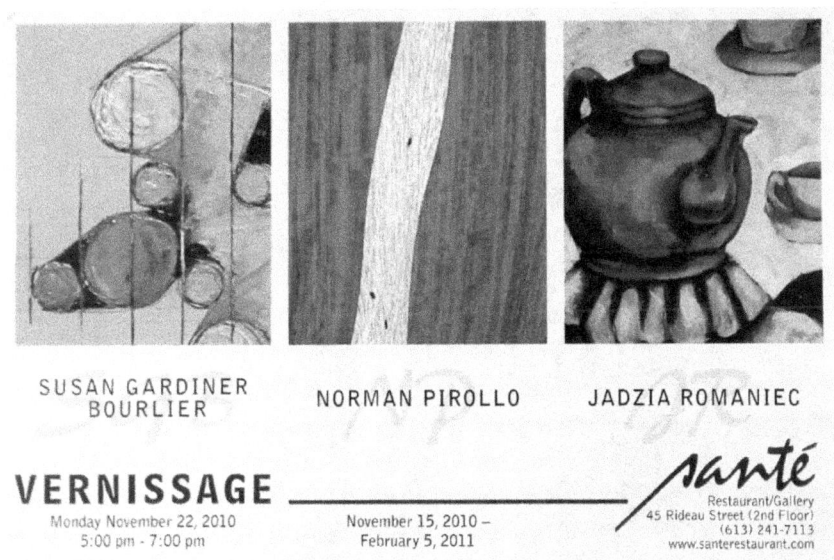

SUSAN GARDINER BOURLIER   NORMAN PIROLLO   JADZIA ROMANIEC

VERNISSAGE
Monday November 22, 2010   November 15, 2010 –
5:00 pm - 7:00 pm   February 5, 2011

santé
Restaurant/Gallery
45 Rideau Street (2nd Floor)
(613) 241-7113
www.santerestaurant.com

Santé Gallery group exhibition card, November 2010

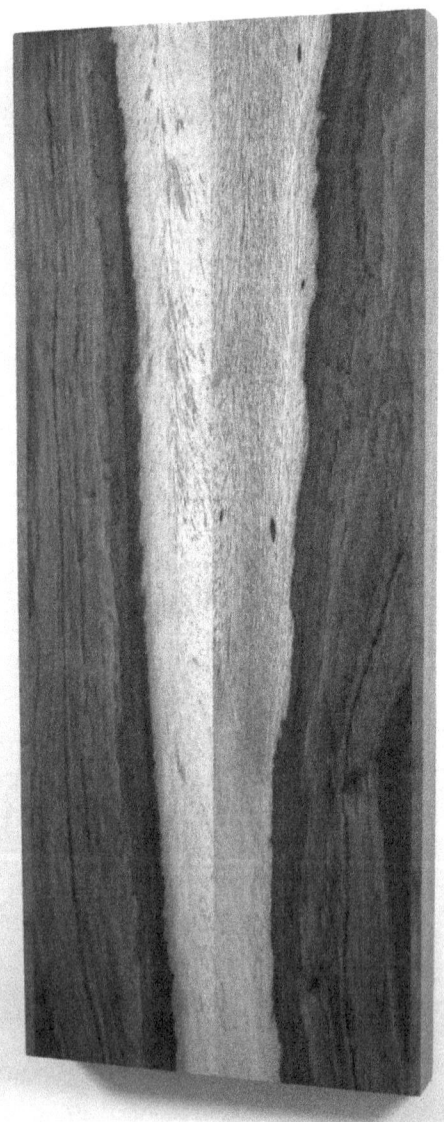

*"**Geyser**"*, 2010. Padauk (book matched heartwood and softwood)

Needless to say, I was both flattered and overwhelmed by the invitation. Art cards were designed and printed for the exhibition by the gallery curator. My role was to supply a diverse body of work consisting of my wood wall art. The wood art would be shown alongside the art of the two other visual artists.

The opening night was busy with many visitors and invitees in attendance. I enjoyed discussing my work and the resulting dialogue with visitors to the exhibition. The art was displayed very prominently with accent lights over most of the art pieces.

Following these experiences, I began to truly feel like an artist. It felt as if I had come of age in the art world. Slowly being acknowledged for my wood art, I was at the juncture where recognition was received as both a sculptor and a visual artist. In light of this, the title of wood artist became more appropriate. This title would cover both the wood sculpture genre and my wood art. The title was short and to the point and this appealed to me.

Another opportunity presented itself in early 2011. An opportunity to be profiled by a leading Ottawa magazine **Ottawa Life** came up. The magazine was interested in profiling me and writing a story about my evolution as a craftsman and wood artist. My furniture and wood art would be shown alongside each other. Seeking exposure for my work, I enthusiastically agreed to this opportunity. After meeting with a magazine writer and provided photography of my work, the well-written story was published in the April 2011 edition of Ottawa Life.

I continued to create wood art using the techniques referred to earlier. Woods of different colors and graphics were combined to create interesting compositions. Any flaws or imperfections in the woods used were instead featured as focal points. Since most domestic wood species are either light or dark woods, tropical or exotic woods were also introduced into the equation. These woods are available in more colors, from light reds to deep reds to striped black and white woods. Other exotic woods such as cocobolo had varying shades of brown in a single piece.

Due to the nature of these woods, exposure to light and air would often either lighten or darken the wood. The original color of the wood would, therefore, change over time. The **lightfastness** of wood is low and color change is almost impossible to prevent. There were UV resistant finishes available which slowed the color change process but unless the wood is kept in a dark environment, it would be susceptible to change color.

The lightfastness presented a problem since the appeal of the wood combinations in several of my wood art pieces relied on the color of the woods. If a client were to purchase one of my art pieces that included colored, exotic woods and the color changed over time, this could present a problem. In light of this, an explanation was provided to people interested in acquiring my wood art of the likelihood that this would occur. Many steps were taken to prevent this but the nature of wood being what it is precluded me from offering any guarantees that the colors would never change. A few clients had no issue with this after explaining to them what shade the wood would become over time. In some cases, a darker wood would provide better contrast with the lighter wood in the wood art.

I also selected a pure white wood, "holly", to provide contrast against darker woods. Holly does not yellow over time. Another favorite wood was cherry, which actually darkened beautifully over time. The combination of holly and cherry was to be seen. The problem involved wood species in colors or shades other than light or dark, specifically woods with red tones. These woods rarely ever remained red and more often than not turned either reddish-brown or brown. The process could be delayed by keeping the wood art away from direct or even indirect light, but the color change was inevitable. This problem turned into a dilemma for me, as some of the more colored wood art pieces being created would likely not retain their colors over time.

Early in 2011, I was invited to participate in an exhibition of two artists. My wood art would be alongside the work of another established artist. The curator also agreed that I could have my sculptural work included in the exhibition. This gave me the opportunity to design and create a series of plinths or stands for the sculptures. The exhibition was held at the **AOE Gallery** in July 2011 over a period of three months. Over the summer, a large number of visitors were introduced to my wood art and sculptures. My wood art with natural wood tones contrasted well with the colorful, abstract work of the other artist. Considerable exposure was gained from this exhibition and the positive feedback inspired me to further pursue wood as an art form.

Exhibition Interaction Exposition

AOE Gallery · May 30 to Aug 26, 2011 · Shenkman Arts Centre · Orléans, ON

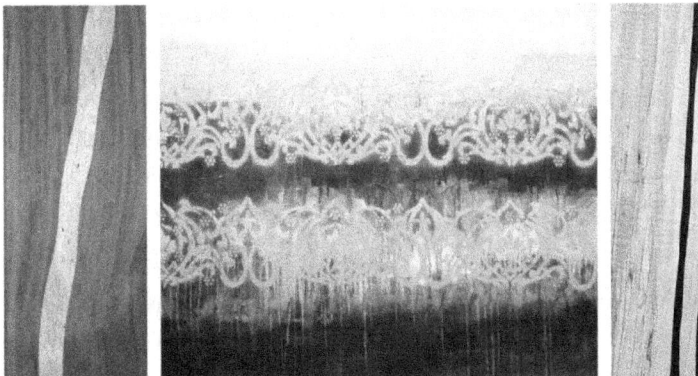

Norman Pirollo: Wood Art/L'Art du Bois · Rola Bleik: Mixed Media/Média Mixtes
Galerie AOE · 30 mai au 26 août, 2011 · Centre des Arts Shenkman · Orléans, ON

When I hung my wood art pieces alongside other art in an exhibition, the variety of colors and hues in other artwork was very apparent. My work was limited to the natural colors of the woods with a subdued red as the more dramatic color. This observation was of concern to me. Visitors to the exhibition would easily be drawn to more colorful art and unless they admired wood as a medium, my work would perhaps be overlooked. I noticed this on more than one occasion and began to survey the behavior of visitors to exhibitions. Fine art definitely was the draw, with its variety of colors, texture, and compositions. In light of this, thought was given to adding color to my wood art. I recalled some experiments in the past with aniline or water-based dyes.

This type of dye is absorbed into the wood as opposed to a pigment dye that sits on the surface. Early experiments were performed to add color to my wood products, but I instead decided to leave the woods in their natural color. Coloring wood was never part of my furniture making. With this newfound requirement to add color to wood, I revisited these colored water-based dyes. Water-based dyes would also retain the clarity and depth of the figure in the wood.

This was an important criterion, since the whole premise of figured woods was their clarity and depth. The aniline dyes would not mask this in any way aside from coloring the wood. Over a period of time, an assortment of water-based dyes was acquired and some experiments performed. The woods selected for the experiments had considerable figure as I wanted to determine the effect of translucent dyes on the wood. Different colored dyes were applied on some Tiger maple, Birds Eye maple and Flame Birch. These were the wood varieties most often used in the creation of my wood art. I was pleasantly surprised with the results.

The woods maintained their clarity and the depth of the figure was not masked in any way. There was some concern that although the dyes were labeled as clear, they might exhibit some opacity. The experiments involved off-cuts of figure wood or essentially scrap wood. My next step would be to apply a clear, natural shellac finish to the experimental pieces and to polish the surfaces afterwards. This step would provide me a better indication of the success of the experiment.

I was very satisfied with the results. Showing sample pieces to some friends and family reinforced the idea that coloring the wood panels would be a good one. The feedback received was extremely positive. Viewing the colored wood pieces made me realize how monochromatic the non-dyed pieces were. This new colored wood was made entirely possible through the use of water-based dyes. Use of another more opaque pigment dye would obscure the figure of the wood. The next step would be to create an actual wood art panel using the colored dye process.

Many of the fine art and photo art pieces I viewed at art exhibitions had matting around the art. The matting was typically lighter and uniform in color. A popular mat color was white. The matting would provide a background to the painting or photo print and separate it from the frame. This effect, widely used in art, made the art stand out. Consideration was made of applying this technique to my wood art pieces. After some thought, a thinner wood art panel was designed which would be raised against a white background.

The white backdrop would serve as a mat. The white background layer would be incorporated into a black picture frame. Shortly afterward, work began on this process. I used a standard white board for the mat and reinforced it by doubling it up within a black frame. The black box frame was contemporary styled. A new colored wood art panel would stand out or pop against this monochromatic background, much like a matted art piece. The framing process for the new wood art can be seen in one of the initial pieces, "*Comet*".

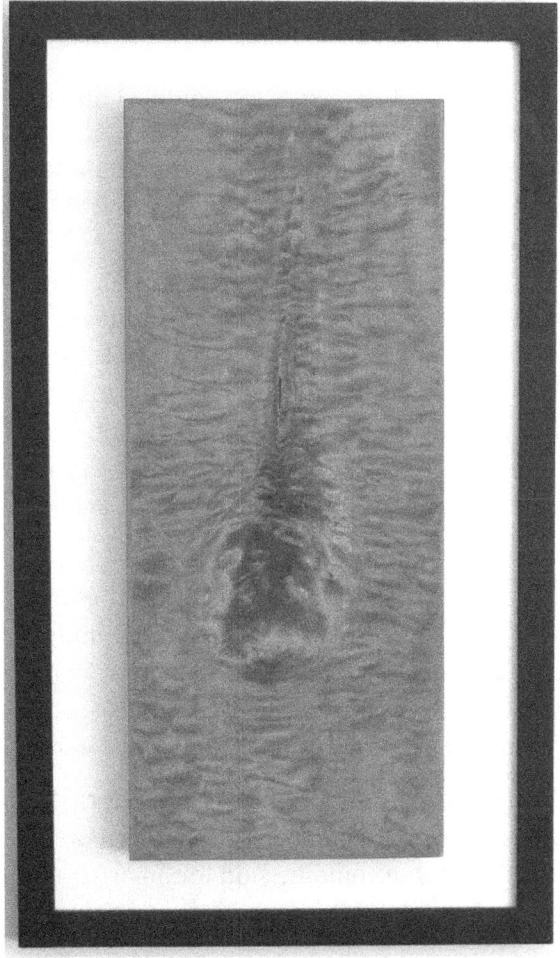

"*Comet*", 2012. Dye-infused wood art, highly figured quilted maple

Developing a body of work of this new art would occur over a few weeks. The white board, picture frames, and mounting hardware would need to be gathered. The wood panels would be considerably thinner since they were now raised against a white background. Creating the wood panels involved some expertise, however, since wood movement was an issue. Wood, by nature, moves with changes in ambient air moisture levels. The thin veneers were attached to a dimensionally stable substrate. Since the solid wood veneers would shrink or expand with changes in humidity, the likelihood that they would bend was high. To offset this, a sacrificial piece of veneer was attached to the back of each veneered panel.

The veneer mounted to the rear of the panel would create equilibrium and balance the effect of expansion and contraction of the veneered assembly. In a few weeks, I was successful at creating a few of these new wood art pieces. The process of creating picture frames was also learned. The new wood art was a dramatic shift from my earlier work. After applying a deep, clear finish to the surfaces of the new wood art panels, the effect of the figured wood with infused color was spectacular. The veneers sheets selected for the wall art were fairly random in graphics as is the nature of wood. This randomness introduced a level of abstraction into the aesthetic. The abstraction in the work was noted in feedback received from fellow artists. It is this experience that introduced me to abstract work and its endless possibilities.

Feeling invigorated as an artist, exhibiting this new art would raise my stature as a visual artist. After creating a substantial body of work, I began to seek opportunities for exhibiting this new work. A small concern of mine was this new genre of work submitted into calls for entry was a considerable departure from my sculptural work.

Only a short while earlier, my wood art was considerably different. Not having been an artist for long, I could only attribute this to my evolution as an artist. The same could be said for an artist embracing a different medium in their work.

Often, visual artists shift from representational painting to abstract work and back again. In research, it was found that this is completely normal during the career of an artist. By alternating styles and mediums, the monotony an artist is faced with can be broken up. Often, a new artistic vision is introduced if a style of work is temporarily abandoned and later resumed. In my case, the timeline was shortened, as the new forms of art created were radical and innovative.

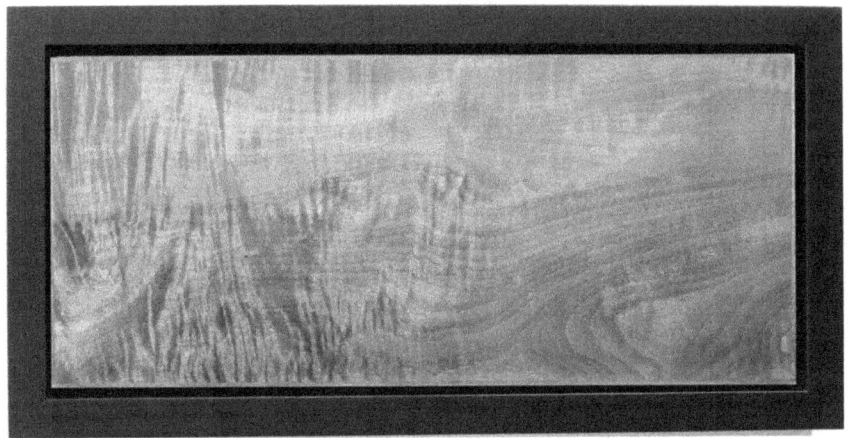

"Sundown", 2013. Dye-infused wood art using figured veneers.

The new colored wood art was intriguing to many people as well as fellow artists. A piece would be entered in select exhibitions to determine feedback. Although the wood art had a distinct appeal, I wondered how it would fare against conventional fine art. The combination of interesting graphics and infused color in the wood would hopefully draw people in. The process of coloring the wood panels also exhibited an interesting side effect. Wood, by nature, varies in density over a certain area. The difference in density causes the absorption of the aniline dye to be irregular. This caused a dark and light effect on the surface of the wood where distinct areas could be either lighter or darker. In many cases, the irregular dye absorption created an image or an abstraction.

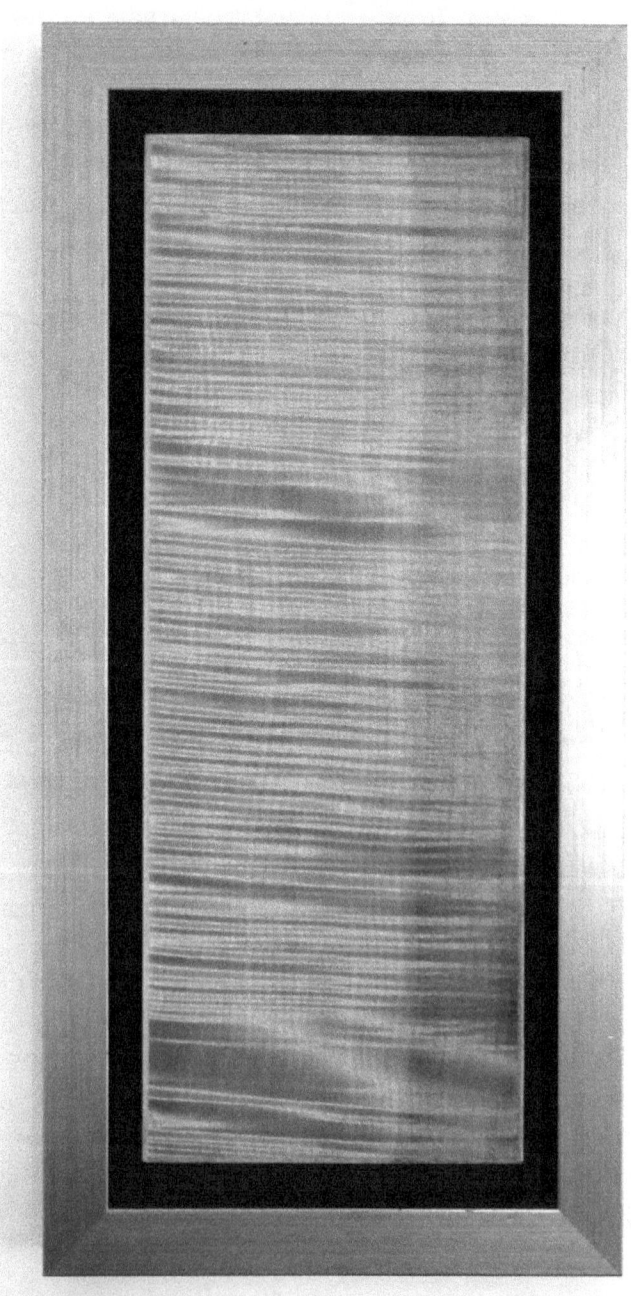

*"**Spring Bulrush**"*, 2013. Dye-infused wood art using figured veneers.

Unless the aniline dyes were applied to the surface, the absorption rate could not be determined ahead of time. This characteristic was intriguing to me. The element of surprise was something I looked forward to in each piece of the dyed, colored wood art. As well as entering this new dye-infused wood art in selective exhibitions; the timing was right for me to apply for a solo exhibition. Solo exhibitions garner the most exposure for an artist as much publicity is generated even before the event. In this early 2012 period, I had already created a substantial body of work of this new dye-infused wood art.

The solo exhibition I applied for was a City of Ottawa exhibition. As part of the submission, one of a selection of municipal galleries could be chosen. Three gallery choices were available and my first choice was a beautiful, enclosed gallery, the **Atrium Gallery**, in the center of the city. The submission process would also involve a very good sampling of my work and extensive biographical information along with an artist resume and artist statement. Another part of the submission asked for a title for the exhibition. The title arrived at was a play on the words **Go Figure!.** The expression, widely used as a cliché, also emphasized the wood figure in my work. I thought nothing more of the submission, as the actual jurying was months away.

Over the course of 2012 many exhibition opportunities became available to me. I introduced my work and myself to the owner of a very prestigious art gallery that had recently opened. The **Michael Gennis Gallery** focused on internationally curated contemporary artwork, both fine art and sculpture. Until this time, I had not seen such a beautiful gallery in my city! On my initial visit I was intimidated to be in the presence of the art of so many internationally renowned artists. The gallery owner **Michael Gennis** agreed to view one of my pieces of wood art and was immediately drawn to the work. This is one of the moments in life where a person feels like they are experiencing a dream. We both agreed that I should bring more art pieces in. The framing was upgraded and the work put on display. The opportunity to show and sell my work for a one year period was provided through this gallery. Later, some of my new contemporary sculptures would also be shown at the gallery.

In early summer of 2012, a local television station contacted me about participating in a new television series, The Artisans. The series would focus on local artisans. Each segment would feature two artisans, usually with complimentary work. Enthusiastically agreeing to this, a date was set for taping of the segment I would participate in. In August of 2012, I attended the taping with a few pieces of my wood art. Having never experienced being part of a television series before, let alone being on television, the process was intriguing.

Prior to the actual taping, I was interviewed by **Sterling Lynch**, the host. I was asked a series of questions about my inspiration, how the wood art was created as well as discussion of art in general. This was done to provide me the opportunity to rehearse the live interview as well as providing a sound and video quality check. Shortly afterwards, the actual taping occurred. The questions were more or less similar as the ones in the rehearsal so I felt at ease with my answers. The television series was aired throughout the upcoming months. Occasionally, friends and acquaintances mentioned that they had seen me on television many months after the taping!

Later in 2012, the City of Ottawa exhibition coordinator notified me that my solo exhibition submission was accepted and the first gallery choice was also selected. This news made me ecstatic! The culmination of my efforts at using wood as an art medium would finally come to pass. I could not be happier.

The process leading up to the City of Ottawa exhibition would involve a series of tasks including art cards, publicity, and determining the placement of my art on the walls of the gallery. This would keep me busy for several weeks in early 2013. The dates of my solo exhibition were also provided to me. Each artist is provided a five-week window for an exhibition. My exhibition dates for **Go Figure!** at the Atrium Gallery were from March 22 to April 22, 2013.

Having my wood art in a prestigious art gallery, the **Michael Gennis Gallery**, dramatically increased my stature as a visual artist. The arts community began to take notice of my work. My confidence level rose where any doubt about the appeal of my work vanished.

Acceptance to a City of Ottawa solo exhibition further solidified my confidence. If a panel of jurors deemed my work suitable for a solo exhibition, how could I harbor any doubt about the quality and uniqueness of the work. In the few short years of entering the art world, I was still considered an emerging artist. The year 2012 was to be my peak year as an emerging artist. There were times where I thought the different genres of work introduced would confuse my audience. However, the common medium was wood. It was also discovered that there is considerable evolution early on in an artist's career.

An emerging artist defines a voice and style that is both rewarding and demands further exploration. Through the evolution of the artist and their work, the form and quality of art typically improves. Participating in the visual arts field brings with it a steep learning curve. Being self-taught and without a formal education in the arts, I learned through my progression that every decision and experience increased my knowledge of the arts. The typical window is five years for an emerging artist to develop a voice, aesthetic and style. The artist seeks a voice and style that is appealing, intriguing and inspirational. I had two more years to go in my probationary, emerging artist status!

Another exciting opportunity presented itself to me in this period. Through my evolving reputation as a wood artist, I received a commission to create a very large piece of wall art for a client. An iterative process was launched where I would collaborate with the client on a design for the wall art. Input from the client was followed with sketches and drawings. The critical elements of the wall art were highly figured, naturally toned wood panels and contrasting metal tubes to join the components of the art. After several consultations, the final design was based on the following scale model where the vertical components would be in metal. This commission provided me the opportunity to explore large-scale wall art.

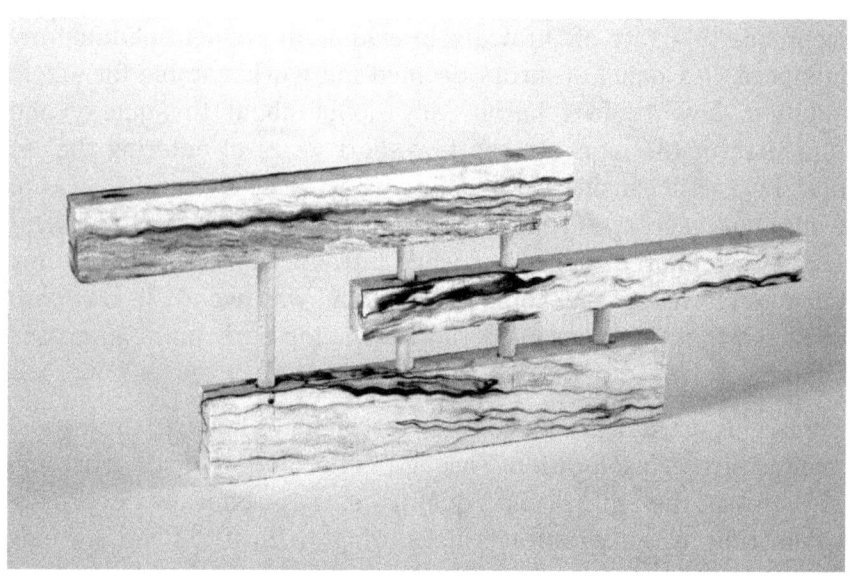

Scale model of wall art commission. Vertical elements would be metal.

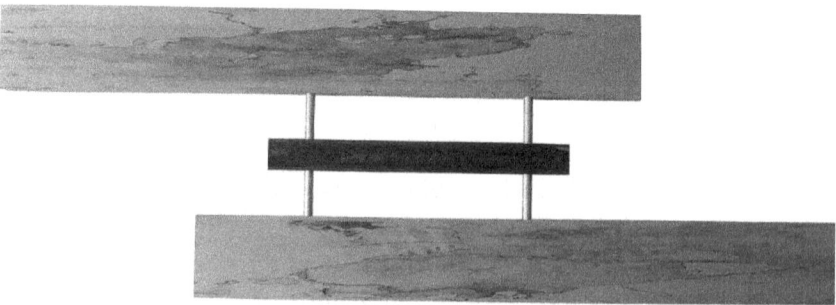

Final wall art commission with 6 ft. wide and 3 feet high dimensions. Spalted elm veneers, metal and solid wenge.

Sculpture Redux

᪲᪲

"Artists rarely do the same thing over and over again. Art is about the new, doing things in a new way"

Eli Broad

DURING THIS PERIOD OF exploration, my sculptural work was languishing. Monthly exhibitions at the arts group **OWAA,** where I was a member, gave me the opportunity to create a series of small sculptures. Although the sculptures were becoming more organic and not as linear and angular as earlier work, I found the appeal lacking and a sense of monotony was developing. My interest in creating sculptures was beginning to wane, as they simply were no longer enticing to create. The small dimensions of the sculptures were fairly similar to one another. The small size was attributed to the limitations of the glass display case at the **OWAA** arts organization. My sculptures were limited in height, depth and width. Since the display case was shared with other sculptors, my work could not occupy anything larger than a standard glass shelf.

With this in mind, my focus shifted instead to my new dye-infused wall art. I could enter a wall art piece in each of the monthly exhibitions at the arts organization as well as one of my small sculptures. The art gallery I was an artist in, **Michael Gennis Gallery**, also exhibited sculptural work. In casual conversation, it was mentioned to the gallerist that I was working on a new series of sculptures.

Due to the success of my dye-infused wood art, a decision was made to experiment with applying the dye-infused process to my sculptural work. Until this time, my wood sculptures were natural wood-toned where I would simply apply finish to the wood. The dye-infused process inspired me to create a series of sculptures using the coloring process.

The possibility arose of another venue, the **Michael Gennis Gallery**, to display my sculptural work. This motivated me to the challenge of creating a new series of sculptures utilizing the dye-infused process. The sculptures at this art gallery were not constrained in display cases. Instead, they were mounted on plinths. Size was therefore no longer a restriction. A focus on a more organic aesthetic was also initiated with the introduction of curves into my new sculptural work. In the spring of 2012, work began on this new series of sculptures.

I also decided to double the height of the new series of sculptures. Due to the organic aesthetic and the introduction of curves in the wood, the additional height would show the shape better. Other dimensions such as width and depth would remain the same. The very first sculpture created was carved from a single piece of highly figured Manitoba Maple wood. It was in the form of a flame with a sinewy shape flowing from bottom to top. As this was the first of the new series, I decided not to be too bold with colors. Instead, the overall color was a shade of deep, light golden brown. The dye applied was water-based and very transparent. This was necessary to not mask the figure of the wood, since part of the appeal of the sculpture was the figure in the wood as well as the organic flame shape.

The final surface of the sculptures would need to be finely sanded and polished to a high degree. The wood would need to impart a perfect, deep clarity. As part of the finishing process, considerable time was invested in the sanding and polishing stage. The results of this effort were pleasantly surprising. The new sculptures were radically different from my earlier work and were stunning! In light of this, I was once again motivated to create sculptural work. I had been applying a broader selection of colors to my wall art so why not use color on the sculptures. It became necessary to get away from natural wood tones and brown shades.

This would hopefully bring a new dynamic to the sculptures. In the next two sculptures, I moved away from a brown shade to alternative shades of red and orange. Since my original wall art was created by applying a veneer over a hollow form, I decided to use this technique for this next series of colored sculptures. The process of applying veneers over a hollow form is similar to that of creating musical instruments such as violins and small guitars. A sheet of figured veneer would need to be applied to both the front and back of the sculpture to both provide dimensional stability and for aesthetic reasons. Since the sculpture would be observed from four sides, each side had to be properly finished. The front and back panels of this particular series were wide whereas the sides were narrow. The veneers used for the front and back were highly figured curly maple. I challenged myself to be able to create this new sculpture series and afterwards apply the dye-infused color process.

The finishing for this new series of sculpture would continue to be the **French Polish** process. This finishing process was successfully used in my wall art, as it imparts depth and clarity to the surface of the wood. It became important to not obscure the figure or graphics of the wood and instead apply a translucent color to it. The French Polish process is applied using shellac, alcohol and a very small amount of oil for lubrication. The shellac is then applied in extremely thin layers that build on one another. Shellac is the most natural of all finishes, it is derived from the Lac bug and formed into shellac flakes of varying color from orange to super blonde, the clearest of them all. Super Blonde shellac is always used in my work as it does not impart any of its own color to the finish. Since color is applied to the wood using infused dyes, the shellac does not interfere with these underlying colors.

After creating two of these new sculptures, color was applied and considerable time invested in the finishing process. The colors decided on were orange and red. This was quite a leap from the earth-tone natural colors of my earlier work. Red and orange colors were successfully used in my wall art and this drew many people to the work. People had expressed intrigue about the translucent wood art.

The colored sculpture was mounted on a base of dark, tropical hardwood. The dark wood contrasted very well with the dye-infused, colored sculpture. Often, when working on a sculpture, I can determine early on if the aesthetic is appealing. This is simply a feeling the artist gets. In the process of creating these two new sculptures, I began to feel a new vibe! The sculptures would be magnificent and unique as I pride myself on creating work that has not been done before. Shortly after completing the sculptures, my excitement grew as the work was shown to acquaintances and friends. The response was overwhelmingly positive. The deep, clear finish that brought out the figured woods became the initial draw. The shape of the sculpture was next in its appeal. The contrast between colored sculpture and dark hardwood base also served to enhance the experience of viewing the sculptures. The veneers sheets selected for both the front and back of the sculptures were random in graphics as is the nature of wood. This randomness introduced a level of abstraction into the aesthetic. The abstraction was similar to that of the wall art I had been creating. It is this experience that continued to enlighten me to abstract work and its endless possibilities.

With a new breath of life in my sculptural work, I began seeking new opportunities to show this work. Exposure is critical to an artists' survival; it is constantly drilled into us to get our work out there. In this period of early 2012, I was enlightened to a group of sculptors in my city. These sculptors had formed a group or network as they called it. The National Capital Network of Sculptors or **NCNS** consisted of sculptors in various media. There were two sculptors in my medium of wood. The group encouraged prospective members to attend one of their meetings to determine if they would fit in with the group and its charter. With the need for exposure of my new series of sculptures and the need for networking with other sculptors in the area, I soon attended one of the NCNS monthly meetings. The meeting was enjoyable and I was impressed with how the group had become established as the premier sculptors association in the Ottawa area. In dialogue with various members, it was discovered that we shared similar challenges in bringing awareness to our sculptural work. I joined the sculptors group and began to attend the monthly meetings.

The NCNS group also prided itself on their annual sculpture show, **Dimensions**, where each participating member would show one or more of his or her latest sculptures. The venue chosen was a very prestigious one and the group had a successful marketing plan in place. Many sculpture collectors, as well as the general public, were aware of this annual show. Through sheer coincidence, the next Dimensions Show to be held was only a few months away, in September 2012. A submission was drafted to include my new series of sculptures. The submission was accepted a few days later and this would provide me the opportunity to show my new work to a broad audience of sculpture collectors. A part of the submission involved volunteering for a task in the preparation and running of the sculpture show. I volunteered to participate in the setup of the show. Each participating member of the show was also tasked with aiding in publicizing the event. My role would be to contact some media and newspapers as well as distributing art cards to certain venues.

Within the same year 2012, I also had the opportunity to show my new sculptures to Michael Gennis of the **Michael Gennis Art Gallery** art gallery. He admired the new work and asked that one of the new sculptures be part of the gallery where he would dedicate a plinth to the sculpture. The exposure that this opportunity would bring was immeasurable. In only a short time, this new series of sculptures was developed, with two prestigious venues to exhibit the work in. The enjoyment and satisfaction derived in creating these sculptures re-invigorated me. I began to feel a breakthrough in my art future.

The dye-infused color process was a success in that it brought out the abstract figure and graphics of the wood in both my new wall art and sculptural work. The dye-infused color process was successfully applied to both genres of work. Applying a thin, clear shellac finish over the colored wood was a process involving weeks of experiments. The French Polish method was commonly used over 150 years earlier but there was scant documentation explaining it in detail. Through a few documented steps and much iteration and experimentation, I began to feel comfortable with the application and process. Proficiency was soon gained in using this finishing method.

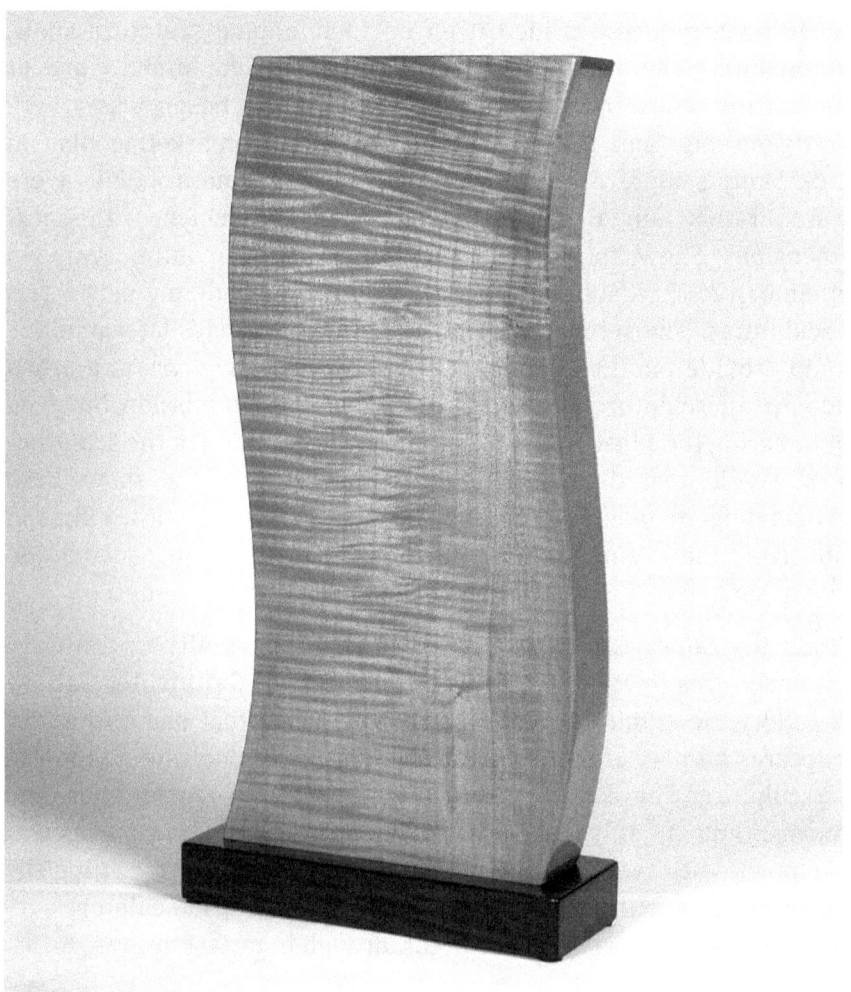

"Inferno", 2012. Tiger maple veneers, solid maple, rosewood base

The NCNS Dimensions 2012 show date arrived and preparations were in place for it to be a success. As with most exhibitions and art shows, there is considerable publicity in the weeks and days leading up to the event. An opening event or vernissage is usually held for the show. The opening night was widely advertised and I discovered that many local sculpture aficionados and collectors attended this opening. As testament to the prestige of the event, the mayor of the city officially opened the event.

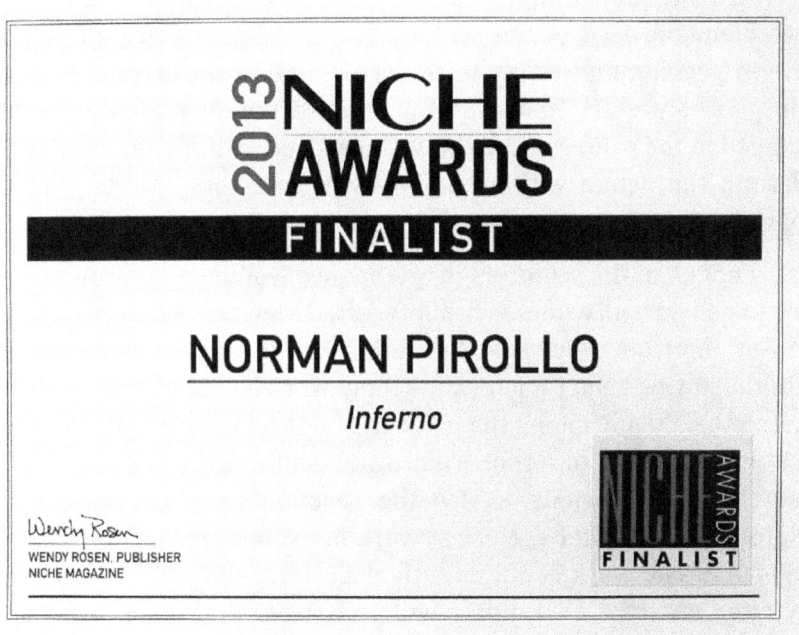

Niche Award Finalist Certificate for *"Inferno"*, 2013

Late in 2012, notification arrived that I was a finalist for a very prestigious **NICHE Award**. The sculpture, *"Inferno"*, had been entered into the competition a few weeks earlier. My entry was one of five sculptures selected from across North America by an elite jury panel. I had also begun to win other art awards in this period of 2012-13.

As with many art and sculpture exhibitions, there are art cards and posters designed and printed to feature the **Dimensions 2012** event. The art cards are widely distributed to local art stores, art galleries and art venues. As well, posters are placed throughout the city to advertise the art or sculpture exhibition. I received a stack of art cards and a few posters to distribute in the weeks leading up to the event. To my surprise, my latest sculpture and entry into **Dimensions 2012** was prominently featured on both the art card and poster. Soon, the setup day for the event arrived. Plinths were transported to the venue and sculptures delivered.

Lighting, a large factor in the success of the show, was strategically set up to highlight each of the sculptures. The plinths were all painted white to provide uniformity to the show and to not detract from the sculptures. My entry, mounted on a white plinth, was prominently displayed in the center of the show. Guests and visitors began to arrive and soon the venue was brimming with sculptors, guests, and the public.

Most, if not all of the sculptors in attendance would hover around their work to generate discourse with interested viewers. I did this, as well as observing from a distance. Since this was my first group sculpture exhibition, I was keen to determine if my work had any appeal and if it generated dialogue among the patrons of this opening event. Since this work was radically different from other sculptural work seen in my research, I was curious to see the reaction received. Artists and sculptors tend to enter their best work in exhibitions and shows such as this one. The work is not only their best but their latest work, and very often an artist or sculptor will go outside their comfort zone to create work for such prestigious shows. It is therefore not surprising to see that many, if not all of the other sculptures, had great appeal with the public. My sculpture drew considerable interest and people were overwhelmingly surprised that it was created of wood.

Great delight was taken in mentioning that the sculpture was indeed wood. A dialogue followed of the choice of figured wood used in the sculpture and the history of both the musical instrument process and the **French Polish** finishing process. It was not merely a sculpture, but an assemblage of exotic woods and period maker processes and techniques. Although it was not necessary to be present over most of the four days of the sculpture show, I decided to spend as much time as possible at the show. This was an exhilarating period, to be able to discuss my new work with visitors and patrons of the sculpture show. The opportunity to interact with the public and gain exposure within my city was greatly appealing to me. Until this time, I had only exhibited small sculptures at the single venue of the OWAA arts organization. The **NCNS Dimensions** show ended a few days later and the show was dismantled.

Over the course of the "Dimensions" show, a few contact names were acquired that I could follow up with over the next days and weeks. On the last day of the show, I recall the anticipation of next year's version of the show and the enjoyment that would be derived in designing and creating a sculpture for that show.

Over the next few months, preparations occurred for my upcoming solo exhibition at a city gallery. The exhibition **Go Figure!,** held from March to April 2013, would involve a large body of work encompassing both my current and early wall art. Only a year separated the different styles, but I felt it was important to show both. The evolution of my wood art from a monochromatic to a colorful palette would be interesting to show visitors to the exhibition. I looked forward to the experience of hosting a solo exhibition. The body of work to be exhibited would need to be my best work in this genre. An opportunity like this demanded my complete focus, as the visitors to the exhibition would help spread the word of my artwork. The work needed to be properly framed and mounted, flawless and appealing!

The **Go Figure!** exhibition opening on March 30, 2013, was very well attended. The NCNS sculptors group I was a member of graciously decided to have the members attend my exhibition opening instead of the regular monthly meeting held on the same evening. As many acquaintances as possible were invited to the opening as well as dignitaries and media.

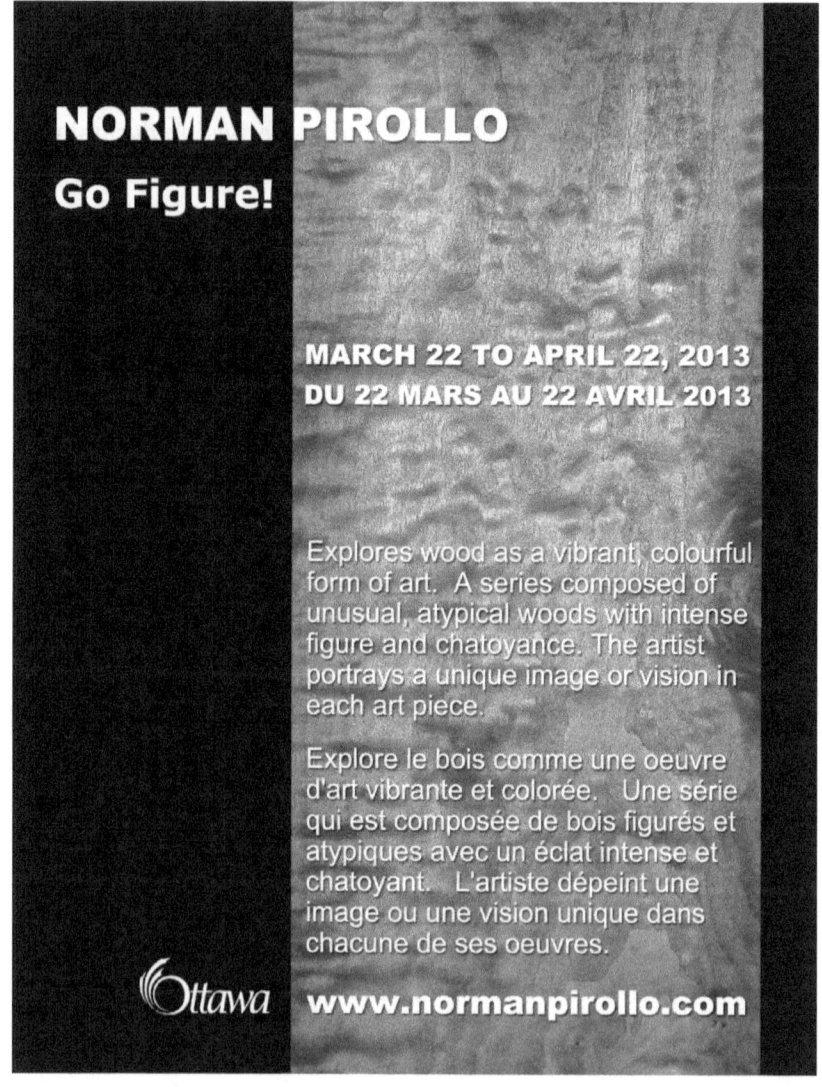

As is the case with art openings, not everyone who is invited attends. It therefore becomes important to draw from every acquaintance, sculptor aficionado, and the public, when issuing invitations to the exhibition. I had weeks to prepare and worked from a checklist of tasks to complete. There were several tasks leading up to both the installation of the exhibition and the exhibition opening. While assembling the body of work to display at the solo exhibition, three extra art pieces were created to substitute for any sales.

Typically, when a sale is made at such an art exhibition, the piece remains up for the duration and afterwards the purchaser picks up the sold piece. The purchaser does, however, have the option to pick his purchase up immediately. Extra pieces would allow for these situations. As well, the art pieces are all catalogued and the list provided to the gallery curator prior to the exhibition. The gallery curator then prints off many copies of the exhibition list for interested visitors. They can leave with the list and quickly identify an art piece they expressed an interest in purchasing.

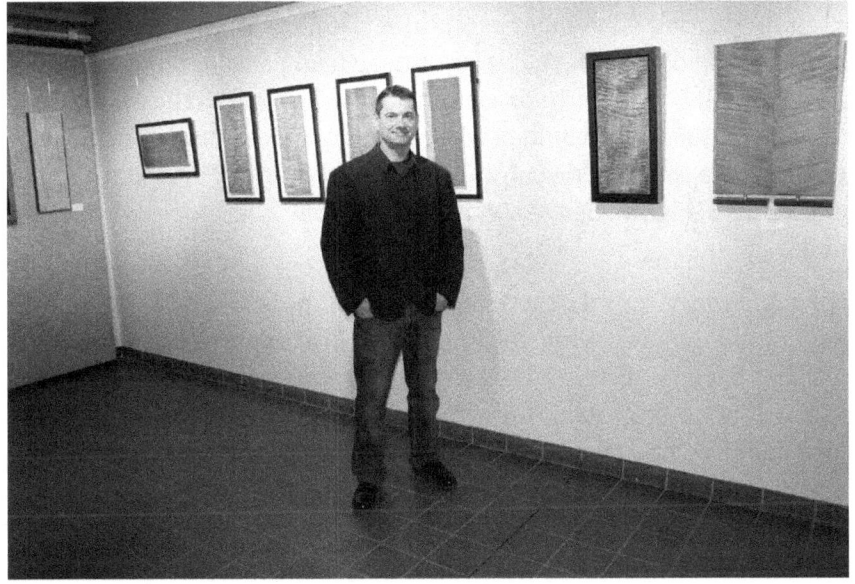

*"**Go Figure!**"* opening night prior to the actual opening or vernissage

In the days and weeks following the exhibition opening event, I had the opportunity to bring people to tour the exhibition. A media reporter asked to tour the exhibition with me where information and background on the wood art was discussed as well as the inspiration for it and the processes used to create the art. Family and friends from out of town attended, it was an opportunity to show the breadth of my work. The exhibition was a glowing success and provided me the confidence to move forward with this genre of art!

In the spring of 2013, I was informed of a possible commission to create a sculpture. The client had seen a dye-infused sculpture of mine on display at the **Michael Gennis Art Gallery** and asked if they could have a taller one created with similar styling. Until this time, I had not considered making a taller version, as my new series was already double in height from the original series of sculpture.

My first series of wood-toned geometric and organic sculptures were on average ten inches in height whereas this new series was close to twenty inches in height. With the commission in mind, I challenged myself in creating even taller sculptures. Designs were drawn and the process begun of creating a new sculpture using a solid block of highly figured wood. This particular sculpture was not only taller but larger in dimensions since it would be shaped out of a deep and wide block of wood. In the previous sculptures, only the front and back were composed of highly figured veneers whereas the sides were solid wood.

Applying veneer to only the front and back of the sculpture worked well, since the sides were fairly narrow in comparison to the wide front and back panels. In this latest version however, the front, back, and sides were of equal width, therefore a greater amount of wood figure could be displayed. It would be necessary to properly finish all four sides of these larger sculptures. The shaping process was slowly begun while being careful to maintain uniformity in width on all sides.

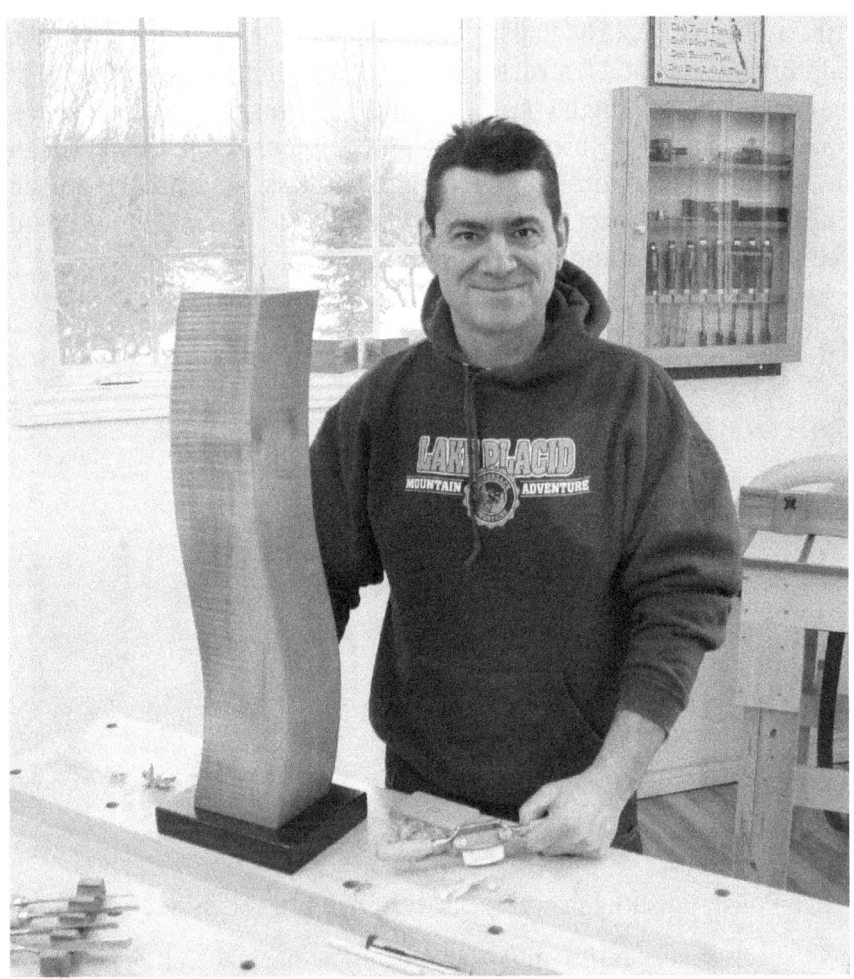

Creating the "*Eternal Flame*" sculpture in my studio, 2013

The 30 inch tall sculpture, *"Eternal Flame",* was an order of magnitude taller than the previous 20-inch sculptures. The creation process was slow, as this initial sculpture of the new series had me delving into uncharted waters. It was necessary to develop new techniques and processes. I had not worked on a sculpture in this style until now. After completing the new, taller and larger sculpture, the time-proven dye-infused coloring process was applied. An orange shade was decided on since the experience of using it in earlier sculptures was positive.

With a French Polish finish laboriously applied afterwards, the sculpture immediately struck me as a beautiful representation of abstract graphics in highly figured wood. Showing it to a select group of acquaintances also brought glowing compliments. It was through this particular sculpture that the decision was made to create all future sculptures larger in size. The organic styling used would lend itself well to a larger and taller sculpture.

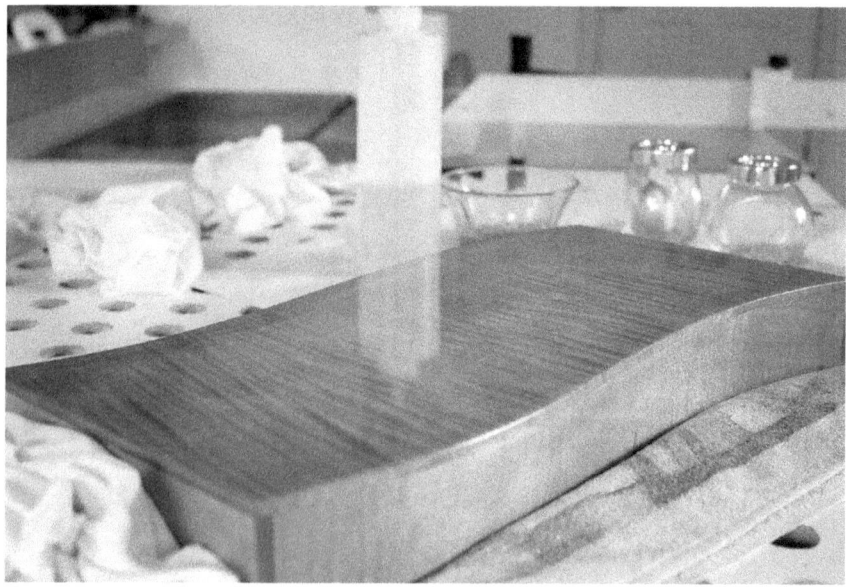

French Polish finishing process, clarity and depth can be seen.

Through this successful and unexpected experience, I decided to create my next series of sculptures even taller and larger in dimensions at approximately 40 inches in height. It was found that there was not much extra effort in moving to larger sizes as the labor intensive part was in shaping and finishing.

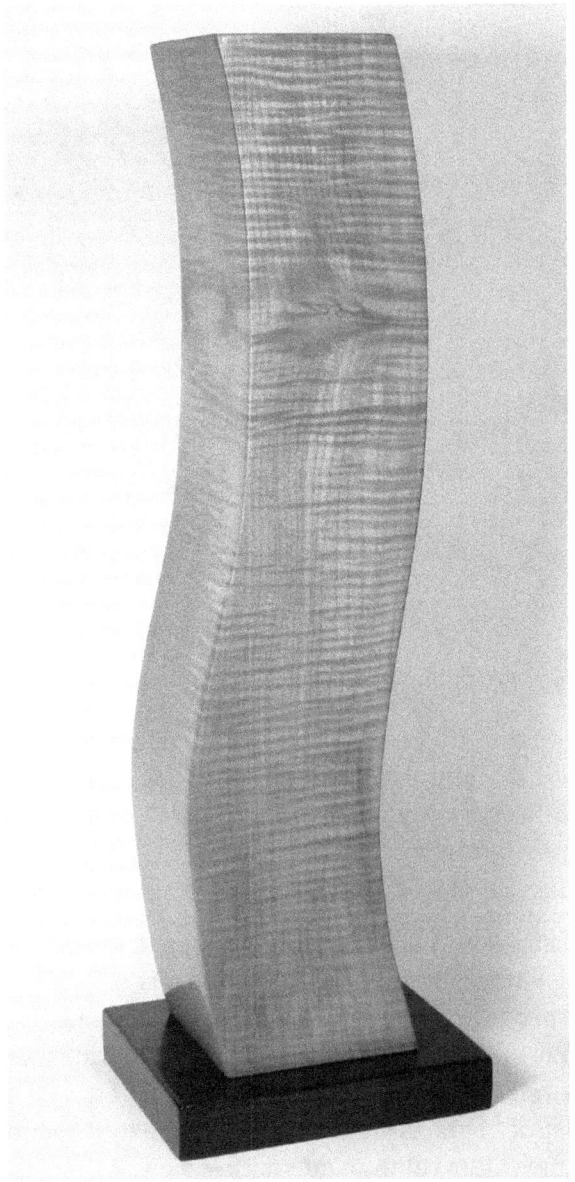

"Eternal Flame", 2013. Highly figured maple with rosewood base.

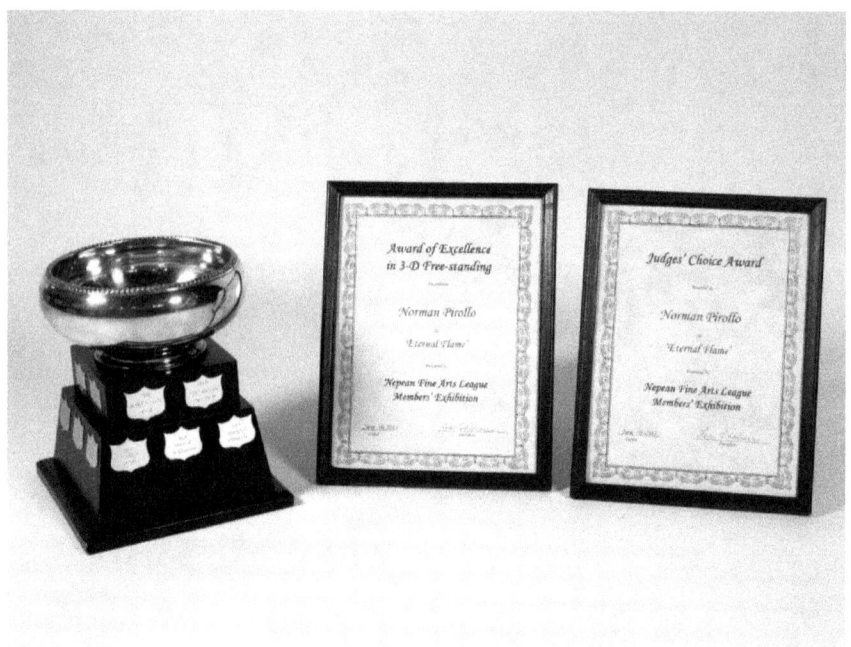

"***NFAL Awards***", received in June 2013 for Eternal Flame sculpture

Since the solo exhibition **Go Figure!** had ended in late spring of 2013, my focus shifted to sculptural work. Having already amassed a large body of wall art in preparation for Go Figure!, there was little point in creating even more work in this genre. I also felt the need to gain more expertise in creating sculptures, especially larger and taller ones.

The next series of larger and taller sculptures proved to be a challenge, however. Working with a similar process used to create the recent 30-inch tall sculpture, sourcing began for large pieces of wood to be able to carve and shape the large sculpture. After considerable searching and visiting wood retailers, large pieces of wood could not be sourced. In my search, a list of contacts that specialized in exotic wood blanks was provided to me. After calling and visiting some of the suppliers, sufficiently large blanks to shape sculptures could still not be located. Since this series of sculptures had an organic shape, it was necessary to have the dimensions of the wood blanks much wider and deeper to allow for shaping of the sculpture.

After a few weeks of searching and looking at alternatives such as joining smaller blanks together, I had almost given up. Assembling a large blank from smaller pieces would also expose unnecessary seams in the woods. As well, bringing different woods together takes away from the harmony of the sculpture since the graphics are no longer flowing but broken up. My thought process at the time was to create a large sculpture from a single blank of wood. In light of the difficulty in sourcing satisfactory blanks, I almost reconsidered pursuing this project and was prepared to drop it instead.

A short time later, it dawned on me to perhaps apply the same process used to create my first series of dye-infused sculptures. This process involved attaching veneered sheets to a hollow form. The process worked well since the sculpture was a few times wider than deep. With the large sculptures envisioned, all sides are similar in dimensions precluding the use of a hollow form. The front and back would be half the width of the smaller sculptures. A hollow form would need to have substantial amounts of solid wood at each corner leaving very little space to hollow out the middle. The large amount of wood at each corner was necessary to be able to shape the organically styled sculpture. The process was therefore not scalable simply due to the large dimensions of this new series of sculptures.

More research and experiments on how to successfully create a larger sculpture continued. The criteria necessary to create a large blank would involve a large amount of wood to shape the form of the sculpture. Since large solid wood blanks could not be sourced, I decided to instead create one from narrow strips of wood. Assembling the pieces together along their length would allow me to build up a blank to the necessary dimensions. Wood movement is always an issue with large pieces of wood. Since my plan was to apply a sheet of veneer to each of the sides of the sculpture, the underlying wood blank would need to be as stable as possible. Wood movement manifests itself with changes in moisture content in the air. By using small pieces of wood in the assembly, the wood movement issue is largely cancelled out if properly done. From studies on wood movement, I also recalled how rift-sawn wood was fairly stable.

If a collection of rift-sawn pieces could be assembled using glue, a large and tall blank from which to carve and shape a sculpture could be successfully created. Experiments began to create a small blank using this process. I recall combining a pattern eight pieces wide and eight pieces deep to create a large, square shaped blank. The pieces were all glued together in four sections; the sections were then glued together to form the final blank. The process appeared to be straightforward enough and resulted in a large, tall blank square. Since the blank was solid and not hollow as originally planned, I also used lighter woods to reduce the overall weight of the sculpture. Having completed the blank, some scrap sheets of veneer were applied to each of the sides and the edges trimmed. This would provide me a better indication of the viability of this new process. The wood movement issue becomes increasingly important as the size of the blank is increased. The results were satisfactory but only time would tell if the inner core of the assembly would remain stable.

The **NCNS Dimensions 2013** sculpture show was coming up at the end of summer 2013. The opportunity to show a new series of much larger sculptures motivated me to pursue the creation of at least two of these sculptures. I was keen on establishing myself as a wood sculptor and any opportunity at exposure helped me in this mission. In discussions with other sculptors and artists, upcoming shows usually motivate them to break out of their comfort zone and create new, stimulating work. The upcoming NCNS Dimensions show would be my opportunity!

Because of the earlier delays in sourcing wood blanks, only two months were available to develop new processes to create the sculptures. Poplar was selected as the wood for the inner core. Working with some rough planks, a series of uniform rift-sawn pieces were cut. Enough pieces were cut to create two large blanks (cores) with leftover pieces. The pieces were assembled in groups of four with alternating grain patterns. The four groups were then glued together to form the large blank **core**.

The alternating patterns of the inner rift-sawn wood strips would cancel each other out and considerably minimize or eliminate any wood movement. The criterion of dimensional stability was critical since thin veneer sheets were being applied to the exterior of the blank.

With any large amount of wood movement, the veneer sheets could crack and tear apart. The next phase would be to shape the form of the sculpture from the blank prior to applying the veneers. This process involved the creation of a template and then using a special instrument to create a fair curve along the length of the blank. The curved surfaces would need to be identical on each of the sides of the blank. I also decided to taper the shape of the sculpture towards the top to reduce the bulkiness of the wood. A tapered, organic shape would also be more pleasing to the eye. With the blanks complete, their surfaces were smoothed and flattened to ensure the veneer sheets would uniformly adhere along the four surfaces.

Applying the figured veneer sheets to the shaped core was the next part of the process. The veneered sheets were prepared earlier. The graphics of the veneers were selected to provide a harmonious, coherent flow from top to bottom. As well, the veneers were matched on each of the sides to give the appearance that the sculpture was carved from a large blank of wood. The veneer sheets were applied in pairs and then trimmed. The remaining veneer sides were then applied to the core with great care exercised. It became critical to ensure that each of the four sheets of veneer adhered properly to the core without air bubbles. As the sculptures evolved, I became increasingly excited!

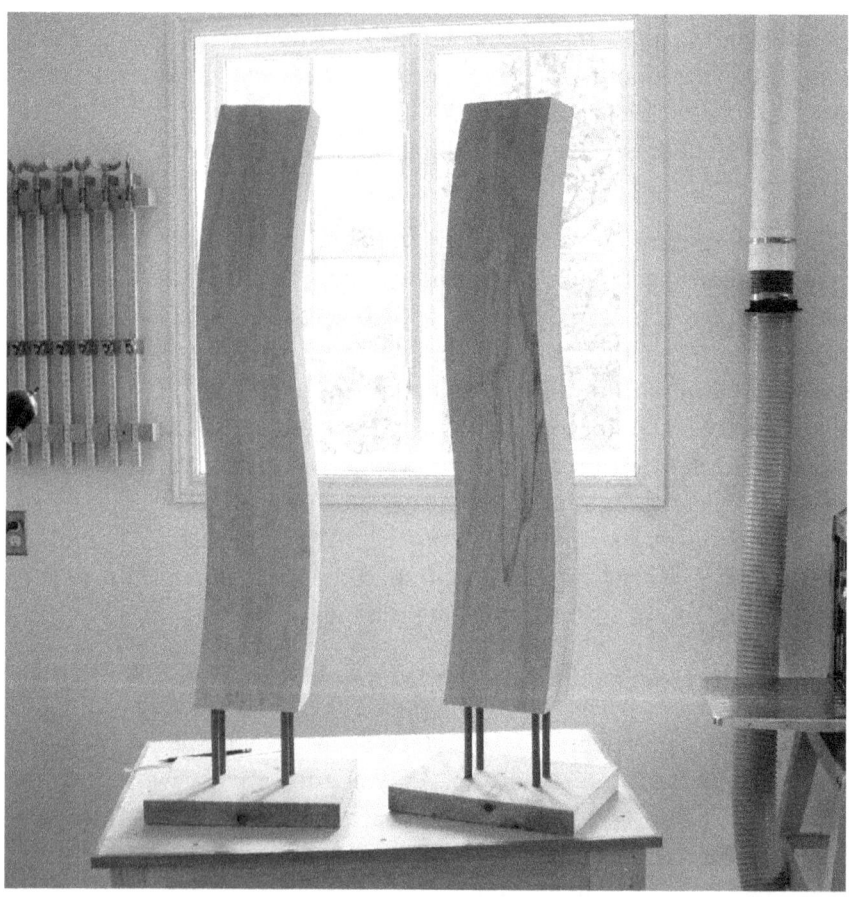

Making of **"On Fire"**. Temporary bases can be seen. Veneers have been applied to the assembled and shaped cores. Finishing is the next step.

It was the sheer size of the sculptures that held me in awe. Since the organic shape was based on a sinewy flame, the extra height of the sculpture introduced an extra curve that added to the appeal. At this stage both of the sculptures were impressive; they had not yet been mounted to their rosewood bases. The next step after sanding and scraping the veneered surfaces to a smooth feel would be to apply the infused dye color. I decided on an orange shade for one sculpture and a red shade for the second sculpture. The dyes were created and judiciously applied along each of the surfaces. A large amount of attention was necessary to ensure the dyes were properly and uniformly applied.

Once the dyes had dried, the veneered sides of the sculpture were once again ever so lightly sanded. Water-based dyes tend to raise the grain of wood and it was necessary to finely sand the surfaces afterwards to regain the smoothness. The last stage of the process was to apply the finish. In this case it would be the French Polish shellac method successfully used on my earlier sculpture series. This was performed over a period of days as each coat needed to be very thin. The clarity and depth of the figure is maintained through application of successive, thinned layers of clear shellac. After application of the finish, the surfaces were polished and rubbed down. A very thin final layer of shellac was then applied. At this stage, the rewards of my work could begin to be seen. The surfaces of the sculptures imparted a glow and sheen reminiscent of a mirror. The graphics of the wood appeared to be translucent with visual depth. The colored wood sculptures were outstanding!

Dark, rosewood bases which had already been prepared, were attached a short while later. I could not be more satisfied with the results. The sculptures were original and very organic in shape. The forty-inch length introduced enough curves into the design to easily distinguish the flame pattern. With weeks to go, creation of these two sculptures was completed, finishing touches applied, and they were entered into the NCNS Dimensions show a short time later. It was necessary for the organizers of the show to know the size and quantity of sculptures each artist brings well ahead of the show. This was to ensure adequate sized plinths were available and set up.

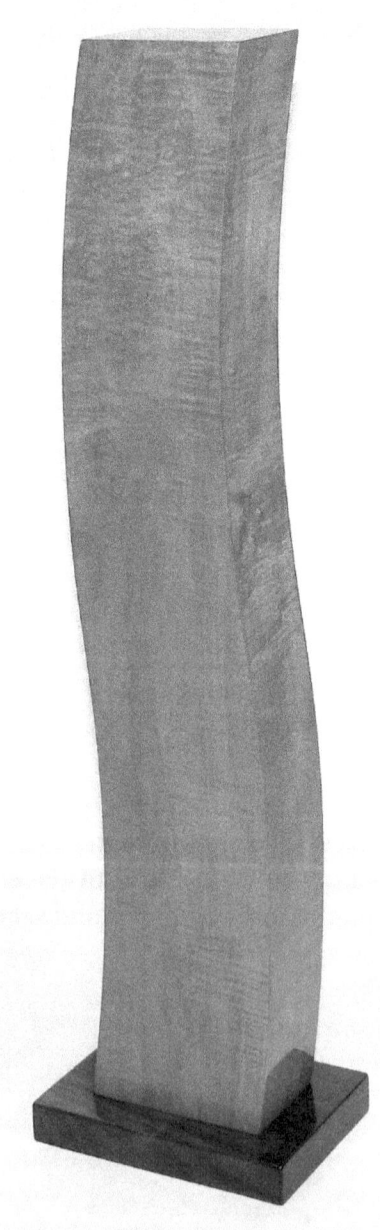

"*On Fire*", 2013. Highly figured dye-infused maple veneers on solid rift-sawn core. Rosewood base. Organic shaped sculpture, 40 in. tall.

The **Dimensions 2013** sculpture show was held in early September and was a success, as always. Attendance was high, especially on opening night. My volunteer task for this show had changed from the previous year. I was now tasked with publicity for the show. This particular task involves considerable timing and establishment of contacts. Accurate timing ensures that media organizations are notified early on of the dates for the event. Each media group has their own lead times for articles and exhibition announcements. The publicity task was performed over the few weeks leading up to the Dimensions 2013 sculpture show. Through my membership in the earlier arts organization **OWAA**, I had gained experience in performing the publicity task, but not on the scale of the Dimensions show. This publicity task allowed me to establish new contacts and to understand the process better. This new expertise could also be applied to next year's exhibition or any other arts organization I was a member of.

Three of my sculptures were submitted as entries in the **Dimensions 2013** sculpture show. The sculptures were all tall and considerably different from my single entry the year before. Each of the sculptures was mounted on its own plinth with adequate light for illumination. The reaction and interest my work generated throughout the show was high. Other sculptors also had their best and latest work on display that also garnered considerable interest. The regular patrons and visitors to this event look forward to it each year, as the work is fresh and exciting. Contacts were made and sales were generated. As well, the dialogue between artists and the public was invaluable. The interaction with the public is great and I enjoy answering questions and talking about my work. Interest from the public of my sculptures and work inspired me to continue in this genre.

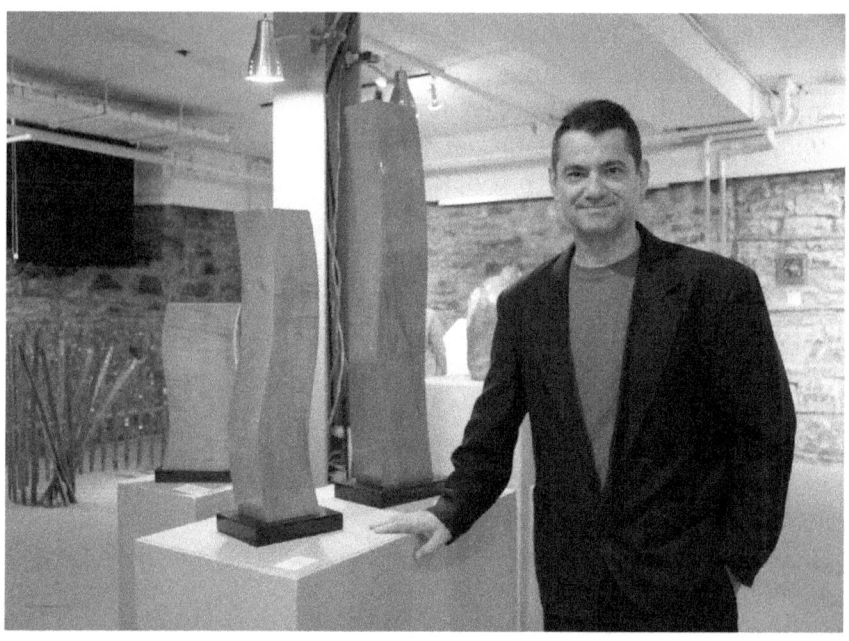

*"**Dimensions 2013**"* opening night, with my new series of sculptures
© 2015 Marc Lavoie – Courtesy Marc Lavoie Photography

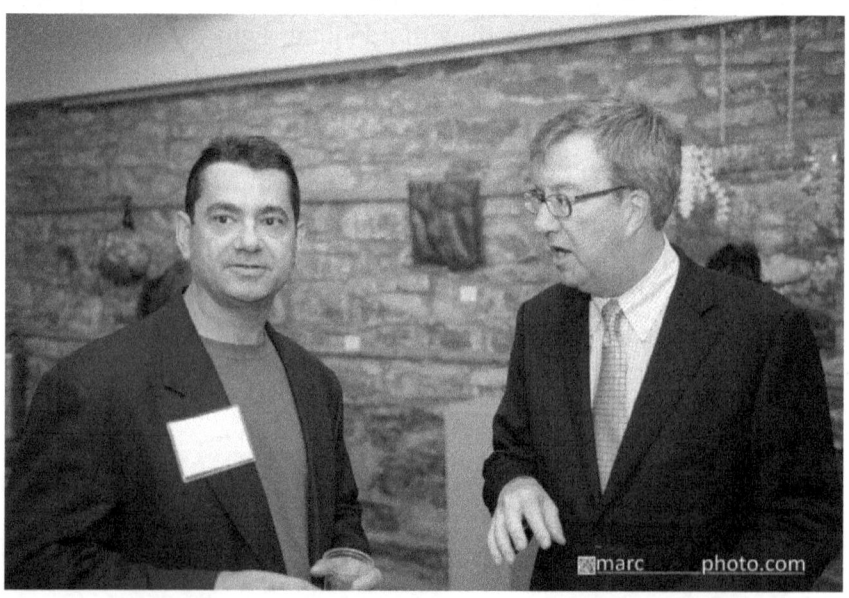

"**Dimensions 2013**" opening night, conversing with the mayor.

MICROSCOPY

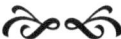

"To keep art stimulating, it's important to open it up to new horizons, which includes showing it in unexpected contexts"

Hans-Ulrich Obrist

DURING THE YEAR 2013, I stumbled upon a different form of art. A televised documentary I was watching featured the analysis of organic structures performed through a microscope. The microscope was an expensive, high power laboratory quality and the resulting images were astonishing. The organisms being examined were not live but thin slices extracted from common everyday food and plants in our environment. Watching in amazement, spectacular abstract images were displayed through the lens of the microscope. In many cases, the images were photographed. Another characteristic of the microscopic images was the wide array of colors visible through the lens. With limited exposure to microscopes aside from a brief interval in high school biology class, I watched and took mental notes. The scientists and biologists in the documentary were obviously professional, therefore making the process appear simple and straightforward.

The random, abstract nature of the images fascinated me as thoughts raced through my mind of using this technique to create a new form of art. The genre of art could be considered micro-organic art. I was willing to invest some time into exploring the possibilities of this micro-organic genre of art.

Through my background in technical research, the next logical step was to set some time aside to further explore this fascinating medium. Research into reasonably priced microscopes was next. The cost of the microscope was critical since investing considerable money into a piece of equipment I might later decide not to use was not practical. Having no access to temporary use of a microscope, my only option was to purchase one. The timing of this newfound interest in micro-organic art was perfect as a new microscope model was introduced around this time. This microscope featured a powerful built-in camera as well as the standard turret style objective lens mounts. The microscope was classified as professional level and the price was reasonable. I convinced myself at the time of the option to resell the microscope if the experiments were not satisfactory. Further research into **microscopy** reinforced my idea of exploring micro-organic photography as a form of art. On a leap of faith, I proceeded to order the microscope, as it was a special order.

Through the built-in camera, I would be able to directly photograph what was seen on the slides. There were questions, however. Was the camera powerful enough? Would I be able to successfully focus on the magnified image, as this was critical? Would the compositions be compelling enough to display as a form of art? How would the public react to micro-organic art? Would there be sufficient compositional difference between organisms to sustain this as a form of art?

All these questions occupied my mind before taking delivery of the microscope. In the meantime, research continued on microscopy and the techniques used to accomplish it. Since high school, I had no recollection of even preparing slides and would need to re-learn this process. Preparing slides and covering organic specimens with a cover glass was a process I would need to experiment with. Another technique to grasp was how and when to use the different objective lenses. In spite of many unknown variables facing me, I delved into microscopy. After receiving the new microscope along with prepared slides, the process began of learning how to view slides and photograph interesting organic compositions at the micro level.

Over a period of days, a few hours each day were spent observing the prepared slides that were packaged with the microscope. I soon found there to be a technique of using the rotating objective lenses. Slides were first viewed at low power (4x), then a higher power was dialed in (10x), and finally the most powerful objective lense (60x) was used to magnify the organic specimen at full power. In certain cases, it was not necessary to use the highest power objective lense as the cellular specimen would completely fill the digital display.

Once satisfied with the composition viewed on the digital display, a photo of it was snapped at the highest resolution. In many cases, a series of photos were necessary to obtain one with perfect focus. A series of colored filters could also be dialed in to change the colors viewed through the objective lenses. The combination of objective lenses and filters provided a few versions of each composition. Over a few days, my comfort level increased with the process. The next logical step would be to create my own slides.

During this experimental phase, research was also performed on the best organic specimens to view through the microscope. One of my criteria was not to have the composition appear to have originated from a microscope. Strange as it sounds, I was seeking an element of surprise when a person would view the image. Mentioning to them afterwards that it was a photograph originating from a microscope was central to the success of this form of art. In other words, I did not want the image to immediately appear to have originated through a microscope lens.

A short while later, a few glass slides of specimens under cover glass were prepared. The specimens were extremely thin slices of everyday fruits and vegetables. The slices were placed between the glass slide and the cover glass with the addition of a very small drop of water to create adhesion. The water would be placed at the edge of the cover glass and was drawn into the glass sandwich through capillary action. The process of creating these slides was largely trial and error with a few notes for guidance. Eventually, I mastered the process and it was then simply a matter of acquiring the best specimens to view through the microscope.

Acquiring exceptional specimens became the challenging part and it equated to panning for gold. It was critical to slice fruits and vegetables to exact thicknesses, dependant on the opacity of the specimen. Some fruits or vegetables were denser than others and thinner slices were necessary. The thickness of each specimen slice determined how much light was let through. The light passing through determined the appeal of the composition. It was critical not to have thick specimens which obscured light passing through.

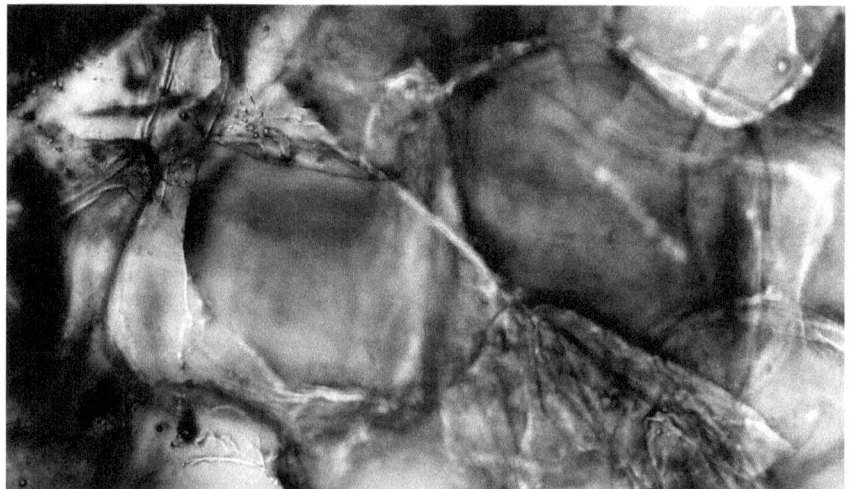

"Tranquility 1", 2013. Organic, microscopic abstract art composition

Although light levels from the lamp beneath the slice were variable, too much light would wash out the composition and remove any detail. I might come across as an expert in the subject now, but it was purely through trial and error that this process was learned. There were a few occasions when I almost gave up on this genre of art. It became frustrating at times to acquire a good composition worthy of a piece of art. The successful compositions were then enlarged and printed on to either canvas or paper. During this exploratory period, I also invested in a professional photo quality printer capable of accurately rendering colors. Printing of the art on to paper would also involve archival quality papers.

The inks in the printer were rated for 100 years longevity or greater without fading when placed in an album. With exposure to light, even if this claim was halved, it would be archival in quality. In a gallery or home setting, the colors would last decades before beginning to fade. The canvas versions of the prints were already archival in quality due to the application of a coating after the print was transferred on to the canvas.

The availability to offer the microscopy images in other media was not explored, as paper and canvas were the most common at the time. It was to be seen if the public would accept this genre of art. A few intriguing, high-quality images were then assembled into a small body of work. This was the very first step taken in order to introduce this form of art to the public. The initial body of work was printed on archival papers and mounted behind glass and then set in wood frames.

The next step was to seek opportunities where this work could be exhibited. To begin promoting the work and acquiring feedback, a few of the images were included at my art web site. The very first opportunity at exhibiting this genre of art occurred in early fall of 2013. A large juried exhibition was held once a year through an established arts organization Arts Ottawa East **AOE** and the exhibition was **Selections 2013**. Two of the first micro images acquired through the microscope were submitted. A few weeks later I was notified that the jury panel had selected one of the images for Selections 2013. A few high quality images were also submitted to a fund raising arts group exhibition, **Timeraiser**. A few weeks later confirmation was also received that the Timeraiser jury panel selected one of the images. Both these acceptances reaffirmed that this new genre of art was both appealing and stimulating. At **Timeraiser 2013**, the print on canvas was auctioned off for time instead of money. In exchange for the art, the recipient of the art volunteered a number of hours over a period of one year to one of a list of official **Timeraiser** charities.

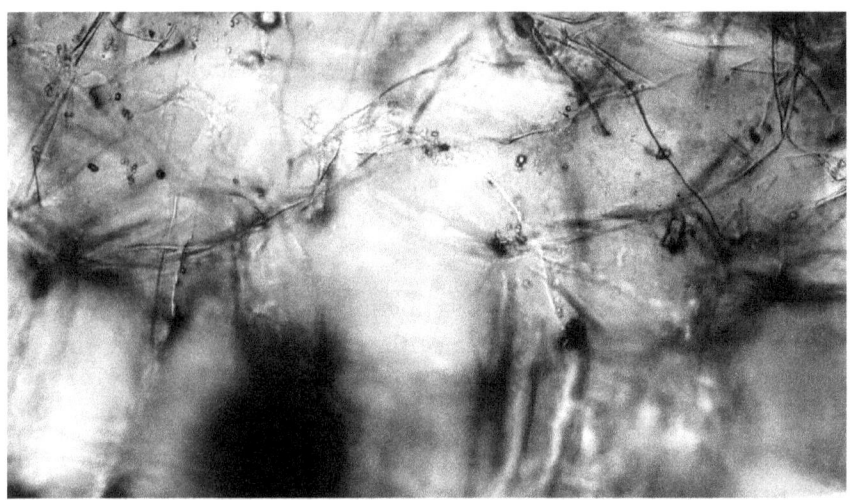

*"**Tranquility**"*, 2013. Timeraiser exhibition winning submission

The **Selections 2013** exhibition was held in late September 2013. The opening night was well attended and awards were handed out. Although my new microscopy artwork did not win an award, it drew considerable attention. The visitors to the exhibition were not sure if it was a photo of a painting or a digitally created work of art. It was neither of course, but instead an image of an organic structure at the microscopic level. The exhibition was held for a period of four weeks from late September to mid-October. Positive feedback from this first exhibition of the microscopy genre of art encouraged me to continue with the exploratory phase.

The **Timeraiser 2013** fundraiser was held approximately two months later. The event opening was a spectacular, classy affair. The presentation of the juried art pieces was very impressive. The venue itself was a large national museum and the exhibition was held in one of the outer foyers. The juried art pieces were displayed and rotated through a large, overhead screen. Bidders had ample opportunity to select which piece they wished to volunteer time for. They could also volunteer for more than one piece, as it was unlikely they would win more than one bid. I was pleasantly surprised, more like euphoric, at the number of bids for my artwork, *"Tranquility"*.

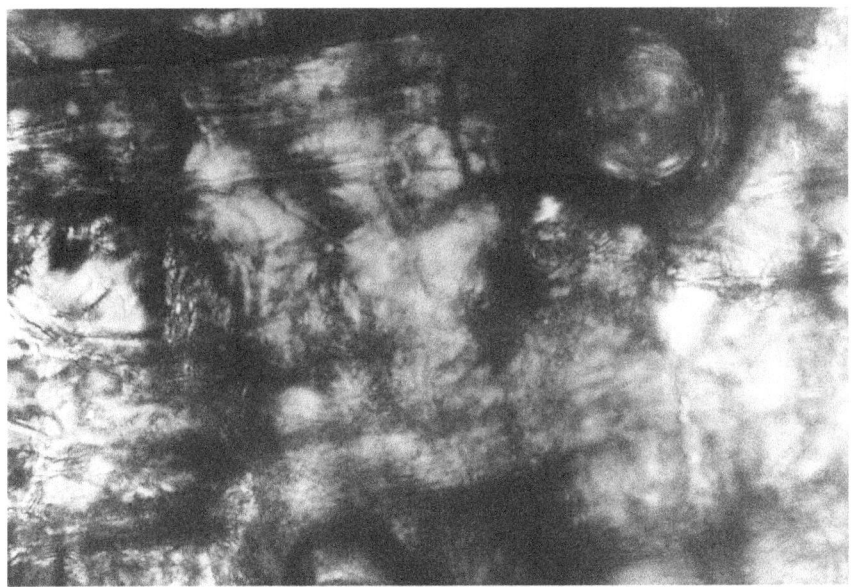

"Wildfire", 2013. Selections 2013 winning submission

Later in the event, winners of the bids were announced. I had the opportunity to see who won my art piece. The winning bidder does not actually receive the art piece until a year later at the same event. During the coming year, the art is hung at one of the corporate offices of a financial contributor to Timeraiser. Over the next year, the winning bidders complete their volunteer hours at the designated charity and are then handed the artwork. I admire and support the concept of this fund raising event.

The artists whose work is selected are also paid for their work at an already established price, relieving considerable pressure about making a sale at the event. Being a part of this event was thoroughly enjoyable and I was extremely glad that my artwork would soon be hanging in someone's home.

During the final months of 2013, further exploration of this form of art occurred and more images of abstract, organic microscopic art were gathered. Notes were taken as I progressed, and organic specimens producing the best results were documented. The best glass slides were also kept aside and marked.

Other glass slides that had questionable compositions were cleaned and reused. As the success rate of acquiring good micro-organic images increased, the body of work of this genre would slowly increase in size.

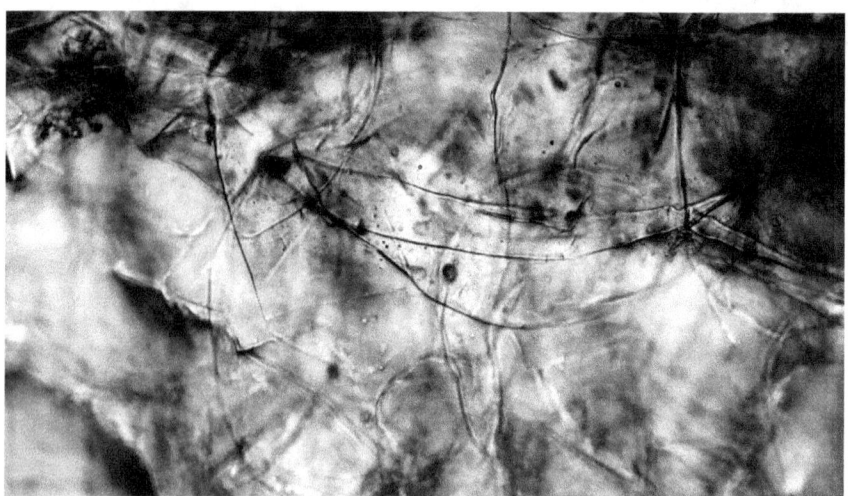

"*Fissure*", 2013. Organic, microscopic art, abstract composition

Over a period of weeks the images increased in depth and complexity. Although the microscope art was intended to be abstract, compositions were also sought which could easily be associated with a representational image. At the time, I was convinced this would raise the appeal of this genre of art. The number of slides accumulated was growing and as a result there were more available to draw from. Each organic specimen on a glass slide presented multiple possibilities of images. The specimens were not uniform in color, thickness or pattern. A thicker part of the specimen would obscure the light entering from under the stage and return a different view than from another part of the same slide.

An example of the compositions I was seeking can be seen in "*Abyss*" and "*Vertigo*". Both these images contain the varied color tones and hues approaching that of art created through painting. Having an abstract image with ties to realism was something I would need to explore further.

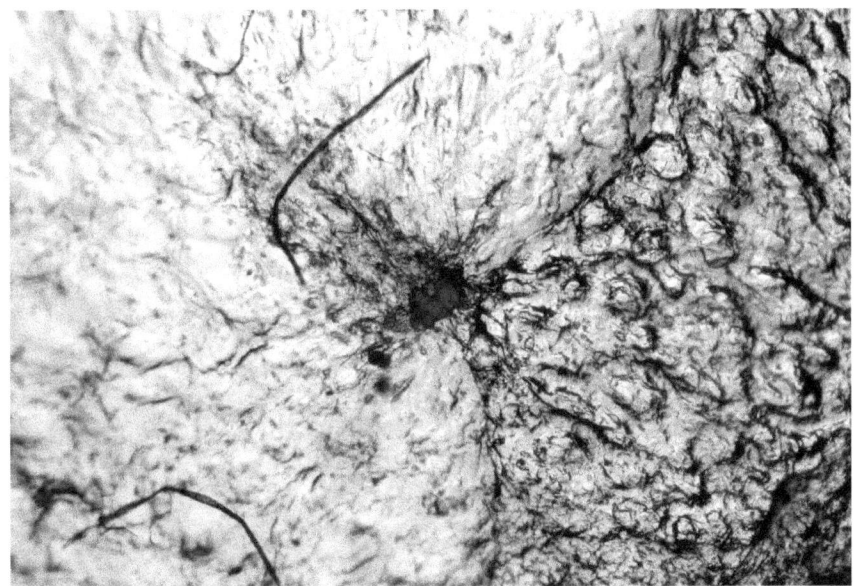

"***Abyss***", 2013. Organic microscope art, abstract composition.

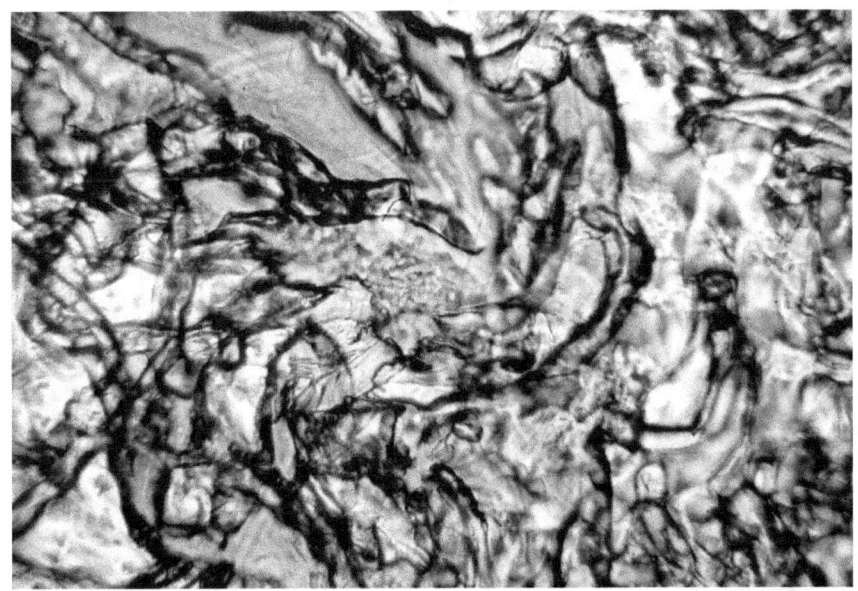

"***Vertigo***", 2013. Organic microscope art, abstract composition.

A specimen under the glass slide is initially damp. Drops of water are then applied for the glass cover plate to adhere to the underlying glass slide. The water is then absorbed by the specimen through capillary action. The specimen eventually dries out. Images photographed from a damp or dry specimen can vary considerably in composition. It was important to photograph as many different images as possible while the specimen was in either a damp or dry state. Tremendous positive feedback was received after posting the images on social media.

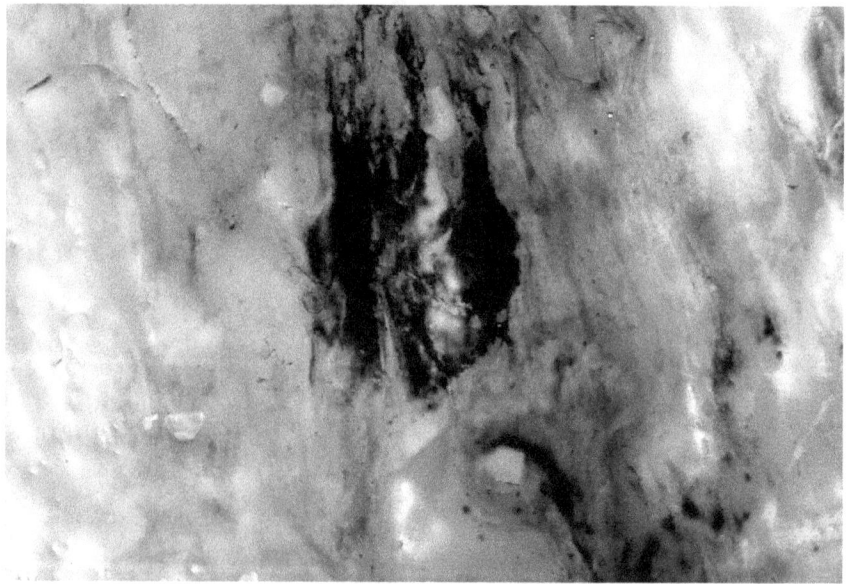

"*Captive In Light*", 2013. Organic micro art, abstract composition.

An opportunity to be part of a large group exhibition at the recently created **Lalande + Doyle Exhibition Space** became available in the final weeks of 2013. Each artist selected would have access to a large wall space where upwards of 8-10 artworks could be hung.

Since the body of work I had accumulated was sufficiently large, a proposal was drawn up and submitted to the jury for this exhibition. Within a few weeks, the great news was received that my entry was accepted. This was to be my third exhibition within months of this new genre of work.

Work began on assembling a dozen or so exceptional images of the microscopy work that were then printed on special archival papers. The prints were then mounted in a series of white frames that were both uniform in size and cohesive in color and style, essentially using similar frames throughout. It was important to not have the frames detract from the artwork. Since the frames were all similar and uniform in size, the focus of the viewer would instead be on the artwork.

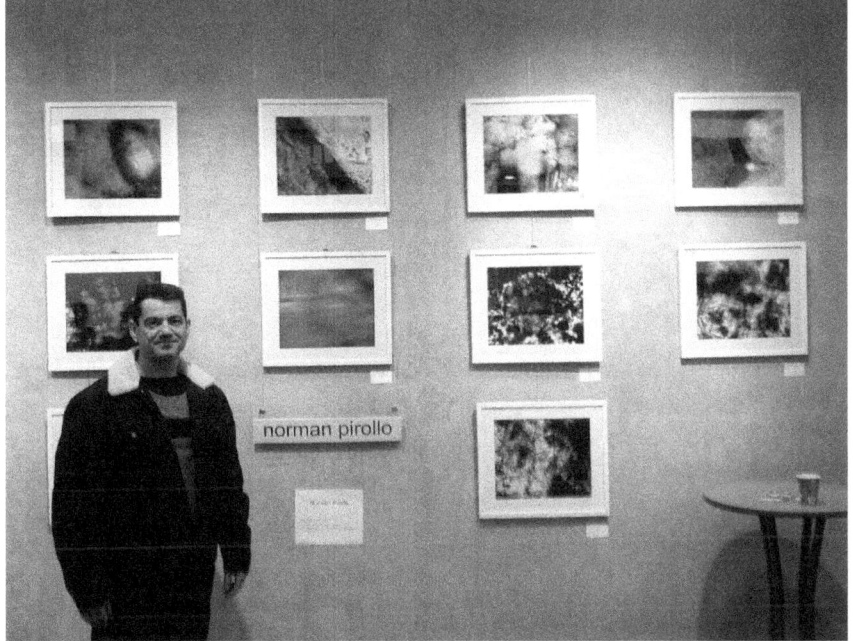

"Lalande + Doyle Exhibition Space" December 2013

Over a period of one week, visitors were able to view the art in the group exhibition. A few people left glowing compliments of my work and I met with several more at the opening event. The exhibition was a great success and inspired me to go further with this form of art. This genre of art was a considerable departure for me as I had entered the same exhibition two years earlier with my wood wall art.

MICRO PAINTING

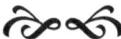

"The art of an artist must be his own art. It is...always a continuous chain of little inventions, little technical discoveries of one's own, in one's relation to the tool, the material and the colors."

Emil Nolde

IN EARLY 2014, although satisfied with the direction of the microscopic art, I felt that acquiring the ideal abstract composition was increasingly becoming a challenge. It was, as I like to say "panning for gold". Although impressive at first, frustration began to set in after a while. Countless hours were spent seeking optimal compositions. In my search, the criteria used were interesting colors, organic shapes, subtle hues and tones, and clarity. Often a feeling of déjà vu was experienced as slide after slide was observed. The lack of control in what was being observed manifested itself more than once. Increasingly, I felt the need to be able to create my own compositions. Using glass slides prepared with organic substances relied heavily on the uniqueness of the subject matter. After many weeks, every slide began to look like I had seen it before.

In light of this dilemma, I began to re-think microscopy as a viable form of art. There were occasions when I threw my hands up and was ready to drop it all. One day, while seeking an optimal composition, I had a revelation. A particular slide being examined did not have a glass cover plate over the organic specimen.

The reason was the specimen was a little too thick for the cover plate to adhere to the lower glass slide and was simply left off. The specimen was transparent enough to allow sufficient light through so this was not a problem. Care was exercised to not let the objective lens come in contact with the slides. In this case, this became even more critical. Objective lenses physically vary in length and when rotating the turret, care must be taken to lower the stage holding the slide to accommodate the lenses. If a glass cover plate is not placed over a specimen, the possibility of contaminating the objective lens increases if it comes in contact with the specimen.

On this occasion, while carefully raising and adjusting the stage, the lense inadvertently did come in contact with the specimen on the glass slide. Not realizing this at first, I proceeded to adjust the position of the slide as I would normally do. The specimen on the slide did not touch the glass of the objective lense but instead the metal casing. As the slide was adjusted from front to back and from side to side, the composition was being modified. The composition was now changing as the slide was moved around. Normally, the composition is fixed and an image is obtained. By moving the slide, a new composition would form. More interesting compositions could now be acquired from each slide instead of the previous limitation of a fixed composition. I was intrigued by this effect and wanted to explore it further.

The effect involved the movement of the specimen on the glass slide. Next, a slide was created and installed on the stage as would normally be done. The difference was the lack of glass cover plate. Without a cover plate, the specimen could be manipulated to modify the image captured. To achieve this effect, a small tool with a needle at one end was developed. The needle would allow me to maneuver or move the specimen. I was now able to successfully re-create the new effect without touching the objective lense to the specimen.

This opened my eyes to a new level of creativity in this form of art. Transforming an organic specimen on the glass slide could essentially create new abstract compositions. Over the next few days, experiments were performed using the tool with the needle at one end referred to earlier. To reduce the viscosity of the specimen to better maneuver it, a small drop of colored dye or water was added.

Using this method, the tip of the needle could be used to lightly re-arrange the composition in order to transform the image. The experiments were a success and the abstract compositions were captivating. No longer was I limited to the image of a fixed specimen. Specimens could be transformed dynamically and new abstract compositions created. By also adding a drop of colored dye to the specimen, this sufficiently changed what was seen on the display. The exploratory phase continued!

An issue that had manifested itself time and again was the resolution of the built-in microscope camera being used. The camera, although powerful, was not a high-resolution camera. It was a camera with medium resolution. The images gathered from the glass slides were intended to be printed onto either fine photo quality papers or canvas. There is a direct correlation between the number of pixels in an image and the maximum size of print that can be created from it. With the built-in microscope camera, I was limited to average size prints. If larger prints were required, more pixels or a more powerful camera was necessary. The camera in the microscope was limiting the size of prints that could be generated. This was going to be an issue since I had planned on marketing my prints in large sizes.

In light of this, other options than the microscope were considered. The only other option would be to search for a microscope with a more powerful built-in camera. After some searching and research, it appeared my microscope was the most powerful microscope and camera combination short of a very high-priced laboratory model. It was critical to get around the megapixel limitation if I wanted to continue with this genre of microscopy and micro painting. The only option that made any sense would be to use a high-resolution DSLR camera to obtain the images. A high-resolution DSLR camera could obtain images an order of magnitude larger than the built-in camera of the microscope. The optics in DSLR cameras were also considerably better than that of a digital camera embedded into a microscope. I had experience using a macro lens in a DSLR camera of mine. A macro lens was used to obtain detailed close-up images of day-to-day household objects. The resolution of the DSLR camera was twice as high as that of the built-in microscope camera.

With all these requirements and options to work with, I was curious as to whether the DSLR camera would be able to take photos of small specimens placed on a glass slide. After further experiments with the DSLR camera combined with a macro lens, it became obvious that the specimen size was too small to clearly photograph. A large, square sheet of glass was instead used as the platform for the slides. Raising the supports for the glass to enable light to enter from below was the next step. Using a small LED flashlight to illuminate the slide from below, I was better able to photograph the specimen. The goal was to be able to use the DSLR with its much-improved optics and high resolution to photograph glass slides. This rudimentary testing was only temporary, as I had no idea whether the camera and lens combination was up to the task.

It was soon apparent that I would need a better setup, one where the DSLR camera was fixed in position with the glass slide below. When photographing at the macro level, focusing on the object becomes extremely important. The slightest movement of the camera could essentially ruin a good image. Handholding a camera for this type of photography can be challenging. For this reason, macro photography is normally performed with use of a tripod. A tripod was temporarily set up to have the camera facing down onto the raised sheet of glass supporting the glass slide. The glass slide was in turn illuminated from below. The images of the specimens being captured were now of much higher quality.

Since the last experiment was a success, a permanent camera stand was considered, one that would allow me to perform both coarse and fine adjustments. Since auto focus does not work well when photographing at an extremely small macro level, the DSLR camera would need to be manually focused. I began to design and make a stand for the camera. The stand would feature a coarse and fine adjustment, and the camera would be attached to the stand through a ball head mount. The ball head mount would allow me to tilt the camera to ensure it is in the same plane as the glass slide. In a further experiment, a small sheet of glass raised on all four corners was installed. Once again, it was illuminated from below. The sheet of glass was a number of times larger than the previous glass slides.

Next, an organic specimen was placed over the sheet of glass and a small amount of colored dye applied to it. The colored dye would allow me to maneuver and transform the image to a level of abstraction that was satisfactory to me.

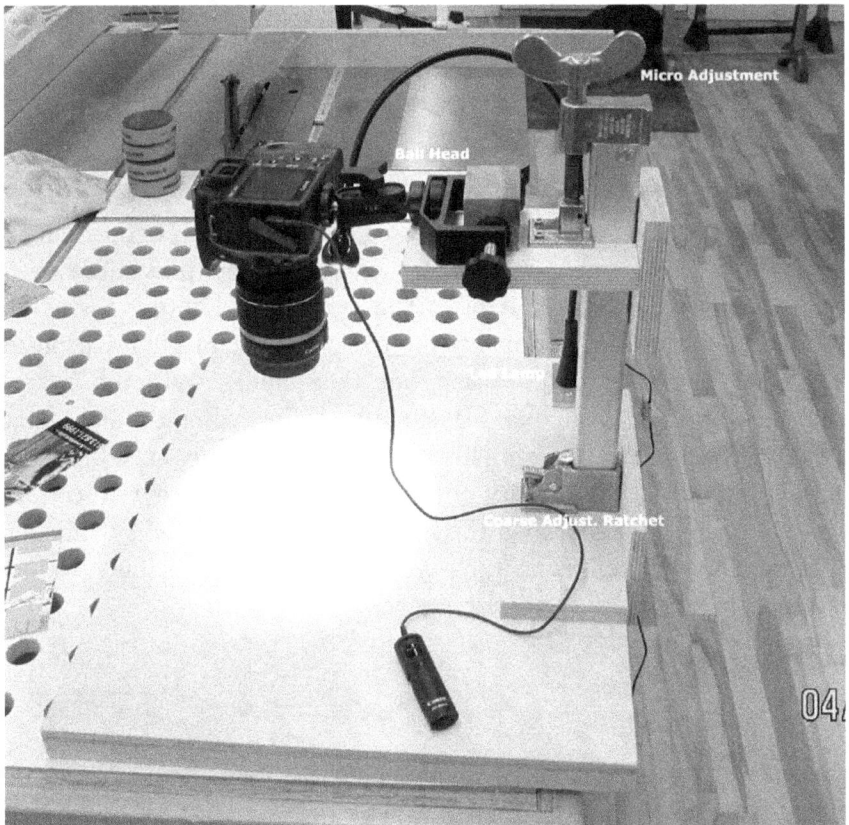

Camera stand with ball head attachment and remote shutter release

The specimen could also be re-arranged afterwards to create a new abstract composition. To perform this, I once again utilized the tool with a long, fine needle at its tip. The specimen placed on the glass was now larger than the earlier specimens applied to the glass slides. With the additional glass surface available, the size of the specimens could also be increased. The increased size would also work better with the camera and macro lens setup. As I progressed through the learning curve, the results were improving with each experiment.

The resolution achieved with the DSLR camera was now high enough to be able to create large prints with great clarity and depth. The excitement around this new process and technique was increasing!

The original images from the microscope were limited to a maximum of 2 Megapixels. Using the DSLR camera, images in the 15 to 17 Megapixel range could now be obtained. This dramatically increased the quality of each image; the size of the images could easily be expanded to create extra large prints. With this all in mind, I set out to create a new adjustable surface or stage for the specimens.

Using my knowledge of woodworking, a small box with built-in illumination was created. The sheet of glass used previously was installed as a cover for the box. The box, with lighting installed, essentially became a light box. I found the LED lamp originally used to be too powerful; it would wash out the images. Without a less powerful LED lamp available, I decided to simply filter the light that emanated from the LED lamp. This was performed using masking tape. The tape increased the opacity of the light and, therefore, reduced its strength. Use of tape softened the light considerably to where images of the specimens taken from above were no longer washed out.

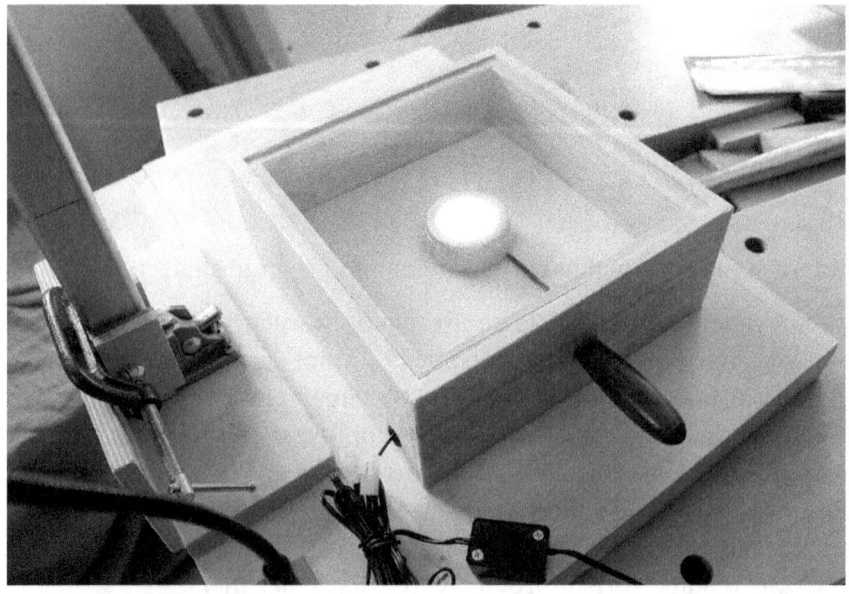

Light box used to create abstract compositions of organic specimens

Further experiments with light levels provided me with improved images. The light was necessary to softly illuminate the specimen from below. Too much light would cause the light sensor in the camera to overcompensate and affect the white balance. Attempts at adjusting the exposure compensation to lower the light sensitivity were made, in the hope that this would overcome the high level of light from below. The only solution was to dramatically reduce the light level coming from below the glass surface by partially obscuring the lamp with tape. Once I felt comfortable with this part of the setup, experiments continued with organic specimens applied to the glass surface.

With the large glass surface, I began to create larger specimens and then adding colored dye to them. The needle instrument created earlier was also used to transform images into intriguing compositions. Since the focus of the camera lense was manually adjusted, a remote shutter was installed to prevent movement of the camera stand while photographing the image below.

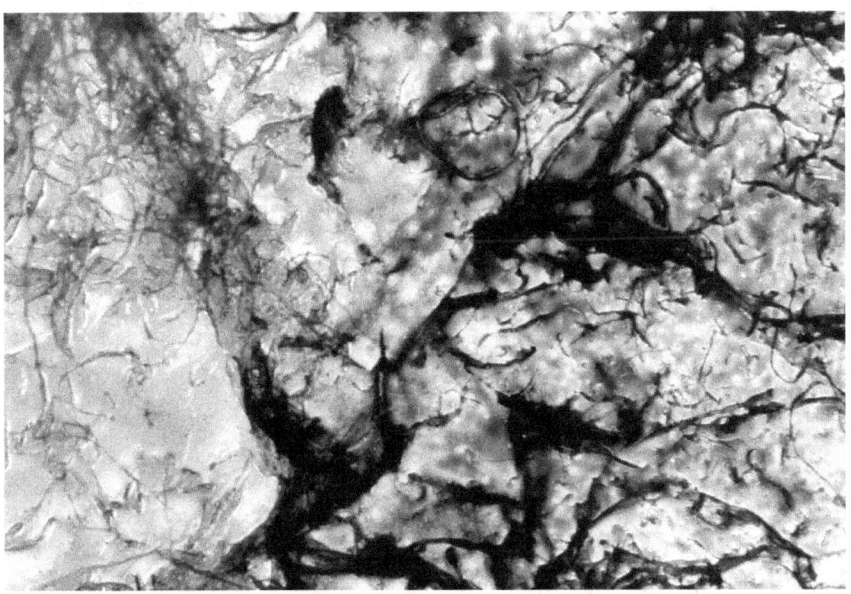

An early image captured using the camera stand and light box

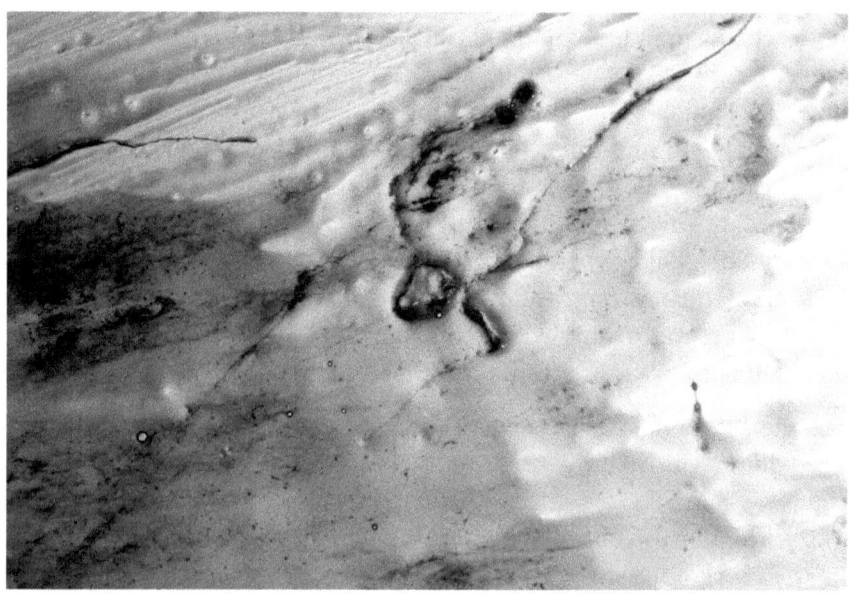

Another early image captured using the camera stand and light box

The images being captured using this setup and method were captivating. Several intriguing abstract compositions could be achieved by merely manipulating the specimen on the glass surface multiple times. The limitation of a unique slide and single composition was no longer an issue as with the earlier microscope setup. Introducing minute fibers into the composition also emulated the fine lines of an abstract painting. The fibers could be randomly arranged to create an abstraction. The wide palette of colors I could now work with was also greatly appealing.

Through the use of colored dyes, both vivid, solid colors and blended colors could be emulated. The process of creating the compositions was very much like painting except a needle was used instead of brushes. At this small scale, maneuvering the needle was similar to working a brush. Exceptional care had to be made not to muddy the composition. If the specimen with colored dyes began to increase in opacity, light entering from below would not permeate the specimen, thereby creating a dark image.

This is a similar phenomenon to blending paints on a canvas, as too much blending can easily muddy the color. I quickly realized a steady hand was necessary to work the compositions at this micro level. The edge of the light box was a very good place to lay my palm down while using the needle instrument. It was interesting how the skills to perform this micro level painting developed with use. As I progressed from composition to composition, my right hand developed a motor skill to steadily control the needle instrument. Being left-handed, the camera stand and light box were positioned to my right where my right hand would guide the needle instrument.

The challenge arose in calibrating the camera to focus the image. As mentioned earlier, there is no automatic focusing at the micro level of photography. It becomes critical to manually adjust the coarse and fine adjustments of the camera on the stand. To further increase the fine adjustment, a long wood lever was installed over the wing nut used for fine adjustments. The long lever would allow me greater precision in raising and lowering the camera and ball head assembly.

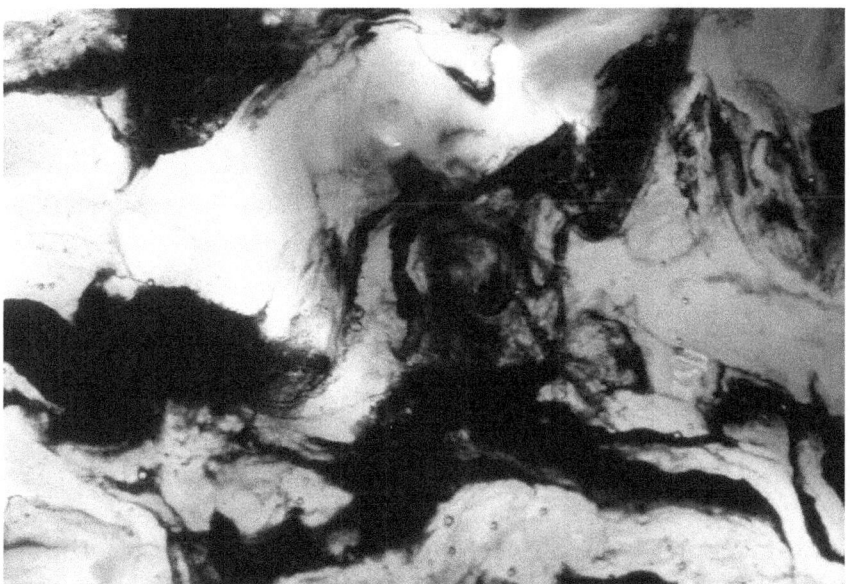

Above, an excellent example of the use of color and dark lines to create an abstract composition. Light from below can be seen permeating the colored specimen.

Since the resulting images from the new DSLR camera stand and light box were of high quality, I decided to experiment with non-organic specimens. The variety of specimens available was limitless. Everything from fibers to oil droplets can be photographed at this level. Photography of the surfaces of shells with concentric patterns, crystals, and other inanimate objects was performed next. The objects would need to allow a certain amount of light to permeate through for maximum effect. The back lighting created a three dimensional effect of the specimen.

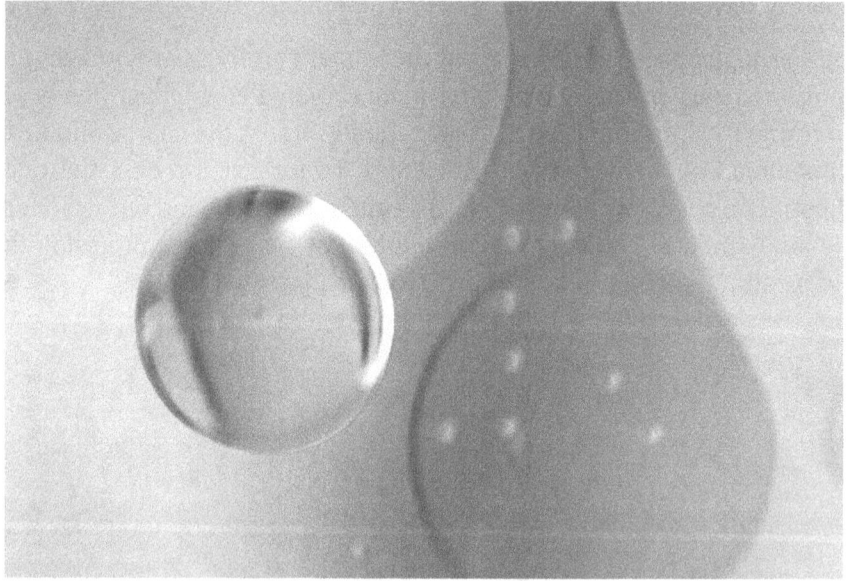

An image of a droplet of oil suspended in a lightly dyed fluid.

The images were extremely captivating and generated considerable interest. As I began to move away from microscopy and towards micro painting, the composition was now in my control. The composition could easily be transformed to my liking. Images of inanimate objects, although intriguing, were ultimately not the direction I wished to pursue. Working with various liquids and dyes to create abstract compositions was my goal. Using this technique, a painting on a canvas could be emulated but on a much smaller scale. The effect of having the composition back lit would create the three dimensional effect I was seeking.

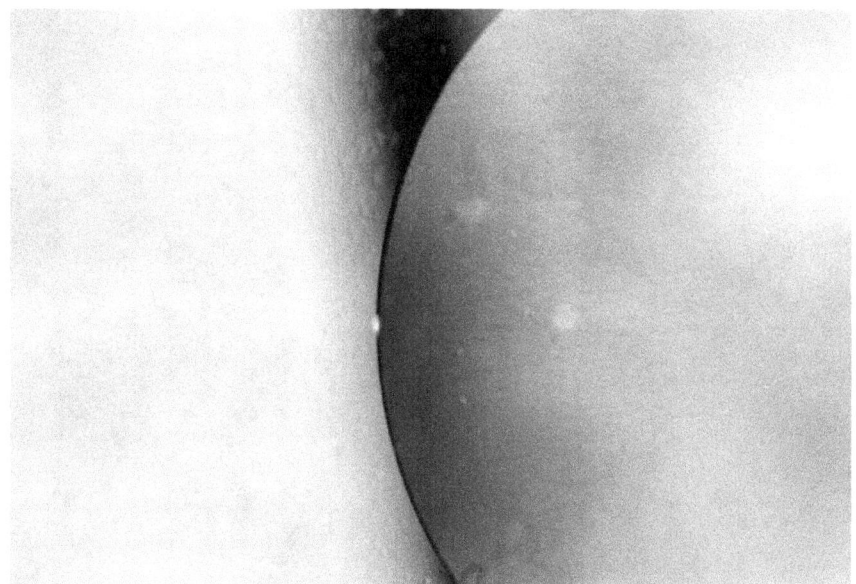

Captivating abstract composition using oil suspended in liquids.

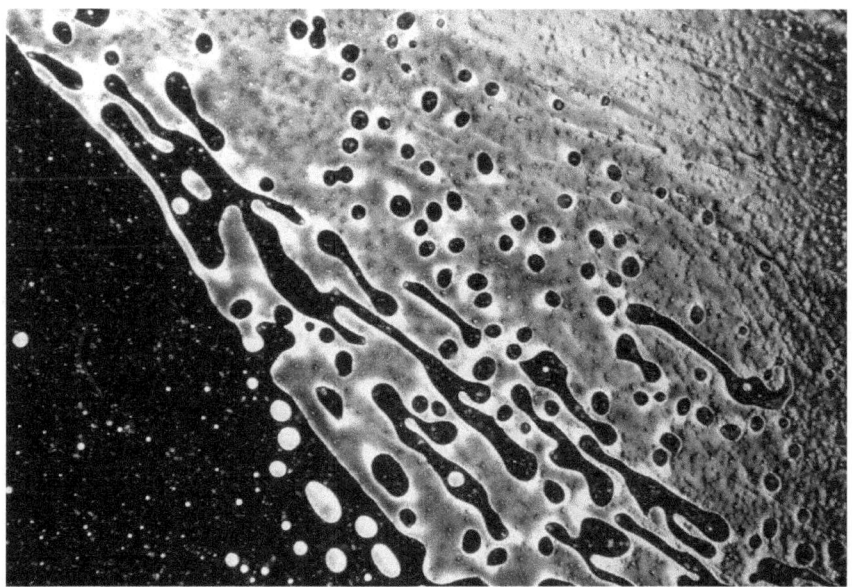

"*Outer Limits*", 2014. Abstract composition using colored dyes an infinitesimally small drop of oil over a glass plate.

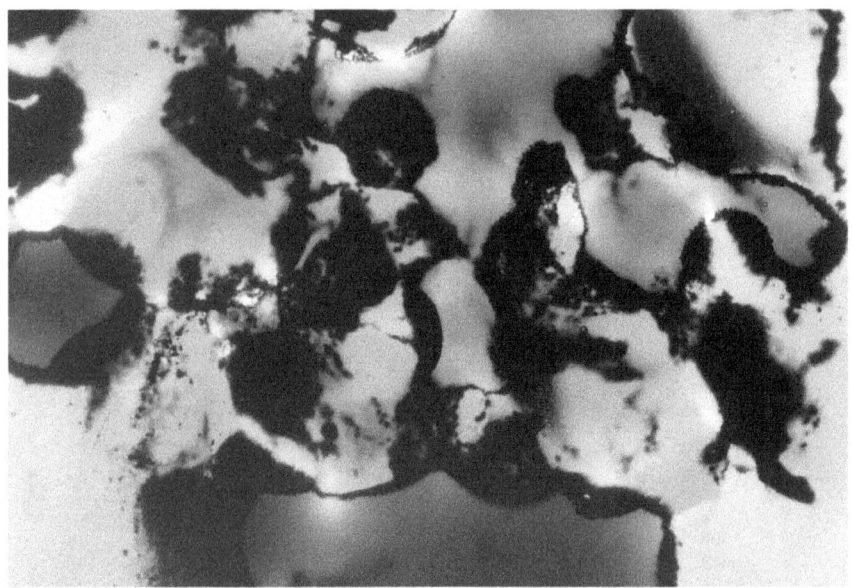

"*Mélange 4*", 2014. Introducing a more colorful palette to the colored dye specimens.

The opportunities available to me with this new form of abstract art creation were unlimited. An immense number of compositions could be created from a palette of colored dyes combined with small fibers. The fibers would delineate colored areas on the glass surface. Developing the skills and techniques to perform this using fine point needle tools was however the challenge.

Next, a tether arrangement was set up where the image seen by the camera was displayed directly on a computer display. This provided a larger viewing area than the small screen on the DSLR camera. With the large computer display viewing size, focusing of the colored dye specimen was also improved. Due to the lack of auto-focus at these macro levels of photography and the resulting low tolerance for even the slightest vibration, the camera stand was reinforced to improve its rigidity. The height of the camera over the light box was fixed and only fine, manual adjustments were then necessary. The camera could therefore be locked in and secured at a pre-determined height over the light box. Acquiring focus through fine adjustments was time consuming but the results were well worth it.

The creation of these abstract images at the micro level encouraged me to explore abstract art further. I began to study the different abstract art movements and styles. Abstract art evolved over time in the form of art movements and periods. Abstract art movements and periods differentiate the various styles of abstract art from one another. It was interesting to discover how abstraction began as an alternative method of viewing an image.

Impressionism (1870-90), one of the earliest forms of abstraction, was essentially a mild abstraction of an objective or representational image. Over the next years and decades, abstract art slowly evolved from the Cubism, Surrealist, Fauvist and Bauhaus "**De Stijl**" movements to its current form. Abstract art today is not objective or representative of an image. In its purest form, abstract art does not represent an actual scene or image. It is up to the viewer of the art to determine what they see in the art. The abstract art genre became the direction I wished to explore further.

The definitive abstract subgenre, which defines complete abstraction, is Abstract Expressionism. In this style of abstract art, the painting is created using gestural movements of the brush and other tools. The gestural movements are influenced and directed through the sub-conscious or unconscious mind. In other words, very little thought is placed into the creation of the composition. The composition instead becomes an extension of the subconscious mind. Through my increasing interest in abstract expressionism, I wanted to apply this new knowledge to painting on canvas. Until this time, only micro level scale images were created which were then transferred to either fine papers or canvas. The act of creating a full size painting intrigued me. I decided to explore painting and began the process of learning as much as possible about painting on canvas. Painting at full scale on a canvas would satisfy my ambition of becoming a well-rounded artist. Delving further into abstract expressionism, the urge to paint abstracts increased. My curiosity grew as to where this would lead me. Perhaps painting full size abstract artwork was to be my destiny after all?

PATH TO EXPRESSIONISM

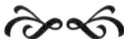

"The vitality of a new Movement in art must be gauged by the fury it arouses"

Logan Pearsall Smith

MY ADMIRATION FOR ABSTRACT or non-objective art had its origins in my microscopy and micro painting work. In a short time, I began to realize that abstract art is not what it appears to be; it is not simple and straightforward to create. Creating an abstraction that draws a viewer in is a skill involving considerable expertise and a liberated mind. Having been in the art world for a relatively short time precluded me from experiencing the creation of representational, objective art. Instead, I began my journey into the creation of art of the abstract genre.

It might be said that this was advantageous since it was not necessary to switch from a previous genre. Had I been painting objective art and made the decision to instead create abstract work, it would perhaps be a difficult transition to make. Since this was not an issue, I enjoyed the freedom to explore abstract painting to its fullest. Immersing myself into the different abstract art periods, I read how many well know abstract painters were formerly representational painters. As I became informed of the various abstract art movements and periods, it was the evolution of abstract, non-objective art that intrigued me. The Abstract Expressionism genre had drawn me in and motivated me to create art.

In the following pages, a series of art movements considered to be modern art movements, are discussed. The evolution of art in these modern art movements shifts from the very mild abstraction of Impressionism to complete abstraction in the later Expressionist movements. The progression of these modern art movements is discussed to provide context for my own abstract artwork. This series of modern art movements had an influence on **Abstract Expressionism**, the movement on which my current art style is based. In my art history studies, it was the modern art movements that fascinated me the most. It was typical for each of these movements to react against earlier movements. In some cases, it was the same artists of a previous art movement who then formed a later movement. The later art movement reacted against or repudiated an earlier movement. Needless to say, the latter decades of the 19th century to the first few decades of the 20th century were a dynamic period in the art world!

Until the late 19th century, all art was figurative or objective. In the final decades of the 19th century a new art movement was formed. The **Impressionists** sought to create a new style of art, which was not purely representational. The artists that formed this movement wanted to break away from creating accurate, realistic depictions of scenes and figures. Instead, their goal was to depict a slightly blurred image, one that might be seen from the corner of an eye. The introduction of lighter palettes, loose brush strokes and ambiguity in the composition created an abstracted view of a realistic scene instead. The paintings were purposely created to be vague and not to be clear and defined. It was up to the viewer to complete the composition and form a realistic image. It was as though the impressionist artist wanted a quick painting of a scene, one that lent itself well to "**plein air**" painting with quickly changing light conditions. Another school of thought advocates that Impressionism was a direct result of the introduction of photography. Until the advent of photography, painted depictions of scenes and figures were common since there was no other method to record a scene or image. The advent of photography changed this. With the introduction of photography in the final decades of the nineteenth century, it was possible to capture images without the need for a drawing or painting.

Impressionism, a new modern form of art, was designed to create an abstracted view of a scene or figure. This genre of art was thought to once again bring excitement to art. Claude Monet was perhaps the most well-known of the Impressionist painters. **Impressionism** is considered to be the precursor to the abstract art movements that followed. It was the first modern art movement which distanced itself from accurate and clear depictions of images. It was left to the viewer of the art to establish a connection between the art and a realistic scene. Using the optical effect of light and the viewer's perception, the viewer could complete the image in their mind. Impressionism was very controversial in its time. Until it was introduced, art was expected to clearly depict a scene or figure. The subject matter of Impressionist paintings was also controversial, where everyday scenes of people were painted instead of contrived images. The paintings depicted the underclass as much as higher-class society. The Impressionist movement, which included Claude Monet and Paul Cezanne, was seminal in changing the face of modern day art. Once the movement became established, reluctance to accept this genre of art was short-lived and Impressionism was embraced.

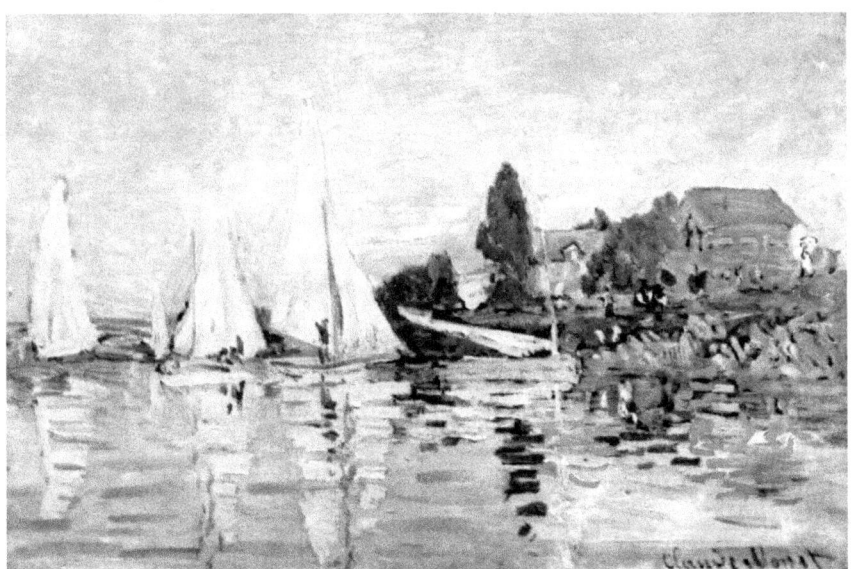

Claude Monet, *"Régate à Argenteuil"*, 1872. Impressionist painting.

The art movements that followed Impressionism continued to distance themselves from reality. Instead, reality became juxtaposed as in Cubism and Surrealism. Art movements of the late nineteenth and early twentieth century came fast and furious. It was though the Impressionist movement opened the door to new, radical forms of art. Realism, objective and representational forms of art had existed for centuries. Art movements leading up to Impressionism slowly improved upon the depiction of realistic scenes and figures. Technical advances in the Renaissance period brought realistic art to new levels through the introduction of perspective and vivid, rich colors.

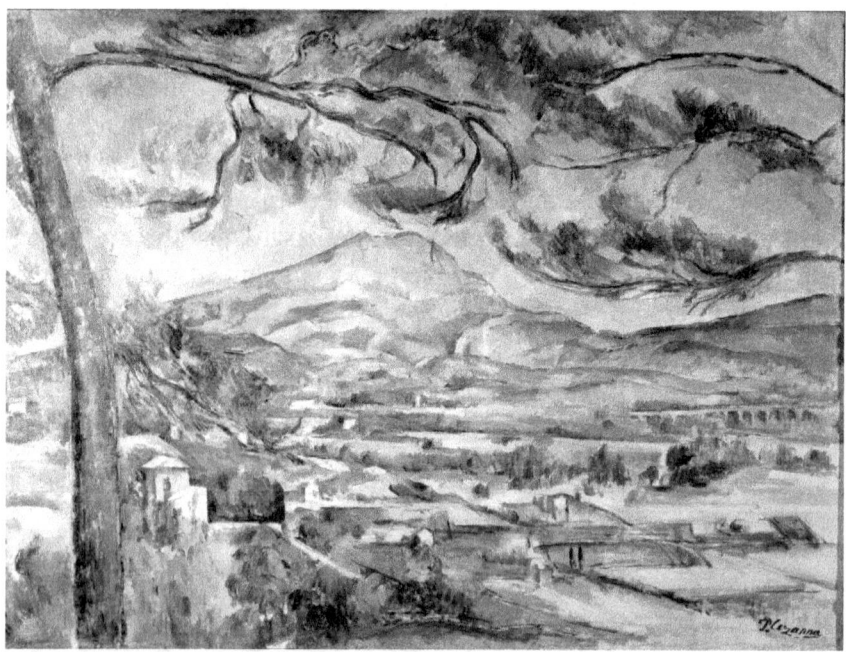

Paul Cézanne, "*Mont Sainte-Victoire*", 1887. Impressionist painting.

Until the advent of Impressionism, it can be said that there were no further advances possible in the depiction of realistic scenes and figures. Conventional art movements had plateaued. People were perhaps seeking a new form of art and the Impressionist movement filled this desire and need. A wave of art movements beginning in the early twentieth century built upon the radicalism of Impressionism. Symbolism was the first of the movements to follow Impressionism.

In this movement, Impressionist brushstrokes were combined with symbolism and patterned backgrounds. Through Symbolism, depictions of reality became even more distant. The **Post-Impressionism** movement quickly followed at the turn of the nineteenth century and into the twentieth century. The Post-Impressionism movement was created in reaction against Impressionism. The tenets of Impressionism, light and atmosphere, were instead replaced with color theory and feelings. The series of art movements, developed in quick succession, were relatively short-lived as artists continually explored new styles and forms of art. The best known painters of the Post-Impressionist movement were perhaps Edward Munch, Vincent Van Gogh and Cezanne. The art of Edward Munch and Vincent Van Gogh was considered to be the earliest form of Expressionism, an art form which embodied art as a form of expression. Post-Impressionism art moved away from the embodiment of nature to a more expressive form of art, one which was based on emotions within the artist.

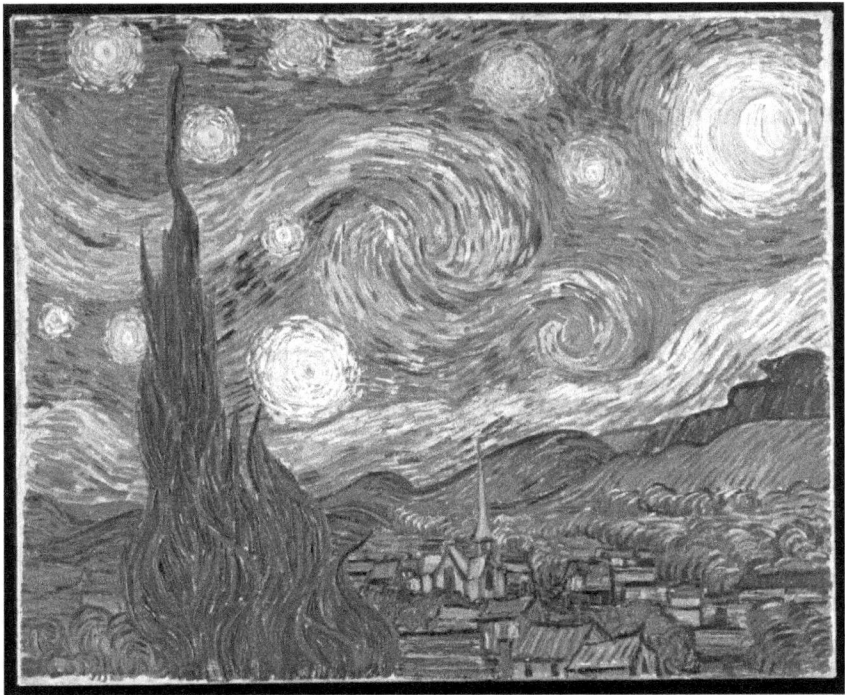

Vincent Van Gogh, **"*Starry Night*"**, 1887. Post-Impressionist painting.

At the turn of the 20th century, photography began to gain momentum as an acceptable medium. It became quicker to have a photograph taken of an image than to have it created using a paintbrush. Due to the advent of photography, the distortion of painted images on a canvas became more appealing as a form of art. Since this technique could not be performed through a camera lens, it once again raised the appeal of art. The language of art slowly evolved into providing an alternative, distorted view of nature and figures. The various art movements that followed Post-Impressionism all sought to create a unique, alternative genre of art in opposition to realism.

Successive art movements, which followed in the early part of the twentieth century, embraced the developing trend against realism. At this point in history, there was such a preponderance of representational and figurative art in circulation that perhaps people demanded a new, different form of art? Were artists themselves getting bored with the accurate depictions in representational painting? Had the development of photography become the tipping point for artists? Was the creation of art similar to the art of a few years earlier no longer stimulating and rewarding?

In my view, these forces came together to spur change in this unique period in history. Art would need to grow within the new, modern era that was upon the world.

The first of the 20th century movements was Fauvism. **Fauvism** (1898-1906) used color to differentiate itself from other art movements. An intense, artificial color palette was used instead of realistic, natural colors. The mix of colors in a painting often clashed and served to dramatize the other elements of the painting. The approach to painting in Fauvism was bold, using pure colors. One of the better-known founding members of the Fauvist movement was Henri Matisse.

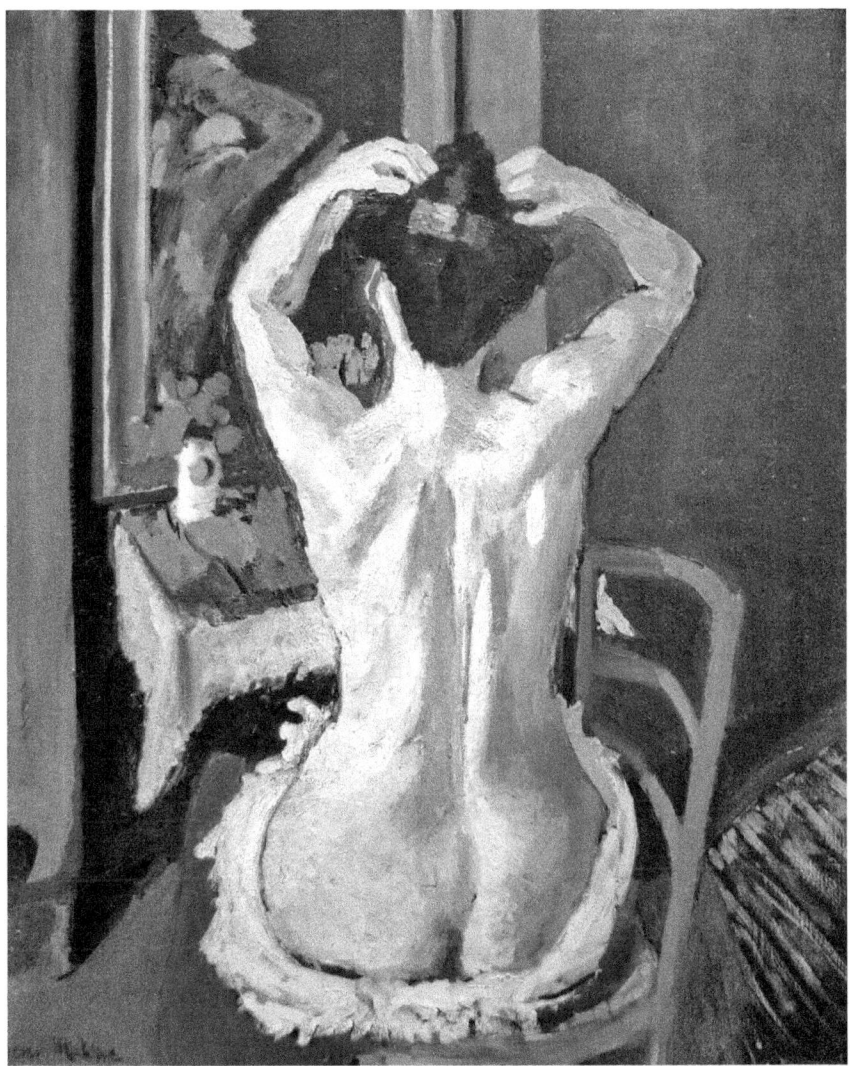

Henri Matisse, *"La Coiffure"*, 1901. Fauvist painting.

The next art movement to follow Fauvism (1905-1918) was the **Expressionist** or Die Bruck movement. This movement, with origins in Germany, was created in reaction to Impressionism. The Expressionist movement featured distorted images emphasizing spiritual and emotional feelings within the artist. This style of art was the earliest manifestation of Expressionism, where art further distanced itself from the depiction of realistic scenes and images.

In **Expressionism**, images and figures were portrayed merely as vague outlines, to be filled in with non-representational colors. In later depictions, the art was completely removed from reality. Instead, the artist combined symbolism, color and emotion in the creation of art.

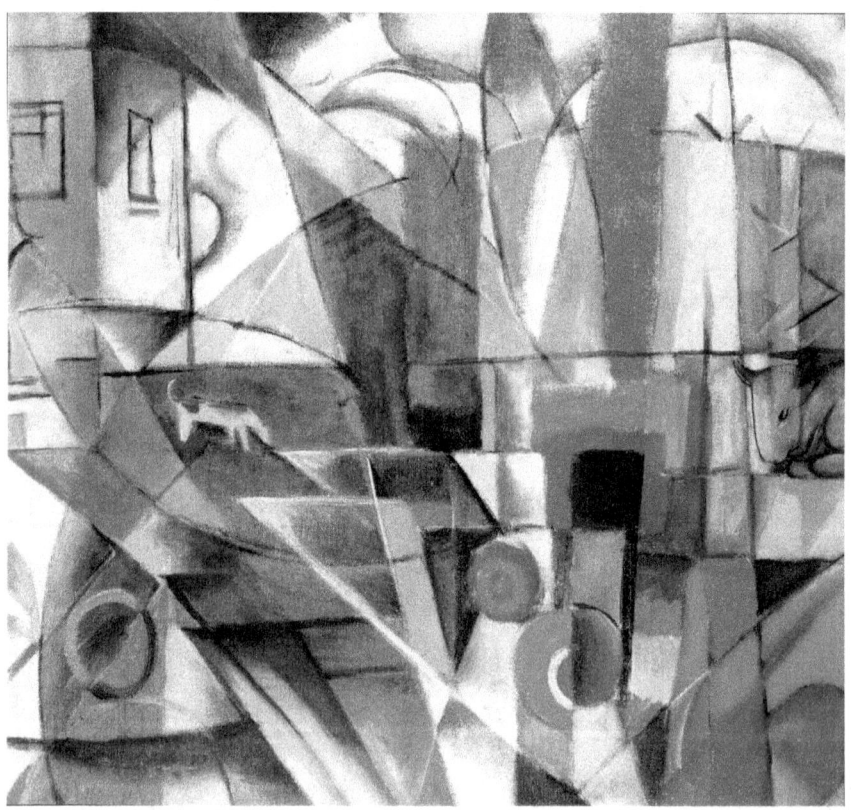

Franz Marc, "*Landschaft mit Haus, Hund und Rind*", 1914. Art of the German Expressionist movement.

Cubism, an art movement formed in 1907 and lasting twenty years or so, was founded by Pablo Picasso and Georges Braque. The Cubists work involved angular, often geometric components of a scene or figure. These linear and angular components were representative of a scene and were then juxtaposed for further dramatic effect. Cubism also embraced the multi-dimensional representation of objects and images. The use of analogous and complementary colors was also prominent in cubist art. Linear perspective was substituted with multiple perspectives, forming a combination of multiple views.

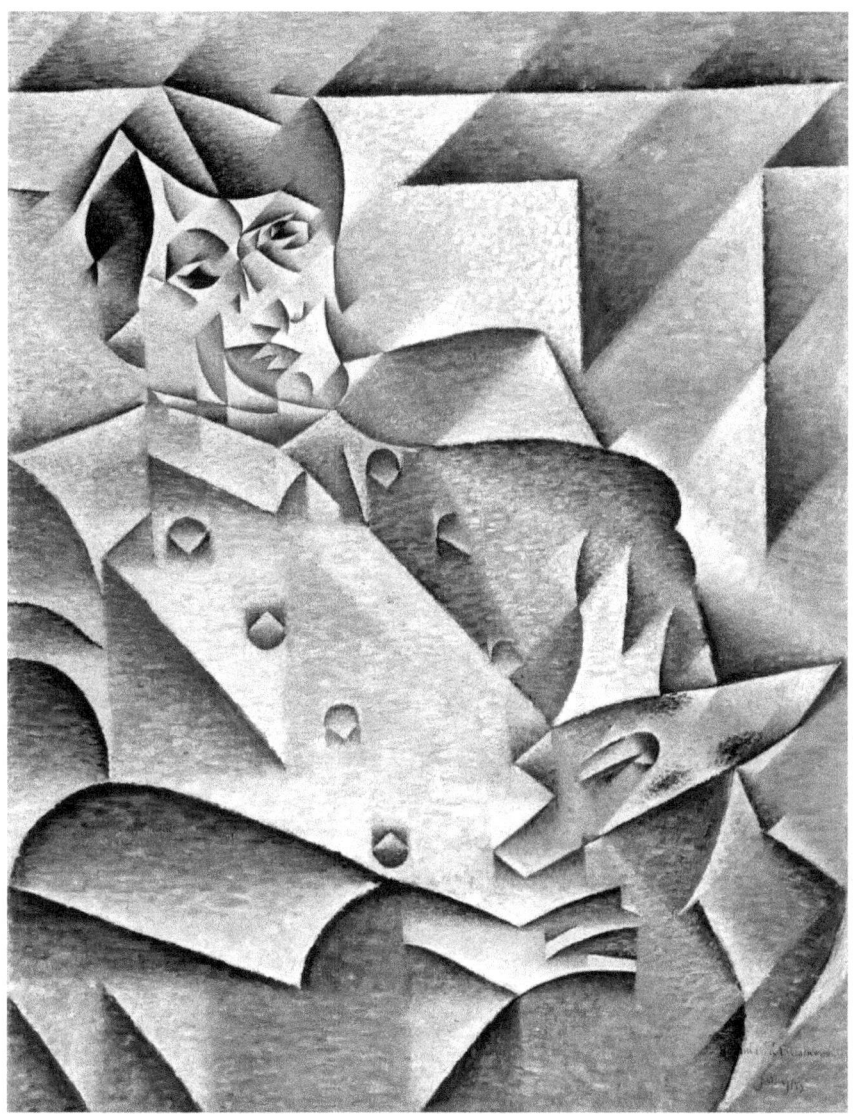

Juan Gris, "*Portrait of Pablo Picasso*", 1912. Cubist genre painting.

In **Cubist** art, representational objects were converted to basic geometric forms. Objects were overlaid onto one another to create the final painting. To interpret a Cubist painting involves standing back and re-arranging its components in one's mind. Full abstraction of the human form and inanimate objects was beginning to take hold in the Cubist genre of painting.

Futurism, a short-lived Italian art movement, was formed in parallel to Cubism. The movement only lasted a few years (1910-1917). The founding members, Umberto Boccioni, Gino Severini, and Giacomo Balla, formed the idea that art should embrace technical and scientific advances of the 20th century. This form of art would highlight the tenets of the modern age, namely industry, speed, vehicles in motion, machines and technological change. The Futurists practiced in every medium of art including painting, sculpture, ceramics, graphic design and industrial design.

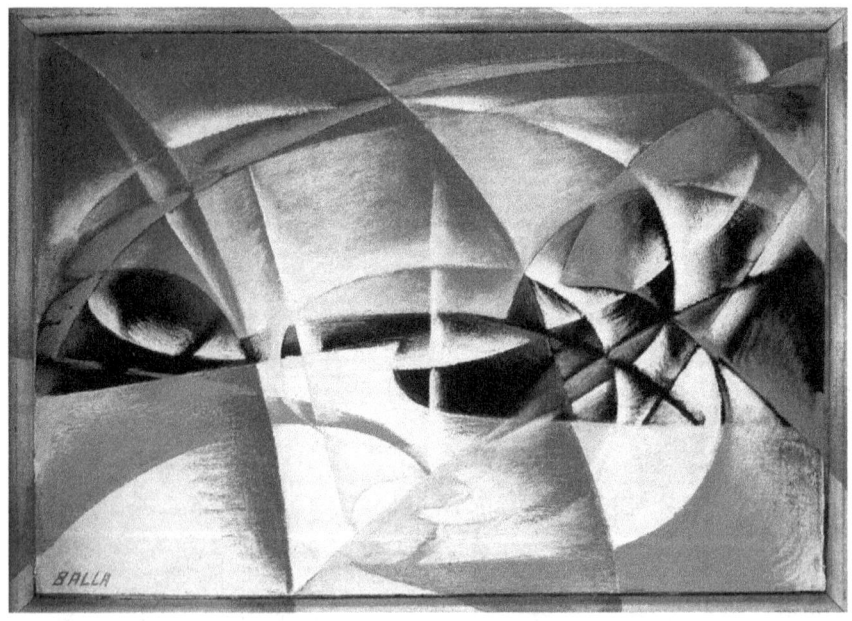

© ESTATE OF GIACOMO BALLA / SODRAC (2015) Giacomo Balla, "*Landscape*", 1913. Example of Futurist Painting.

The **Bauhaus** was an art school based in Germany that combined crafts and fine arts and operated from 1919-33. It was founded with the premise that the creation of total works of art, including the fine arts and decorative arts, would be brought together. The Bauhaus style later became one of the most influential currents in modern design and Modernist art, architecture and education. The Bauhaus Style was promoted by its founders as an approach to design and art.

The Bauhaus Style gave an equal ratio to form and function without the need for unnecessary frills and decoration. Well-known Bauhaus founders include Walter Gropius, Piet Mondrian and Wassily Kandinsky. Piet Mondrian began as a representational artist, primarily painting landscape scenes. Through the Bauhaus school, his work evolved to that of "pure abstraction". As a founding member of the **De Stijl** (The Style) modernist movement, he began to embrace geometric, rectangular shapes and forms delineated through the use of lines. Piet Mondrian's subsequent art, for which he is well known, embodied the abstraction of lines and squares.

Piet Mondrian, "*Tableau I*", 1921. Bauhaus "De Stijl" style art.

His work was seminal in the evolution of 19th century representational and figurative art to the full abstraction of early to mid-20th century art. The Bauhaus was founded at a time when the defining German spirit had begun to shift away from emotional Expressionism to a **New Objectivity**. The school's founder, Walter Gropius had launched the school with studies in Expressionism, but changed the emphasis and curriculum to a more modernist approach. Gropius embraced modern architecture, art and design and wished to incorporate Modernism into the fields of study within the school. He argued that a new period of history had begun following the end of the First World War. He wanted a new style to reflect this through the new Bauhaus "**De Stijl**" (The Style) movement referred to earlier.

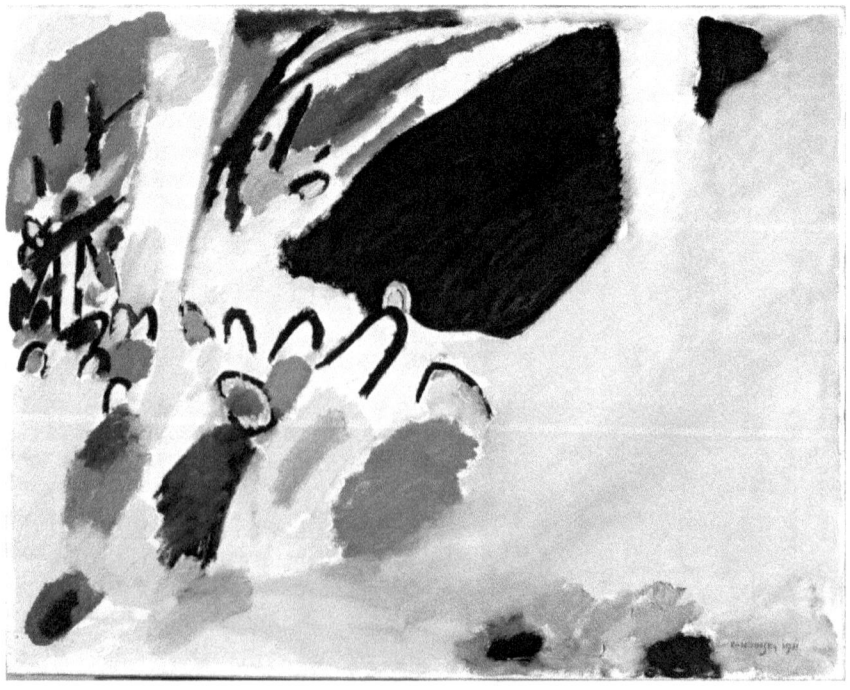

Wassily Kandinsky, "***Impression III (Concert)***", 1911. Bauhaus style.

Surrealism was a new art movement which began in the early 1920s. Surrealism developed out of the Dada Movement during WWI. The goal of this art form was to bring together dreams and reality. Artists in the movement created unusual, non-realistic scenes which accentuated and distorted people and objects.

The painting philosophy and technique of Surrealism was to let the subconscious express itself. The philosophy of Surrealism was largely driven through the open and imaginative arrangement of ordinary and depictive expressions. This technique later became instrumental in other genres of abstraction, notably Abstract Expressionism. Juxtaposed objects and scenes characterized surrealist artwork. Photographic quality, dream-like images combining symbolism and imagination were the mainstay of Surrealism. Several artists of the era participated in this movement, the most well known was Salvatore Dali.

In 1931, Dali painted one of his most renowned art works, "*The Persistence of Memory*". This painting introduced a surreal image of soft, melting pocket watches. The images of soft watches were to reject the notion that time is rigid and critical. Other images in the art also lend themselves to this soft, lackadaisical approach to time.

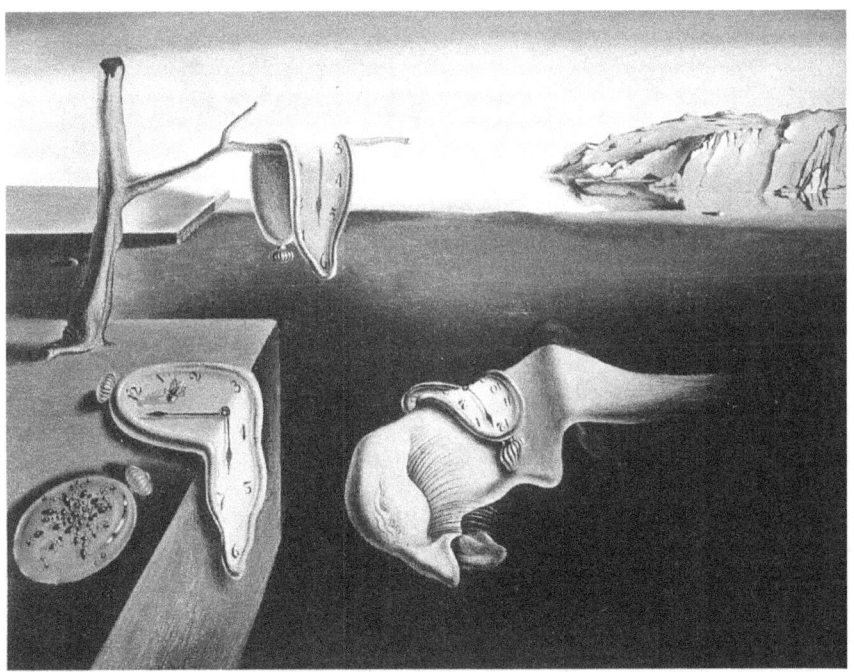

© Salvador Dali, Fundació Gala-Salvador Dalí/ SODRAC (2015)
Salvador Dali, "*The Persistence of Memory*", 1931. Surrealistic art.

Joan Miró was a Spanish painter largely recognized for his Surrealist art. He joined the Surrealist group in the early 1920s. His early work was characterized as "dream paintings". Miró's early work had representational tendencies despite his Surrealist leanings.

From 1940 and on, the focus of Miró's work included iconography with subjects ranging from women to birds. He developed a unique style while residing in Paris, influenced by poets and writers. His work is associated with Surrealism due to his belief in **Automatism**. Joan Miró was an early follower of automatic drawing in order to distance himself from earlier objective painting techniques.

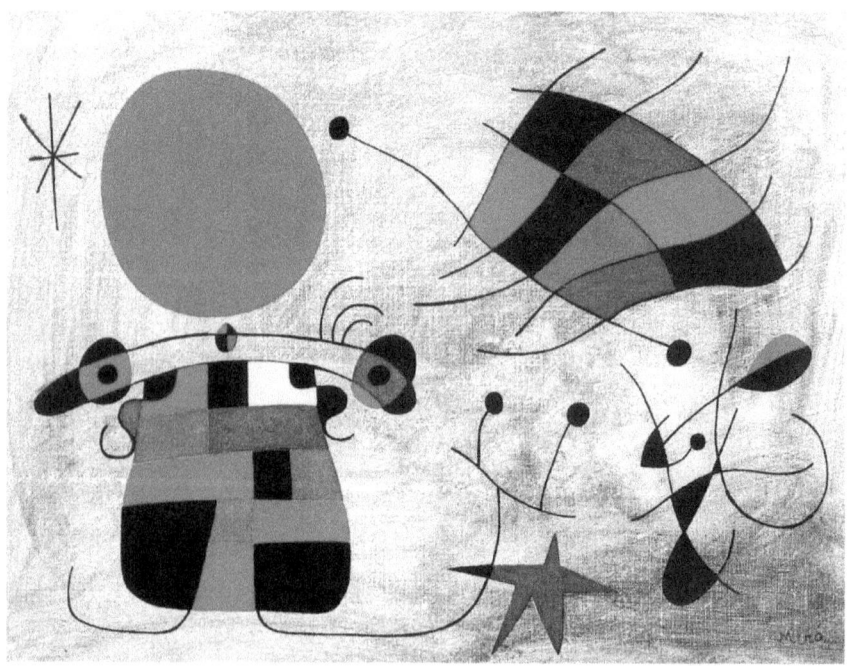

© Successió Miró / SODRAC (2015)   Joan Miró, "*The Smile of the Flamboyant Wings*", 1953. Automatism, Late –Surrealism, Abstractionism.

The creation of the Abstract Expressionist art movement (1945-1959) was heavily influenced by American artists meeting with European Surrealists who were self-exiled to the USA during World War II. The Abstract Expressionism art movement was likely the most influential of the art movements following World War II.

Abstract Expressionism was founded in New York City by a group of former representational style artists. The artists, considered the **New York School**, embraced the introduction of self-expression and gestural brush movements in this style of painting. The gestural brush movements were largely driven by emotion and the subconscious. There is debate as to whether the subconscious is equivalent to the unconscious or merely exists or operates in the mind beneath or beyond consciousness. The abstractions of **Willem De Kooning** were a combination of self-expression, the subconscious, and a commentary on society. His abstract art was primarily biomorphic in nature.

Subconscious - *of or concerning the part of the mind of which one is not fully aware but which influences one's actions and feelings.*

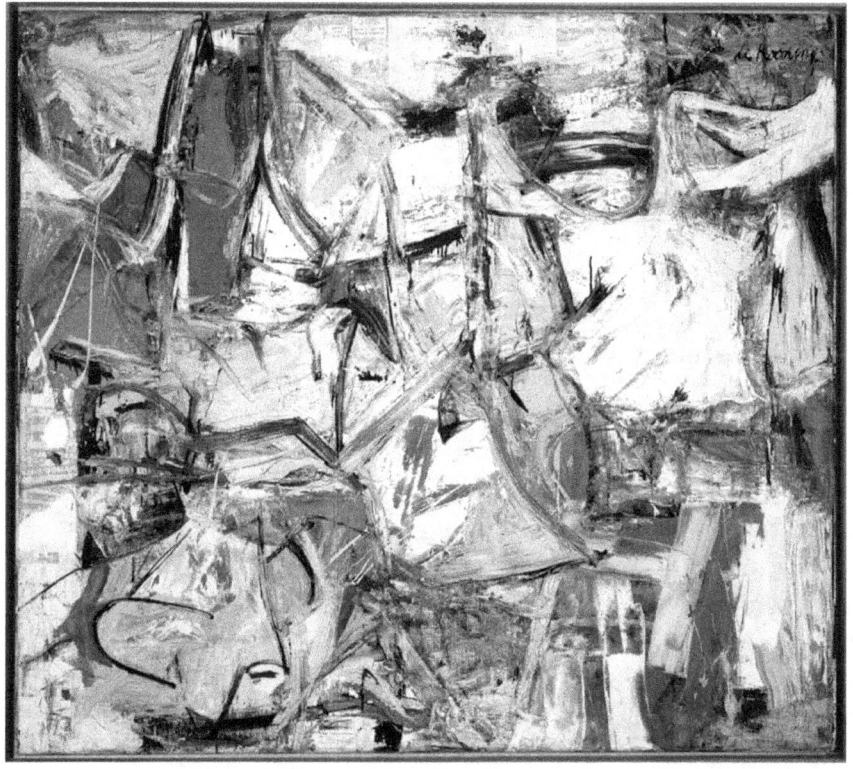

© 2015 The Willem de Kooning Foundation / ARS, New York / SODRAC, Montreal   Willem de Kooning, "*Gotham News*", 1950.

Abstract Expressionism was the first American art movement to achieve international significance. The movement was created to distance American artists from Europe, the centuries old center of art. The members of the Abstract Expressionist art movement were determined to develop a "Made in America" art movement to better distinguish their American art from European art.

The Abstract Expressionist founding members were very diverse in their style of art. Painting techniques ranged from color field work to gestural drip painting and everything in between. The members realized that a central art movement would bring them together since they all had abstract expressionism in common. The painters within the "New York School" explored the notion that color and form were sufficient as elements of art. They wanted to bring their subconscious feelings and emotion into their work. Spontaneous, gestural brush movements were instrumental in how their art was created.

The founding members of the **AbEx** (Abstract Expressionism) movement were Hans Hoffman, Jackson Pollock, Willem de Kooning, Robert Motherwell, Franz Kline, Barnett Newman, Arshile Gorky and Lee Krasner. Each of these artists brought their unique style to the movement. Hans Hoffman was both a teacher and artist. He was a great influence on many artists of the era, therefore propagating the Abstract Expressionist style of art. The style most associated with AbEx was the **action painting** of Jackson Pollock. Pollock moved away from the easel and instead created his art on unstretched canvasses laid out over a floor in his studio. **Jackson Pollock** used techniques such as drip painting, brooms, scrapers and throwing paint onto a canvas to achieve his form of action art. He soon became popular with art critics and the media with his new and unusual form of art. Pollock drew considerable attention to the AbEx movement and raised its stature within art circles and art critics of the era. Skeptics of his style of art were plenty, but the overwhelming acceptance by the art world soon overcame any opposition. The "action painting" style became widespread from the late 1940s to the late 1950s. The terms Abstract Expressionism and action painting are often used interchangeably. During the late 1940s, the radical approach of "action painting" revolutionized the art movements that followed.

Pollock realized that the journey of creating the art was as critical as the art itself. The public's taste and mood in the post-WWII years had changed considerably. There was a general euphoria in the air. People began to embrace liberty and change. Jackson Pollock's radical style of emotion driven abstract art was perfectly suited to the new mindset of breaking away from tradition and embracing modernity.

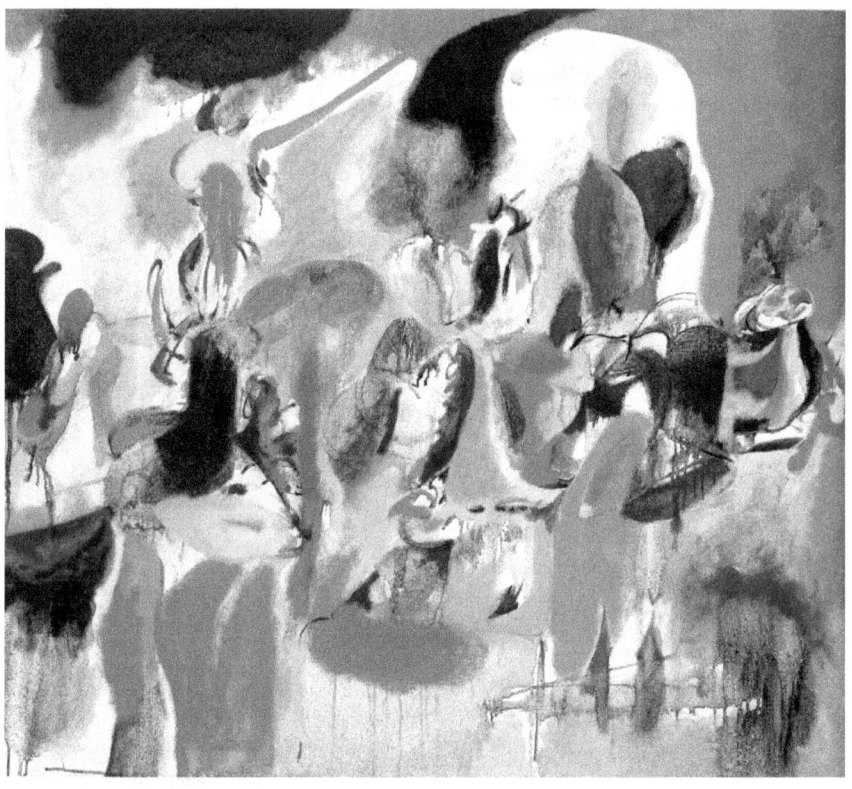

© ESTATE OF ARSHILE GORKY / SODRAC (2015) Arshile Gorky, "*Water of the Flowery Mill*", 1944. Abstract Expressionism (AbEx).

Along with Mark Rothko, Jackson Pollock and Willem de Kooning, **Arshile Gorky** has been applauded as one of the most powerful American painters of the 20th century. His style of work was lyrical abstraction and was considered a new language. He "*lit the way for two generations of American artists*". Arshile Gorky's work had considerable influence on the Abstract Expressionist movement.

Leading members of the AbEx movement have acknowledged his considerable contribution and influence. Arshile Gorky's earlier work was inspired and influenced by Paul Cezanne and Picasso. His art work hangs in several large American and worldwide art institutions.

Franz Kline, an action painter and member of the Abstract Expressionist movement, was known for his large-scale, non-objective, fluid and dynamic paintings. In his earlier years of Abstract painting, his work was monochromatic in black and white.

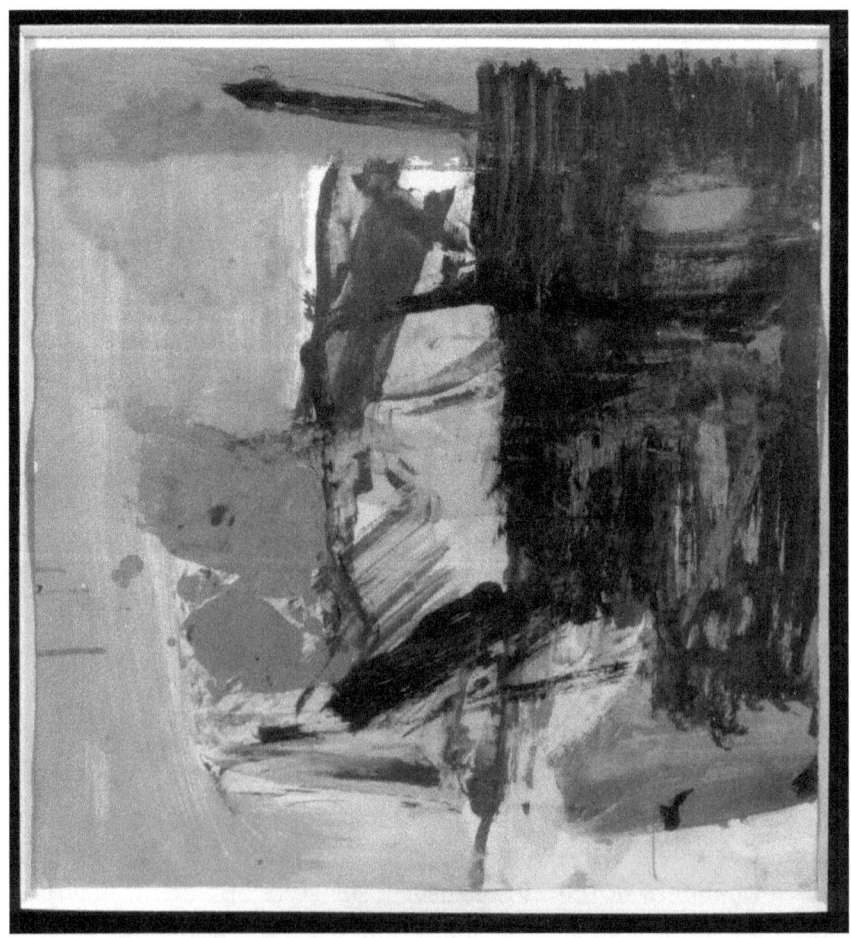

© ESTATE OF FRANZ KLINE / SODRAC (2015) Franz Kline, *"Untitled"*, 1960. Abstract Expressionist (AbEx), Action Painting.

Franz Kline's style and inspiration was thought to have been derived from that of Willem de Kooning. Franz Kline also introduced symbolism to his work in the form of calligraphy. In his later years as an Abstract Expressionist action painter, Franz Kline incorporated color in his work with the addition of colored accents to his black and white paintings. Similarly, Pablo Picasso had reinvented painting and sculpture earlier in the 20th century through the Cubist movement. Abstract Expressionism (**AbEx**) was a term that applied to multiple abstract artists working in New York during the late 1940s to the late 1950s. These artists each had different styles but collectively were part of the AbEx movement. Abstract Expressionism emerged in New York City as a major movement from the late 1940s through the 1950s. In the intervening years, several leading art galleries began to hold exhibitions of Abstract Expressionist artists.

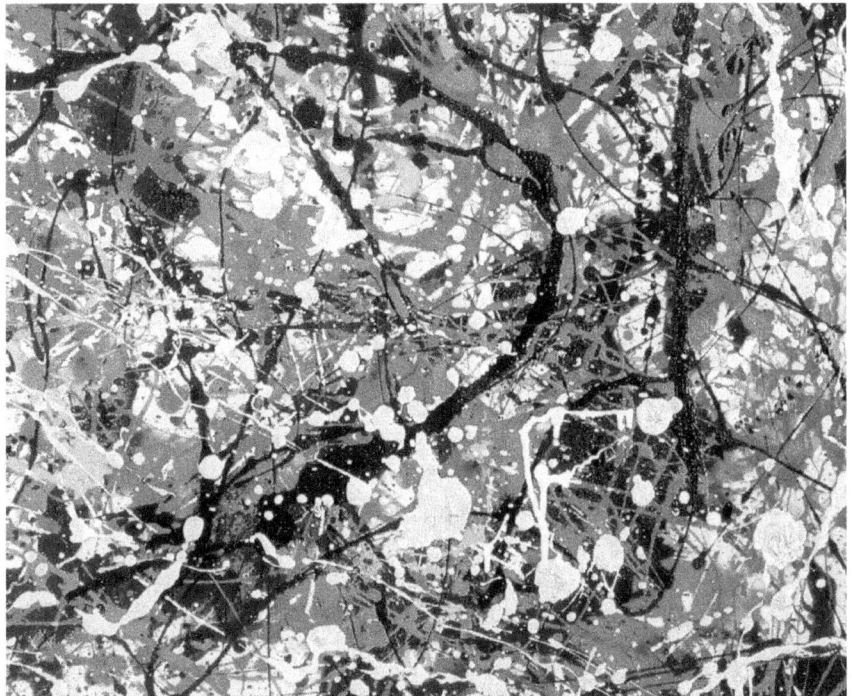

© Pollock-Krasner Foundation / SODRAC (2015) Jackson Pollock, "*Number 8(detail)*", 1949. Action Painting, Abstract Expressionist (AbEx).

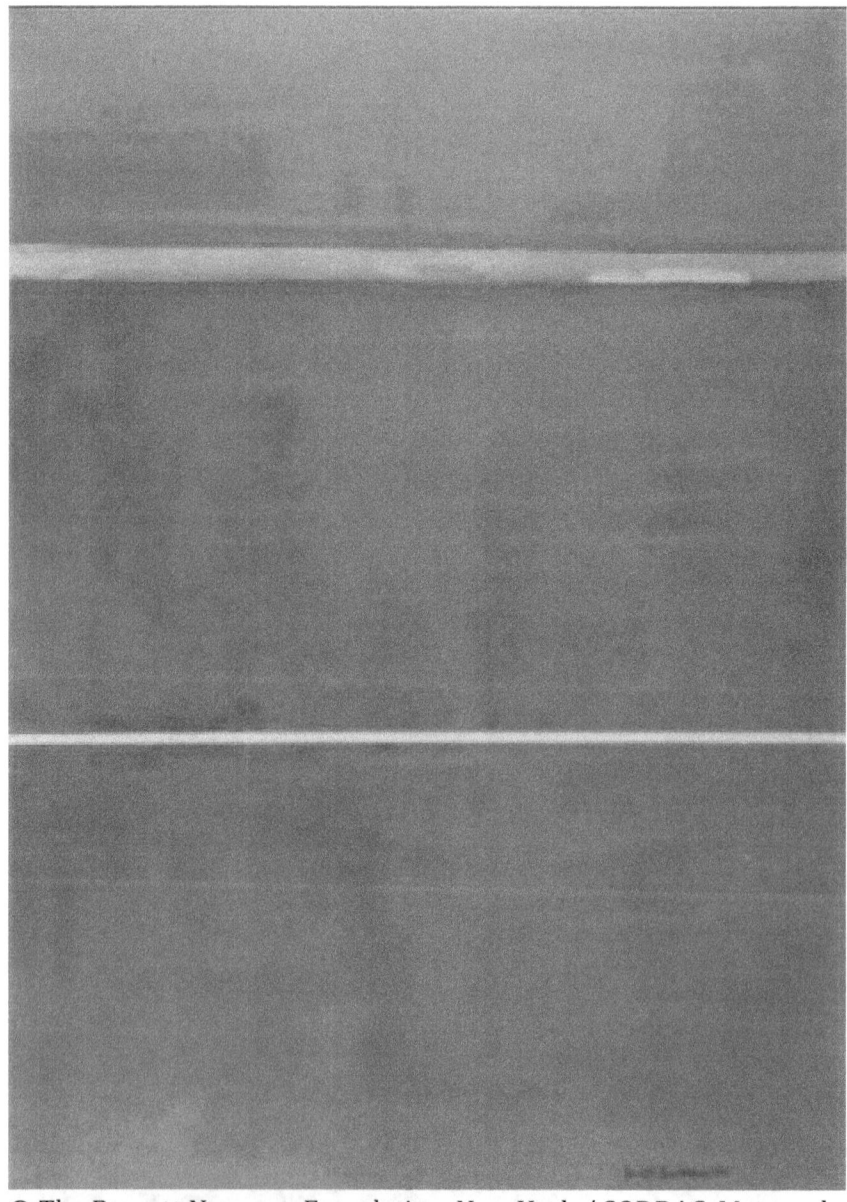

Barnett Newman, "*Dionysius*", 1949. Color field painting, Abstract Expressionist (AbEx)

It can also be said that innovations by the founding members of the AbEx movement highly influenced successive art movements of the 1960s and beyond. **Color field** work was an off-shoot of abstract expressionism and involved the painting of large areas of colors. Some of the large areas or fields of color were analogous, some complementary. The leading color field artists of the era were Mark Rothko, Barnett Newman and Clyfford Still. The philosophy of the color field painters was to remove unnecessary elements in a painting.

Color field abstract artists wanted to present each painting as a unified, cohesive and monolithic image. Large color forms characterized color field art with either soft or hard edges. The large color fields were to be the focal point in the painting. Thin lines or **zips** of contrasting colors typically separated color fields, either in a vertical or horizontal orientation. The emotion, which the color fields conveyed, became a large part of color field painting. The large forms of soft-edged and hard-edged color in color field art were revolutionary in their time. Although considered part of the Abstract Expressionist movement, color field work was the polar opposite of the busy, dense "drip and splatter" style of art at the other end of the Abstract Expressionist spectrum. Color field painting was a precursor or forerunner to a later art movement known as **Minimalism**.

Two parallel movements to Abstract Expressionism occurred in Canada in the same period as Abstract Expressionism. The **Automatiste** movement of Quebec (1943-1960) was founded by Paul-Emile Borduas and later grew to include another founding member, Paul Riopelle along with eight other members. The artists in this movement had origins in earlier genres of art, but were increasingly influenced and informed through the Surrealist movement. Artists of the Surrealist movement practiced automatic painting and drawing. As well, the "Automatism" theory was a large influence behind this group.

Automatism was derived from the term "**Automatic drawing**", a theory and concept put forward by the Surrealist movement. Random movements of the hand best characterize automatic drawing. In Automatism, hand movement is instead guided by the subconscious with little to no thought placed into control. Early forms of Automatism focused on drawing.

Automatism originated and was developed by the early painters Salvador Dali and Joan Miró. Followers of Automatism then applied the concept to painting. Although intended to be purely driven through the subconscious, it was also thought that "automatic drawing" was not entirely automatic. The Automatiste found that there was a small amount of conscious intervention to make the painting or image visually appealing or comprehensible.

Automatism – *the removal of conscious intention in the creation of art.*

"What I have learned, having lived in Canada for so long, is that Automatisme and especially Borduas' manifesto, along with Riopelle's international success, is that Canadian artists have been very influential on the world stage. Borduas and Riopelle also influenced my early career, as I moved toward my Signature series and toward abstract art, eventually returning to figurative and fantasy art" -- **Cristian S. Aluas**, professional artist. Las Vegas, Nevada.

A second Abstract Expressionist movement, **Painters Eleven,** was formed in the Toronto, Canada area by a group of diverse painters practicing abstraction in their work. The eleven diverse painters in this group held their first exhibition in 1954. Members of the group included Jack Bush, Oscar Cahén, Hortense Gordon, Tom Hodgson, Tom Gorson, Alexandra Luke, Kazuo Nakamura, William Ronald, Walter Yarwood, Harold Town, Ray Mead, Jock Macdonald and Alexandra Luke with Jack Bush as the pre-eminent artist of the group. Although the artists in the group had differing artistic visions, their commitment was to advance the genre of Abstract Expressionism in Canada. Several of the members of this group had origins in advertising, freelancing and as art teachers. They brought in leading members of the AbEx movement of New York to teach workshops they had organized in the Toronto area.

Canada lagged in acceptance of the American Abstract Expressionism movement of the 1950s. Even though the **Painters Eleven** initial exhibition of 1954 received negative acclaim and poor acceptance from the public, several art critics spoke highly of the exhibition as a breath of fresh air into Canadian art.

Until this time, the Group of Seven was the only influential Canadian art group with widespread appeal. The **Painters Eleven** group went on to create an exhibition in New York in 1956 and by 1957 the group had successfully established Abstract Expressionism as a genre of art in Canada.

Over the course of my own art journey, I have had the opportunity to make the acquaintance of **Denise Trottier,** the daughter of the late artist Gerald Trottier, one of Canada's foremost abstract painters of the 20th century. I was drawn to the abstract work of **Gerald Trottier** due to his own journey as a multidisciplinary artist.

He worked in the realm of sculptural, stained glass, murals and abstract art as well as liturgical art. Within the fine art genre, Gerald Trottier worked with multiple media to convey his vision and emotion through art. The expression of narratives in his work can be seen in the multiple series of work generated over his art career. His late 1950s to mid-1960s period of Abstract Expressionism paralleled the AbEx (New York School) movement as it carried over into the Canadian art space.

Included are the following paragraphs and images provided to me by Gerald Trottier's wife, **Irma Trottier** and his daughter, **Denise**. The paragraphs detail Gerald Trottier's own art journey and how he traversed genres and media to convey his vision and philosophy of art.

The inspiration derived from other contemporary abstract artists of this period can be seen in some of Gerald Trottier's work. This demonstrates the influence that Abstract Expressionism wielded in other countries such as Canada. The remarkable career of this Canadian abstract artist is also detailed in the following paragraphs.

Abstraction within a diversity of media and subject matter

Gerald Trottier's abstract oeuvres had their roots and inspiration in his studies abroad and at the Arts Students League of New York. In 1953, he was awarded a Canada Foundation scholarship to study medieval art and art techniques in Europe.

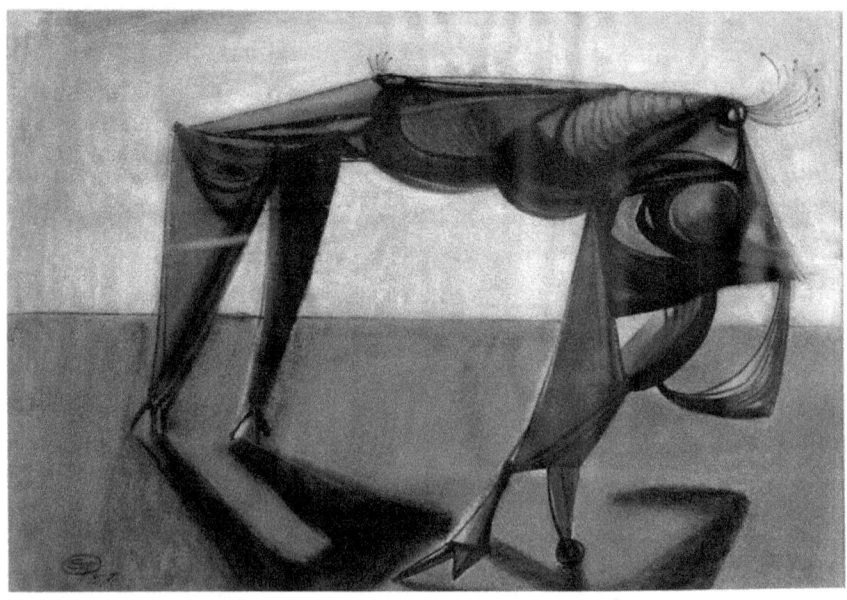

Gerald Trottier, "*Insect in Between*", 1951 © CARCC 2015.
Charcoal and chalk. Photo credit: "Photo by Rod MacIvor".

The impact of this period of culture as well as abstract artists such as Rouault, Joan Miró, Picasso, Sutherland and Franz Kline can be seen in symbols, banners, design, geometric shapes, lines, and liturgical objects; all of which are included throughout much of Trottier's work.

During this European trip, he also studied lithography in Brighton, England. His limited edition litho and lino prints (several appeared on the covers of *Canadian Art* in the 1950s and 1960s) reflect his love of line and symmetry.

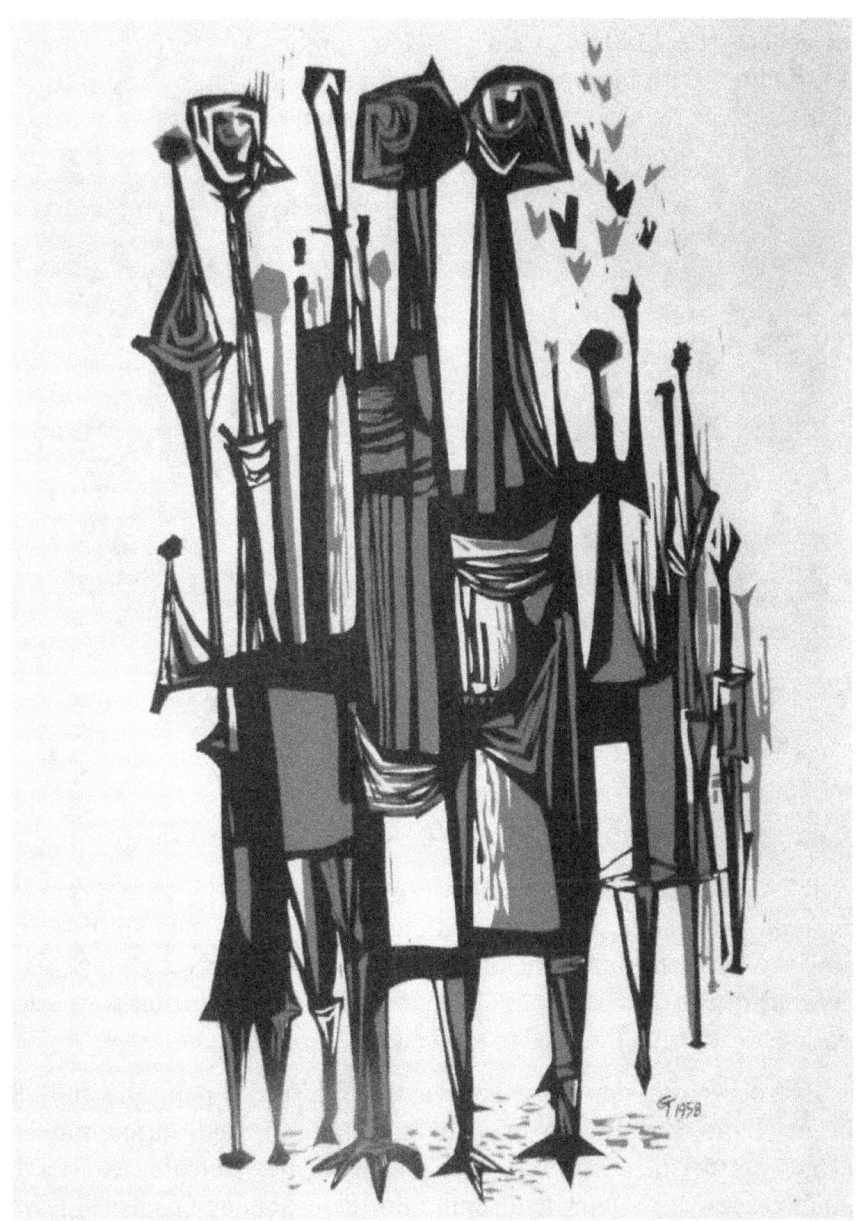

Gerald Trottier, *"Untitled"*, 1950 © CARCC 2015. Lino print.

Throughout the 1950s and early 60s, a number of Trottier's works were painted with large bold lines with red, blue, yellow and purple colours such as those found in medieval stained glass.

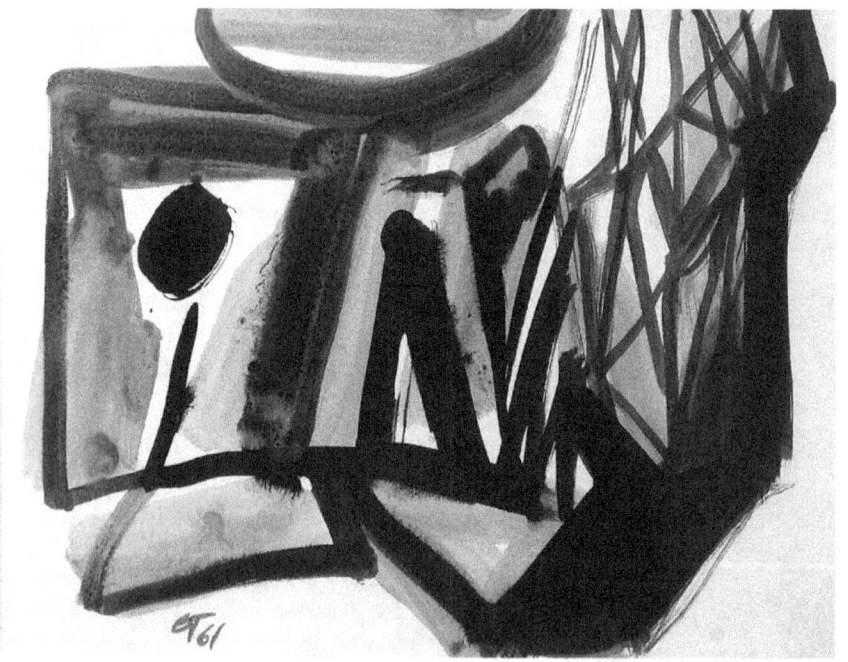

Gerald Trottier, *"**Abstract**"*, 1961 © CARCC 2015. Ink wash.

In 1957, two of his abstract works were chosen for the *Second Biennial exhibition of Canadian Art* at the National Gallery of Canada, in Ottawa, Ontario where the majority of the exhibited works were abstract. However, it was in the late 1950s and mid 60s that Trottier's artistic creations went from national to international recognition.

His abstract expressionism was revealed in large oil paintings full of vibrant colors, thickly applied paint and interspersed with symbols and geometric lines. In 1958, he along with Alex Colville, Jean-Paul Lemieux, Léon Bellefleur, Paul-Émile Borduas, Stanley Cosgrove, Jean Dallaire, Alfred Pelland and Harold Town participated in the *1st Bienal Interamericana de Pintura y Grabado* in Mexico.

Trottier was awarded a Canada Council Fellowship in 1962 and in 1963, the National Gallery selected two colourful abstract works of Trottier for the *Fifth Biennial Exhibition of Canadian Painting,* in London, England.

In the 1964 April edition of Canadian Art, Naomi Jackson Groves described Trottier's recent works as '*expressionistic mystic symbolism which is always convincing in the hands of this dedicated artist.*' In 1965, eight of his large oil paintings were chosen to represent Canada at the 8th Sao Paulo Biennial along with Claude Toussignant, Jacques Hurtubise and Ray Kiyooka. Willem Blom of the National Gallery of Canada described these works as displaying '*the powerful expressionist and mystical range of his painting.*'

Trottier's murals, stained glass and sculptures of the 1960s also reflected abstraction with bold geometric symbols, designs and vibrant colours. In 1962, he submitted a mural design for a large mosaic mural at Carleton University, Ottawa. His design was chosen over 9 other artists, including notable Canadian artists such as Harold Town and David Partridge. This semi-figurative abstract mural, titled The Pilgrimage of Man, is 168 feet in circumference and 10 1/4 feet high. The then President of Carleton University, Davidson Dunton, wrote: '*I am completely convinced in my own mind that it is one of the very great pieces of permanent art in this country.*'

In 1964, Trottier designed an imposing 28 pound brass ceremonial mace for York University. The relief work of the shaft is full of symbols, and geometric shapes. Trottier's sculptures (bronze, and limestone), mosaic and stained glass liturgical works in churches reflected the artist's life long preoccupation with his own spirituality and love of abstraction and line. Several of Trottier's landscape watercolour paintings of the 1970s were also painted in an abstract expressionistic manner, reminiscent of Joseph Mallord William Turner. While Trottier used abstraction as one of the means of conveying his ideas, his work is multi-dimensional and multi-faceted. He used a multitude of media: oil, acrylic, pen and ink, chalk, conté, charcoal, pastel, pencil, stained glass and watercolour. Trottier painted, drew, was a printer, graphic artist, sculptor, illustrator and muralist and designed postage stamps. He was a true Renaissance man.

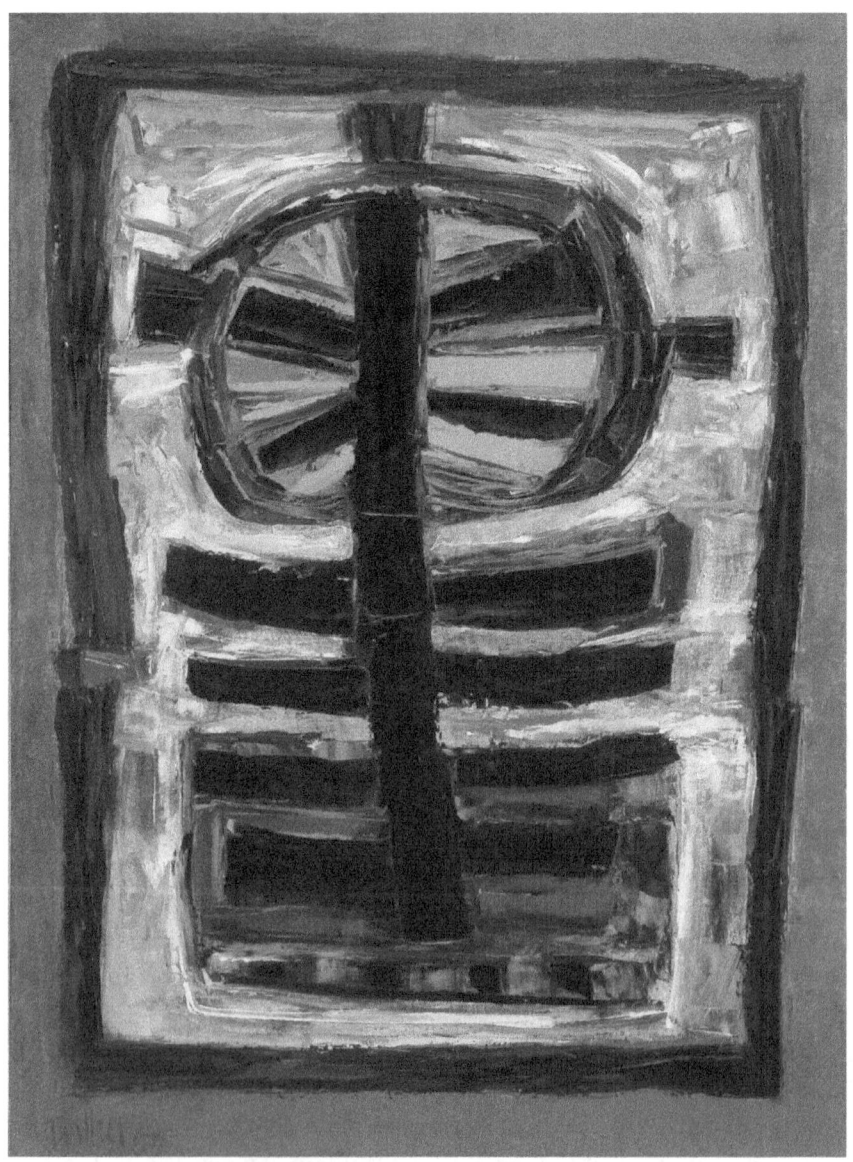

Gerald Trottier, *"Christogram"* at CUAG, 1963 © CARCC 2015.
Oil on linen. Photo credit: "Photo by David Barbour"

ABSTRACT BEGINNINGS

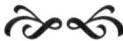

*"No great artist ever sees things as they really are. If he did,
he would cease to be an artist"*

Oscar Wilde

THE GENESIS OF MY current style of abstract art has its origins in the Abstract Expressionist movement. The revolutionary impact the AbEx members had on art history has had a positive influence on me. The AbEx founding artists took a leap of faith and against all odds decided to pursue an alternative vision and philosophy of art. Each of the AbEx members brought their individual style to the group, but they collectively came together to advance this new, fledgling movement. I recall reading that certain art critics of the time were overwhelmingly negative to this new form of expressionist art and this was understandably so. Abstract Expressionism was considerably different and driven by reaction to the conventional fine arts of the era. Other notable art critics of the period looked favorably upon Abstract Expressionism.

Lincoln Kirstein, an influential New York City art connoisseur, was a detractor of Abstract Expressionism. Kirstein struggled with the relevance of Abstract Expressionism. He argued that with the repetition of basic forms and colors, the body of the artists work would also become repetitive. He also put forward that the simplicity and ambiguity of modern art removed it from purpose or successful content altogether.

In *"The State of Modern Painting"*, a 1948 Harper's Magazine publication, Kirstein wrote about the demise of modern painting. He describes how the modern painter is extremely invested in his own personal statement and style, to the extent that his body of work becomes repetitive and uninteresting. Lincoln Kirstein wrote that *"modern painting was now about shapes and strokes instead of figures and portraits"*.

"This personalism, which is rarely even comparatively original, is just as rarely interesting for long. Usually it gets attention simply because it is easy to recognize its provenance or because it differs stylistically (somewhat) from the work of other similarly 'original' personalities" -- **Lincoln Kirstein**

On another front, the two most influential art critics of the late 1940's to the early 1960's period, Clement Greenberg and Harold Rosenberg, generated an intense positive dialogue of Abstract Expressionism. It was this dialogue, eventually turning into an intense rivalry between the critics, which brought AbEx art to the forefront and helped to make it mainstream. The art critics, Clement Greenberg and Harold Rosenberg, held opposing opinions of Abstract Expressionism. Although the relationship between these two art critics began amicably, it eventually became adversarial.

Both Rosenberg and Greenberg espoused unique and opposing views of how Abstract Expressionist art should be viewed and interpreted. Clement Greenberg maintained that the art should be accepted at face value, regardless of the methods used in its creation. He also referred to the history and evolution of modern art movements, where Abstract Expressionism was simply the next movement in the progression. While AbEx art was radical, it was not more radical than earlier movements when they were first introduced. He wrote about how abstract expressionism included the requisite elements to distinguish it from traditional art. Through the elimination of depth and representation, and by flattening the picture plane, AbEx work instead focused on the transference of emotion to the canvas. One of the tenets of the AbEx movement was also the pursuit of non-geometric abstraction.

Instead, Harold Rosenberg was of the opinion that Abstract Expressionism was a complete departure from earlier modern art movements. The creation of the art was as much if not more of a departure as the art itself. Rosenberg maintained that in **Action painting**, the process of creating the art should itself be considered a form of art. This new, radical process of creating art should be clearly emphasized as being revolutionary and worthy of dialogue. Rosenberg wrote about the emotion and gestural actions that AbEx artists used in their art creation as a radical shift from earlier art movements. This new **action** process of transferring subconscious activity to the canvas was in itself radical. The activity of an AbEx artist expressing their individuality onto a canvas could be likened to an event.

The rivalry between these two influential art critics carried on for years, where each would publish articles promoting their philosophy and opinion of how the AbEx art movement should be defined and interpreted. The widespread publicity generated by this intense dialogue fostered critical discourse and ultimate acceptance of this new genre of art. It was interesting to note that both these critics looked favorably on Abstract Expressionism and only had a difference of opinion in its interpretation.

It was interesting to note that the majority of AbEx members were formerly representational or objective painters; they created very little abstract work earlier in their art careers. The group also understood the need to form a distinctly American art movement.

Until this time, fine art was largely Eurocentrist, where art was viewed from a European perspective. It was also intriguing that a few of the AbEx founding artists had emigrated from Europe. These artists had embraced America as their new country and had no hesitation in distancing their art from that of European art. European art was associated with centuries of history; it was classic art, Renaissance art, figurative and landscape art. Through abstraction, the AbEx group members were able to separate and distinguish their art from European art. After studying a few of the individual members of AbEx, their unique, different styles of abstract expressionism were revealed. I would look at their art work and visualize myself painting in a few of these styles.

The various styles of the AbEx members were so diverse that only abstraction was the common element. After further research into this art movement and its individual members, my confidence increased at creating art in the Abstract Expressionist genre.

The challenge I gave myself was to be able to create Abstract Expressionist work and develop my own voice and style within this genre. Having a limited amount of experience at painting, a better understanding of the techniques of painting in this genre became necessary. Which medium would I feel most comfortable working with? Which medium would be best suited to this type of work? Should I paint on stretched canvas or wood? What type of brushes would I need? How to paint using pure emotion?

Through an earlier experience using oil paint as a medium, I was not particularly fond of the long drying time involved. The fumes from oil paints were also a concern, especially in a confined space. Although oils could be laid onto the canvas thickly and in layers, a side effect of this would be long drying times. Having seen watercolors being used, I found them to produce a somewhat flat rendition of an image. Preferring a thicker paint, one that introduced a small amount of texture into a painting, limited my choice to acrylic paints. Reading about acrylics and talking to other artists that used acrylic paints in their work, I became convinced this would be the right medium for my art. Acrylics were fast drying, were relatively free of fumes, and could be mixed to a consistency approaching that of oils. These features would lend themselves well to abstract work.

Of course, each artist using their preferred medium would heap praise on their medium of choice. Oils, for example, had an inherent luster, which precluded the use of applying varnish after the painting was complete. Oils could also be laid thick on the canvas, using an impasto technique. Watercolors were very fast drying and fairly inexpensive. The artists that preferred acrylic paints extolled the virtues of this medium. Acrylic paints are fast drying, generated virtually no fumes, and could be laid on thick and in layers. These traits were all enticing and supported my leanings towards acrylic paints. With this new knowledge, the decision was made to invest in acrylic paints along with a very good set of brushes specifically for use with acrylic paints.

Further research and consultations with other acrylic artists made me aware of the difference in the quality of acrylic paints available. Acrylic paints are available in multiple grades, from student to professional grade. The student grade acrylic paints tend to have more filler mixed in with the pigment. Higher grade professional acrylics have a larger concentration of pigments. Having more pigment in the paint increases the luster of the paint, as the colors are purer.

Although one would assume that professional grade paints are the only choice in professional art, student grade paints do have a place. When a large canvas needs to have both a colored ground and an underpainting of a certain color applied, it is more economical to simply use student grade paint since there needs to be so much coverage. Professional grade paints can instead be used to block and paint the composition. I found that the quantity of paint used on a canvas is directly related to the style of the artist. If working in thick layers, a considerable amount of paint is necessary. If blending in a single layer, less paint is necessary. Acrylic paints are typically available in tubes and larger jars. The tube paints vary in cost relative to their quality. For a large canvas, the amount of paint can be considerable and it becomes important to use the paints judiciously.

With this in mind, the decision was made to use student grade paints for a few of my initial abstract compositions. As my work progressed and evolved, I would alternate between professional and medium quality acrylic paints and use less student grade paints. After all, I had not even developed an Abstract Expressionist style at this time and could be considered a "developing abstract artist". A few of my first paintings were created using large brushstrokes and a palette knife. The palette knife is often referred to as a painting knife. A large palette knife created a different aesthetic with broad swaths of color overlaying each other. Other paintings were created strictly using a smaller painting knife. A smaller painting knife allowed me to add multiple smaller areas of colors in a concentrated, colorful composition.

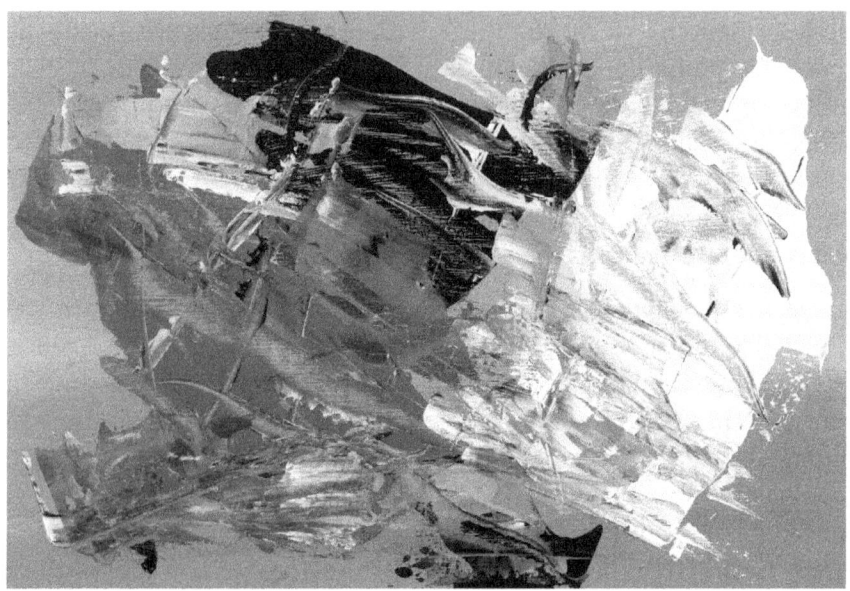

Norman Pirollo, "***Demographics***", 2014. Expressionist painting, colored ground, large palette knife.

In my first compositions, I enjoyed working with the layered effect as opposed to blending colors together. With layering, pure colors were used, although some colors were mixed afterwards and used instead. My initial abstract paintings were colorful, vivid compositions using a pure color palette. Later on, I began to soften the colors in the palette to enhance the visual drama in the composition. Through my initial work, it was found that I was drawn to colors. Further research discovered that there is a category of artists considered **colorists**, whose art is characterized through the use of intense color. The intense colors then become the dominant element of the art. Having unknowingly stumbled on to this style of work, perhaps this was the direction I should pursue?

While exploring the different styles of expressionist art, each piece created would feature elements of that style. This exercise helped me to understand the complexity of creating such an art style as well as determining its appeal afterwards.

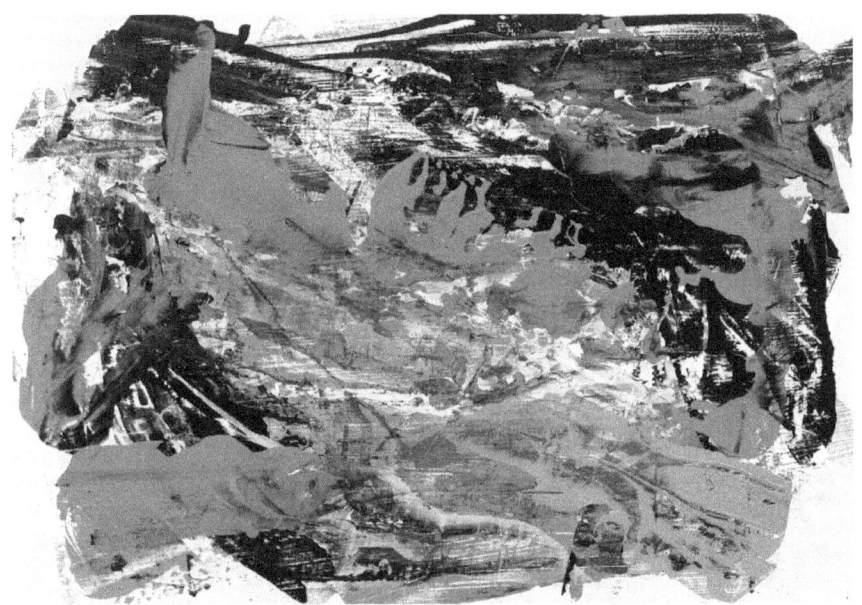

Norman Pirollo, "*Wildfire*", 2014. Expressionist painting, colored ground, large palette knife.

Working with large canvases involved a much greater quantity of acrylic paint. Using a given amount of paint for maximum effect became important. I also became concerned with the texture of the open weave in the large canvases. The canvases are typically manufactured on machines that weave fine threads of cotton material in an interlocking pattern. A textured weave is an inevitable result of this process. Stretched canvases are usually pre-gessoed where a gesso application is applied to the surface of the canvas.

The gesso is much like a paint primer and aids the acrylic paints in adhering to the canvas. The gesso application also has a secondary effect of filling in the weave of the canvas material. Some artists apply another layer of gesso to the canvas to further fill in the weave. Once the gesso layer is dry, the canvas is lightly sanded to remove any ridges, hollows and imperfections on the surface.

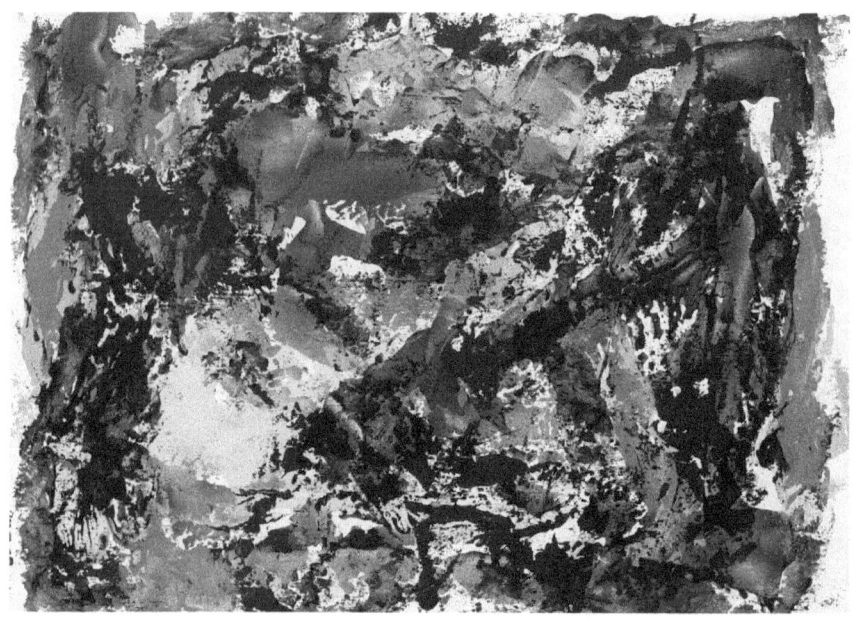

Norman Pirollo, "*In The Wild*", 2014. Expressionist painting, colored ground, small palette knife.

I experimented with this and found a second application of gesso did indeed smooth out the open weave of the canvas. The result was appealing to me and I have since performed this extra step on all my canvases. In my work, filling in the weave also creates a nicer, smoother substrate to work on. An unfilled weave gives the appearance that not enough paint was applied to the canvas. The applications of gesso also provide good adhesion for the layers of acrylic paints that follow. Once the gesso layers were completely dry and lightly sanded, a tonal ground was applied to the canvas.

The tonal or colored ground is a base color that serves as a background for subsequent layers of paint. In my experience, a gessoed canvas creates too harsh of a white color on which to apply paint. I much prefer a softer background of a light earth tone color or a contrasting color to the layers of paint applied afterwards. Other steps followed were to tape the edges of the stretched canvas in preparation for painting. Afterward, once the tape was removed the edges were painted black. The black color creates a framed, gallery like appearance for the canvas.

Creating a series of abstract compositions was the next challenge. Using color charts and guides to complimentary and analogous colors, I worked to create a harmonious collage of colors in each composition. The initial palette of colors applied consisted of pure, rich colors straight from the tube. Later, I would mix colors to achieve softer, subdued colors. Since the second set of colors was mixed, shades and tints of primary colors could be created. This greatly expanded the repertoire of color possibilities in my work.

Norman Pirollo, "*Kaleidoscope*", 2014. Expressionist painting, small palette knife.

With this early work, I would often post images on social media to determine the appeal of the art. The feedback received was critical to the direction I should pursue in my work. The feedback would be in the form of **Likes** or **Shares**, either on Instagram, Twitter or Facebook. These were and continue to be the most popular social media methods of communication. Feedback on new artwork has become fairly instantaneous through social media. In earlier times, an artist only had galleries or exhibitions as venues to display their work and seek feedback.

Visitors would visit a gallery or attend an exhibition and the gallerist or curator determined the popularity of art works through visitor feedback. Social media has added another opportunity for an artist to determine the appeal of their artwork. Social media has no boundaries, unlike a local gallery or exhibition. I would often post new artwork on several social media channels to determine its appeal. In this case, photographing the art became a critical step. Through my developing expertise in photographing art on a micro scale, it was not too difficult to transition to photographing full-scale art. I had my preferred room and wall location for hanging new art and would set up a tripod and camera to photograph it. Light conditions in the room were an important factor in a quality and accurate photographic rendition of the art.

It was interesting to see the amount of feedback that different art pieces received. Since art appreciation is subjective, each art piece would appeal to a particular group of viewers. With this understanding, certain art pieces had broader appeal and this brought the greatest value to me. It was in my best interest to develop a style of abstract expressionism with broad appeal. Although I thoroughly enjoyed creating the art, it was also important to create art that could be successfully marketed. Marketing leads to sales and every sale would motivate me to continue to generate more art. Without sales, I would probably languish and lose the urge to keep creating. Artists are all wired differently, and some artists create art regardless if there is a market for it. Their ambition is to simply continue to create art.

My personal ambition was to be a self-sustaining artist. The sales of my art would finance the further creation of art as well as provide me some financial freedom. Not worrying about financial support would clear my mind and allow me to continue creating good, quality art. The expression "art begets art" holds true for me where the creation of art becomes a life-long endeavor. Through the creation of successive bodies of work, financial independence would hopefully be achieved. Financial independence would relieve the stress and pressure of supporting myself at my passion. Most people, including myself, are not very creative when under pressure or stress.

I am a firm believer in "inner peace" and make every effort to clear my mind of any "daily grind" issues before standing at my easel to create art. Financial support is likely one of the most important issues an artist struggles with during their art career.

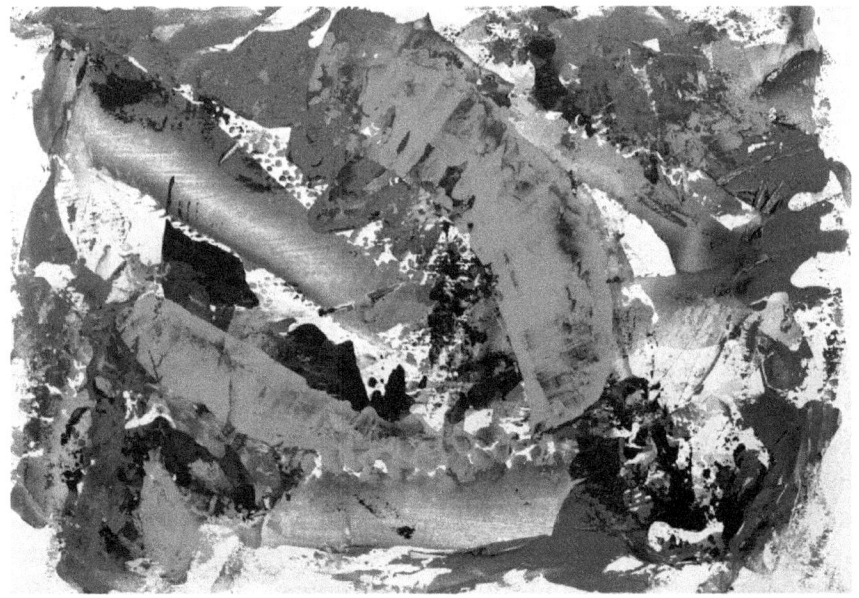

Norman Pirollo, "***Shattered***", 2014. Expressionist painting, mixed palette knife.

I soon began to feel at ease at painting with a palette knife. Occasionally, paintbrushes were used to blend areas of paintings but my overwhelming tool of choice had become the palette knife. I discovered how easy it was to muddy or overwork paint when a brush was used with wet paint or **wet on wet**. It became necessary to occasionally stop and let the paint dry somewhat. When a paintbrush was used to soften areas, I would use the brush sparingly. This would ensure that there was minimal mixing on the canvas and subsequent muddying of the area. I could see that this process would improve over many paintings; it would become an acquired skill. In my research into abstract expressionism, I sought to learn about as many painters of this period as possible. Although the goal was to develop my own voice, it was critical to look back and examine the various styles of artists of the AbEx movement.

Some Abstract Expressionist styles were more appealing to me than others. With an affinity to the palette knife as a tool with which to paint, I would seek art that had been painted primarily using this method. While most drawn to this type of work, I also realized that the paintbrush was necessary for both the creation and completion of abstract art compositions.

The Abstract Expressionist movement was a complete departure from previous art movements. Previous art movements would incorporate images of realism, either in pure form or distorted. Instead, Expressionism introduced no realism whatsoever into the composition, it was mainly created through emotion and subconscious gestural movements. Until the Abstract Expressionist movement appeared, the trend in Modernist art was slowly distancing itself from realism. **Surrealism**, the movement that directly preceded Abstract Expressionism, provided distorted and exaggerated images of reality as elements in compositions. It is this spontaneous and subconscious element of creation that first drew me to Abstract Expressionism. I wanted complete autonomy in my work without any link to realism. At one point, an attempt at abstracted landscapes and scenes was made, but this was a struggle and the experience was not rewarding. I can definitively say this is part of an artist's journey, to explore and experiment with different styles. How else can an artist determine which style of painting they gain the most satisfaction in creating?

The New York School, synonymous with Abstract Expressionists, was a diverse group of artists who came together to pursue the new art movement known as Abstract Expressionism. Working collectively within this new group, the New York School of Abstract Expressionists (**AbEx**) provided artist members with the power and influence to stage their own art exhibitions. The artists work was otherwise condemned to a modern version of the "Salon des Refusés" of the Impressionist era. In the early AbEx period (1945-52), Abstract Expressionist art did not yet have widespread appeal and people were left scratching their heads as to the direction of the artists. We see vast amounts of abstract art today and think nothing of the compositions, since abstract art has become an established and mainstream genre of art.

However, in the post-WWII era, abstract art was in its formative stage and considerably radical for the period. In this period, the public was used to seeing social realism in paintings. Surrealism, the movement preceding Abstract Expressionism, came close to abstraction but was merely a stepping-stone to pure abstraction.

It is necessary to always place the development of art styles and periods in the context of the era. What were the established norms of the era? What was considered radical? What did people expect of visual art? How much of an influence did politics and societal issues have on art?

Social realism was developed in the 1930s to place a realistic face on the life and rigors of the era. North America was in the midst of a depression. The American government of the 1930s decided to engage artists in creating art that drew attention to the working conditions of laborers and the plight of the poor. Social realism was an art form the general public could easily relate to and comprehend. A few New York School (AbEx) artists had their origins in these government-sponsored programs, **WPA** or "Works Projects Administration", of the mid-1930s, whose mission was to create art in the social realism genre. The American government essentially dictated to these artists what they should paint. Once the depression ended and WWII began, the US economy began to grow again and become prosperous. The **WPA** government sponsored art programs were then discontinued. A few of the AbEx artists are on record saying they grew tired of creating the **social realism** style of art and longed for a style of their own. After years of working at art in the social realism genre, I can see how they wanted to instead create non-representational art.

The AbEx movement, although unfavorably portrayed by a few critics, had its proponents and followers. Influenced by their background in creating social realism murals of a monumental scale, the AbEx group was also recognized for creating large-scale works on canvas. Early AbEx art (1940s) was characterized as biomorphic and organic in nature, whereas later work (1950 -) was either **action painting** or **color field** work.

The noted New York art critic, Clement Greenberg, advocated Abstract Expressionist art as "pure" painting that only featured what was essential to art, the making of marks on a flat surface. The AbEx movement continued to gain traction as the 1940s became the 1950s.

Large magazine spreads of Jackson Pollock and his work helped to propel abstract expressionism into mainstream art. Abstract Expressionism had finally come of age. The early to late-1950s period was the heyday of this movement during which the collective members of the AbEx group created a prolific amount of work. Artistic censorship following WWII was another reason for the growing acceptance of Abstract Expressionism. Conventional art of the era was scrutinized by the government for suggestive political leanings and left wing symbolism. Abstract Expressionist art was considered apolitical and safe since the subject matter was abstract. In the eyes of the American government, Abstract Expressionism was an art movement that could be both supported and exported to other countries as a **Made in America** art movement. The American government supported and promoted the AbEx movement as a reflection of American democracy and individualism.

The AbEx artists worked independently of each other where each artist developed their own style of abstract art. This is the inspiration I was seeking, to develop an individual voice within a collective genre of art. I admired the Abstract Expressionist artists of the New York School and wanted to follow in their footsteps. Flaunting the rules of art and simply pursuing their own vision of art was to be applauded. The fact that there are no rules in abstract art liberated the artists from tradition. Perspective does not exist in abstract art, at least not in the "pure" interpretation of abstract art. Scale, perspective and anatomical guidelines have no use in Abstract Expressionist art. The artist simply needs to develop a method to transfer emotion and subconscious thoughts to a canvas using gestural movements. Conscious thought directed at the composition would instead take away from the abstraction. Detail work became unimportant and irrelevant. Painting became a pure form of expression without limitations.

California Abstract Expressionist Jay Meuser, a non-objective style painter of that era, was quoted as follows when describing his painting "**Mare Nostrum**". "*It is far better to capture the glorious spirit of the sea than to paint all of its tiny ripples*".

Jackson Pollock, a founding member of the AbEx movement, brought a radical style to Abstract Expressionist painting. Pollock believed that the creation of the art was just as important as the art itself. Jackson Pollock used the floor as his easel, utilizing various techniques to apply paints to an unstretched canvas. His painting style was known as **action painting** where he would use various non-conventional methods to transfer paint onto the canvas.

Pouring paint, drip techniques, sticks, syringes and large brushes were all used to cover the canvas with paint. His best-known technique was "drip and splatter painting" where splattered streams of paint were thrown or dripped on to a canvas creating broken lines. The lines were fairly dense and organic in shape, randomly crossing each other. Application of the paint was performed through gestural, subconscious movements with no actual composition in mind. Instead, the composition evolved as paint was applied to the unstretched canvas. Pollock attacked the canvas from four sides and without obstructions or restrictions. From the late 1940s to the late 1950s, Pollock succeeded in popularizing **action painting** into an acceptable technique used to create art. Abstract Expressionist art had reached its pinnacle through Jackson Pollock's' style of painting. Expressionism had now become the antithesis of realist or objective painting.

"*I don't work from drawings. I don't make sketches and drawings and colors sketches into a final painting*" – **Jackson Pollock**

Although the **drip and splatter** style of painting was popularized by Jackson Pollock in the mid 20th century, it is not often seen any longer as a form of abstract painting. As with several abstract styles of art, it only lasted a few years. The death of Jackson Pollock was also instrumental in the demise of this style of painting since "drip and splatter" was directly associated to him.

Inspired by this style of painting, I created "**Opposites**". Elements of action painting are implemented into the art in the form of drips and splatters. Alternative methods of applying paint were also explored.

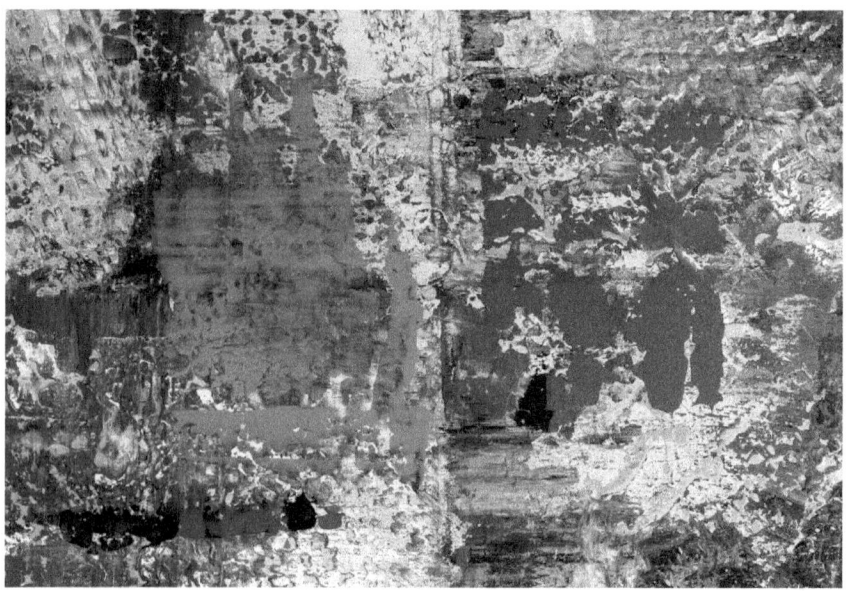

Norman Pirollo, "**Opposites**", 2014. Abstract Expressionist, drip painting, splattered paint, color field, palette knife.

"I continue to get further away from the usual painter's tools such as easel, palette, brushes, etc. I prefer sticks, trowels, knives and dripping fluid paint or a heavy impasto with sand, broken glass and other foreign matter added." – **Jackson Pollock**

Color Field painting was another style of Abstract Expressionism developed in the late 1940s to late 1950s. A few AbEx members painted in this style. Color Field painting had its origins in Modernism. Large fields of solid color distinguish color field art from other styles of abstract expressionism. The large areas of solid paint were spread across the canvas. This style of expressionism embraced form and process instead of the gestural movements typical in other styles of abstract expressionism.

In the color field style of painting, *"color is freed from objective context and becomes the subject in itself"*.

Clyfford Still, an AbEx member, was considered a leading Color Field painter. The composition of his non-objective paintings featured juxtaposed colors. **Mark Rothko**, also an AbEx member, was a colleague of Clyfford Still at the California School of Fine Arts. Rothko developed his own style of Color Field painting. Robert Motherwell, another AbEx artist, dabbled in both abstract expressionism and color field painting. His work was characterized by loose, open fields of color combined with loosely drawn lines and shapes. Another member of the AbEx movement, **Barnett Newman**, was considered one of the leading color field expressionist painters. Areas of pure color separated by thin vertical lines or **zips** can distinguish his art.

"Feeling must have a medium in order to function at all; in the same way, thought must have symbols. It is the medium, or the specific configuration of the medium that we call a work of art that brings feeling into being, just as do responses tot the objects of the external world... ...The medium of painting is such changing and ordering on an ideal plane, ideal in that the medium is more tractable, subtle, and capable of emphasis (abstraction is a kind of emphasis) than everyday life." — **Mark Rothko**

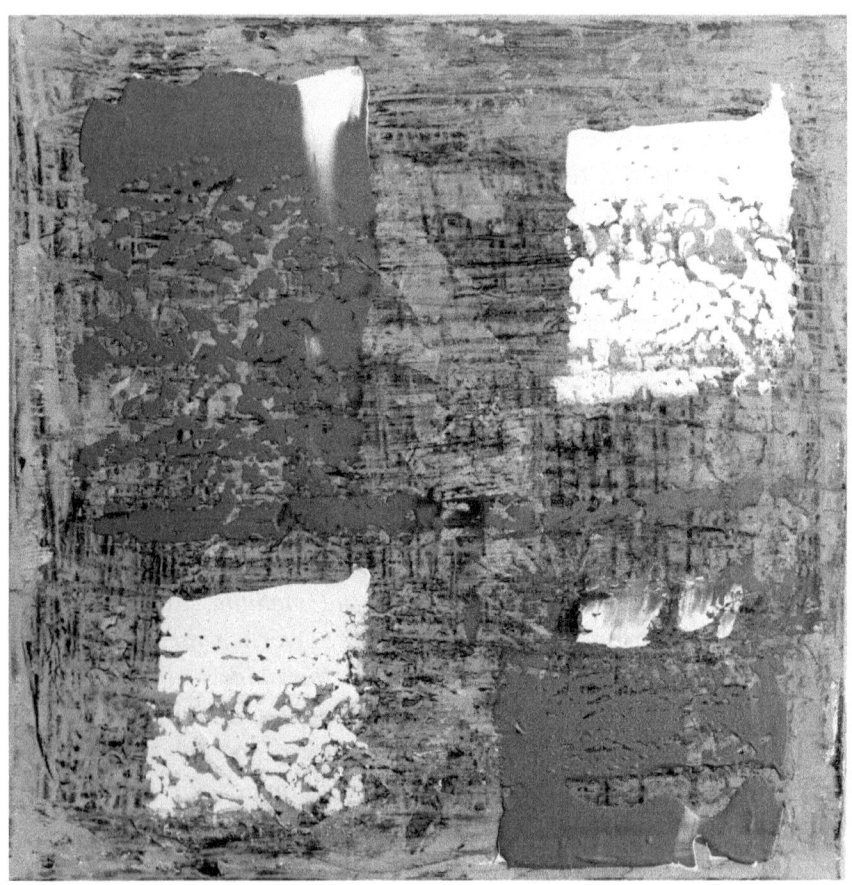

Norman Pirollo, "***Diversity I***", 2015. Abstract Expressionist, color field painting, palette knife.

"Like your phrase that I am concerned with the immediate and the particular without using a general formula for the painting process...
...My concern is with the fullness that comes from emotion, not with its initial explosion), or its emotional fall-out, or the glow of its expenditure. The fact is, I am an intuitive painter, a direct painter. I have never worked from sketches, never planned a painting, never 'thought out' a painting. I start each painting as if I had never painted before."
— **Barnett Newman**

LEAVE NO STYLE UNTURNED

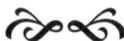

"I founds I could say things with color and shapes that I couldn't say any other way – things I had no words for"

Georgia O'Keeffe

MY TAKEAWAY OF THIS formative period was that it was necessary to further explore the different styles of Abstract Expressionism. Art appreciation can be very subjective as quickly realized in my few short years in the art world. A painting could be applauded and enjoyed by one person and not appreciated or disliked by another person. I discovered if there is a balance between people that applaud and people that dismiss, the art is good. This critical feedback meant that an equal number of people appreciate the work as disapprove of it. If an overwhelming number of people enjoyed the painting, it became clear to me that the right direction was being pursued with my art. This was an excellent manifestation of subjectivity.

I continued to create individual art pieces containing elements of the different AbEx styles researched. The process of creating these art pieces helped in my comprehension of the complexity of the individual art styles. As well, the appeal of each of the expressionist styles could be determined by acquiring feedback. Since my tenure in the art world was fairly short at this time, I did not have years of exhibitions and shows to draw from in my quest for a style. It became critical to seek a voice and style that I enjoyed creating and was appealing to the public.

In my experience, the **journey** can be as rewarding and enjoyable as the goal. Creating art and gaining feedback was a process I enjoyed. People would be asked to give their honest opinion of my art. In asking for this critical feedback, the subjectivity of the art was a determining factor. Abstract art is unlike objective or representational art where a viewer can judge the quality of a painting from the accuracy of the rendered image. Abstract art evokes emotions based on personal experiences and values. In abstract art, the adage "the end justifies the means" often applies. Since elements such as perspective and realism are not determining elements of the quality of abstract work, the viewer can only determine the appeal of the work by what they see on the canvas. There are no other elements to judge an abstract work, except for perhaps color balance.

The excitement intensified that the journey would introduce me to areas of the art world I had never anticipated being a part of. In research and conversations with other artists, it was found to be fairly normal for an artist to seek a style or genre of work they would be at peace with. The exploratory journey would not be a time-consuming chore, instead it allowed me to gain experience in creating abstract work and grow as a visual artist. Creating different styles of abstract art would remove any doubts I had of pursuing alternative directions in art. It can be frustrating for an artist to be attached to a style of art without exploring other styles. How else can an artist determine which style or genre they ultimately enjoy working in?

The AbEx movement had a direct influence on my developing abstract art. I pored over the work of the individual AbEx members to determine which direction to enjoy and pursue. Since this movement occurred in the mid 20th century, there were copious amounts of original film footage and interviews of the AbEx artists. As well, there were many magazine articles and excerpts from books that profiled a few of the individual AbEx artists and their work. It would be both interesting and educative to listen to and read about what they had to say about the origins of their style of work. I looked forward to understanding why this group of artists selected this particular genre of art and how they arrived at their individual styles.

James Brooks, a fairly late adopter of the Abstract Expressionist genre, had origins in the figurative world. One of his later art pieces, "***Untitled, 1952***" inspired me to create a similar work, "***Primeval, 2014***". The palette knife was used by James Brook to paint his art. This gave me the opportunity to experiment using a palette knife. My color selections and composition are considerably different although similarities can be seen in the art works. In creating this art, I was able to improve my palette knife techniques. The goal was not to imitate James Brooks work but to use it as a basis for the development of my own voice and style in this exploratory phase.

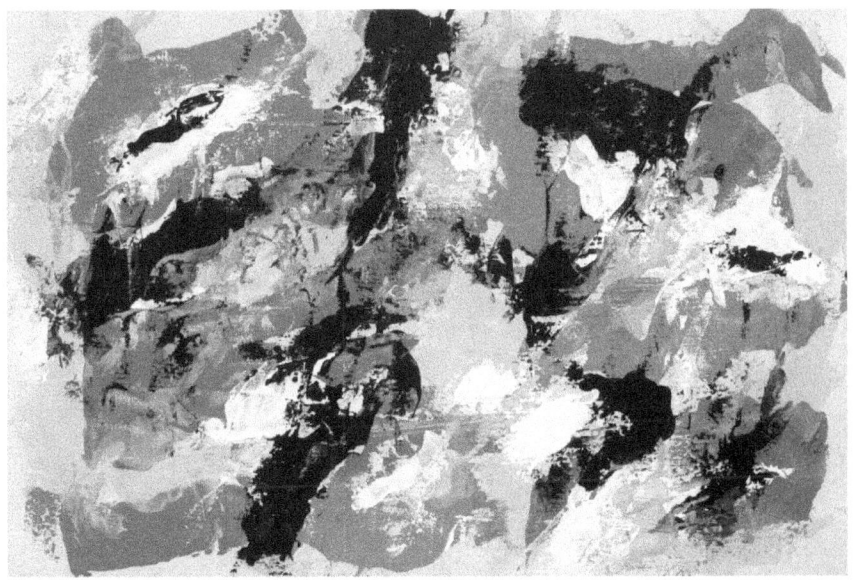

Norman Pirollo, "***Primeval***", 2014. Abstract Expressionist, gestural action painting, palette knife.

Taking this style one step further, I created a subsequent art piece using a larger palette knife, "***Turmoil, 2014***". The larger palette knife enabled me to cover larger areas of the canvas to create wide swaths of paint. The inspiration for this piece was James Brooks work but in a more complex composition. This art piece had broad and long knife strokes that appear to be sweeping across the canvas.

The palette knife was also worked to create a mottled effect on certain color swaths. The swaths of color overlaid each other to create a textured surface. The use of multiple, varied colors created complexity in the composition. There is a critical juncture where a layer of paint just applied is allowed to slightly dry or skin over and to sufficiently thicken. This allows the next overlapping layer to not muddy the colors. As can be seen in my painting below, the colors cross each other without picking up any of the underlying colors. To be able to add layers of paint to a canvas without muddying colors is an acquired skill. This can be viewed as a form of "wet on wet" painting.

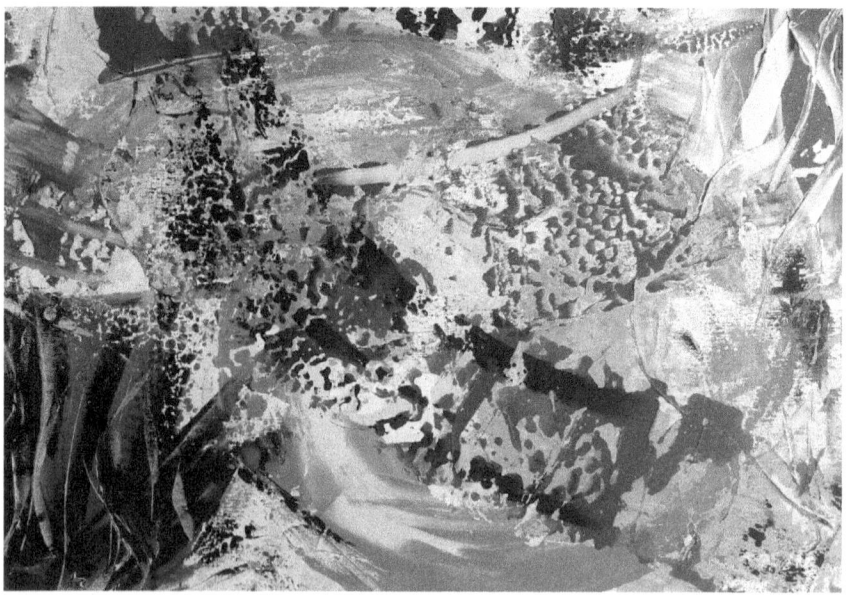

Norman Pirollo, "*Turmoil*", 2014. Abstract Expressionist, gestural action painting, palette knife.

In the next art piece of this series, "*Transcendence, 2014*", I went further with the wide swaths of paint. The composition is somewhat more organic than the earlier work. The technique of adding two paint colors to a large palette knife and then applying to the canvas was also introduced. This technique provided the streaked effect of two colors being mixed while they are being applied.

The amount of color mixing occurring on a palette knife could also be controlled to create a partially broken effect. In this art piece, a very light blue background or ground was introduced to contrast with the colors laid over the ground.

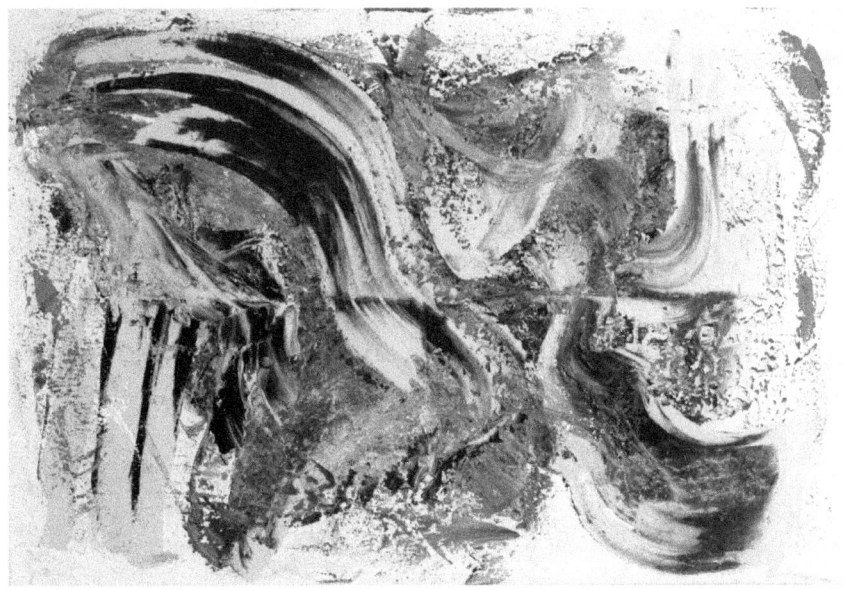

Norman Pirollo, "*Transcendence*", 2014. Abstract Expressionist, gestural action painting, palette knife.

Through my first few expressionist paintings, I soon realized that gestural movements to convey emotion were essential to the success and allure of the composition. It was important not to create a composition with a contrived appearance. The palette knife and brush movements need to come from within. I would often begin work on a blank canvas with a colored ground already applied. The colored ground would be a fairly neutral or a soft color ensuring that layers of paint applied over the ground would be highlighted to project depth and color.

Since abstract work uses shape, form, color and line instead of a visual representation, an emphasis on these elements became important in the creation of a composition. In "*Ikon, 2014*", I overlaid a series of colored shapes onto an underpainting and colored ground to depict early symbolism.

"Ikon" was informed through the work of **Franz Kline** and his art of symbolism in the form of calligraphy. Symbolism preceded modern languages; it was an early form of communication among people. Symbolism was also created as a method to record thoughts and messages. The *"Ikon, 2014"* painting of my exploratory period was a departure, where representation was introduced into an abstract painting. In essence, my departure was comprised of the addition of symbols involving conscious thought, much like the symbolism of early man. Technically, abstraction refers to a departure from reality in the depiction of art. The departure can be partial or complete. In this painting, a slight amount of representation was combined into an abstract composition. Although pure abstraction removes any reference to visual reality, partial abstraction can be viewed as a compromise. I chose to explore the addition of recognizable elements in this work.

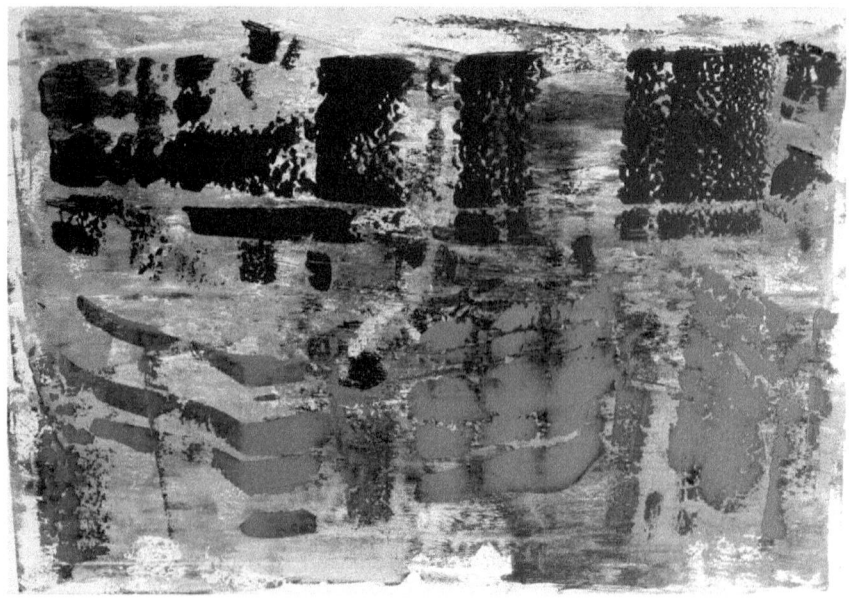

Norman Pirollo, *"Ikon"*, 2014. Abstract Expressionist, representational reference in an abstract composition, palette knife.

In my next work of this style, I went further in combining representation into an abstract art composition. *"Alpine, 2014"* became my first experience in creating an abstract landscape scene.

Typical of representational landscape art, the painting is based on a real scene or image. The image can originate from a photo or it can be created in "plein air", painted outdoors live in front of the scene. In this work, there is no reference to an actual or photographed scene; instead it was based purely on my conscious visualization of this particular scene. The palette knife was used to create the composition, where elements of the scene were overlaid onto one another creating a semblance of depth and perspective, much like a realistic view. A few of the colors used in this composition also lent themselves to a landscape scene. Other pure colors were included to dramatize the scene and to emphasize that it is in fact an abstraction and not based on realism.

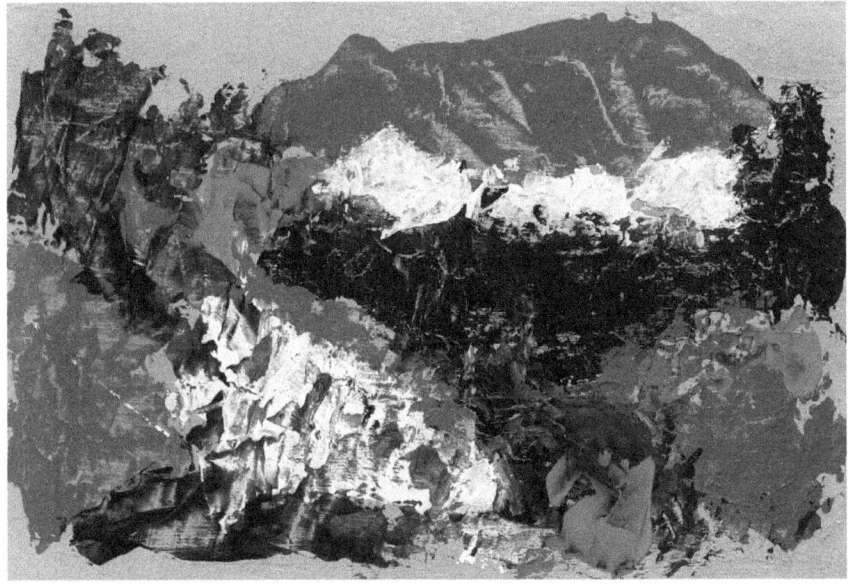

Norman Pirollo, "**Alpine**", 2014. Abstract Expressionist, palette knife, representational reference in an abstract composition.

In "**Transference**", I experimented with different shades of color to introduce an effect of depth into the composition. The colors created in the palette were complementary to one another. Vivid colors overlaid onto one another in a random pattern created the unique effect of each layer appearing to be separate from the one below. This particular painting surprised me as to how powerful layering can be.

The middle, dark color created a transition between the vivid blue and red layers. The layers appear to be floating at different depths. Although one of the tenets of abstract expressionism is that the picture plane is flat and without depth, this painting exhibits depth without deliberate intention. The acquired skill and timing of applying one layer over another layer of paint became critical; since I was striving to not have the colors mix between layers. The "wet on wet" technique with some modification was used. The title for the artwork is deliberate and reflects an illusion of transference of the common "blue" medium between the layers.

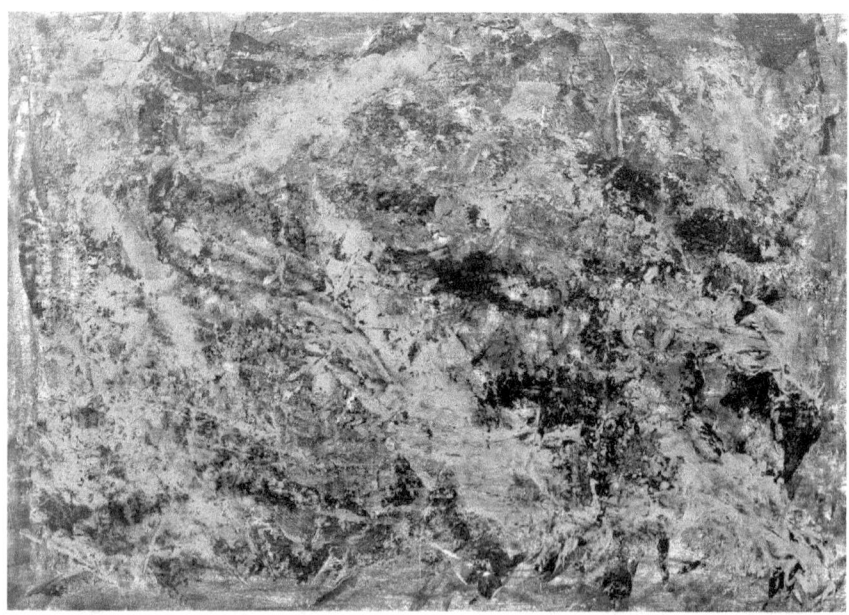

Norman Pirollo, "***Transference***", 2014. Abstract Expressionist, gestural action painting, palette knife.

Hans Hoffman, a founding AbEx member artist, was one of the émigré artists from Europe to the USA. He was highly regarded as an arts teacher and informed many students of his methods and philosophy. A large component of his teaching style was to have students determine their own style and not simply work in the style of another artist. Many of Hoffman's students became successful artists and he made a significant impact in the art world through his teaching efforts.

Hans Hoffman stopped teaching in the late 1950s and instead focused completely on the creation of art. He would amass a growing body of Abstract Expressionist art over the following years. Hans Hoffman's later work, in the Abstract Expressionist years of postwar-WWII, was influenced through emotion and the subconscious. Gestural actions driven by emotions were instrumental in the creation of his Expressionist art. Using colors overlaid onto one another, he juxtaposed rectangular areas of color into fascinating abstract compositions. For this series, I created a unique palette of colors to apply to the canvas.

Norman Pirollo, "*Diversity 3*", 2015. Abstract Expressionist, gestural action painting, rectangular forms, palette knife, brushes.

In "*Diversity 3*", I accentuated the negative spaces on the canvas. After application of a colored ground, adjacent colored areas of color were applied to slightly overlay each other. This particular piece was a departure for me in its balance of negative space, colored forms and areas. The palette was a combination of analogous and complementary colors to emphasize the delineation between the forms and to accentuate the negative spaces on the canvas.

Formerly a representational painter, Hoffman's departure from realism can be seen in his work over the decades from the 1930s through the 1960s. It was in the 1960s that he introduced a new body of work focusing on geometric forms and colors as symbolism for landscapes and objective realism. Hoffman also introduced the **push-pull** theory where instead of representational forms; color and form were instead used to create movement and depth in a painting. It is this series or style of work that influenced me to create my own series of art using rectangular forms as a basis. I enjoyed the process of juxtaposing these areas of color onto a canvas in a spontaneous and subconscious driven process.

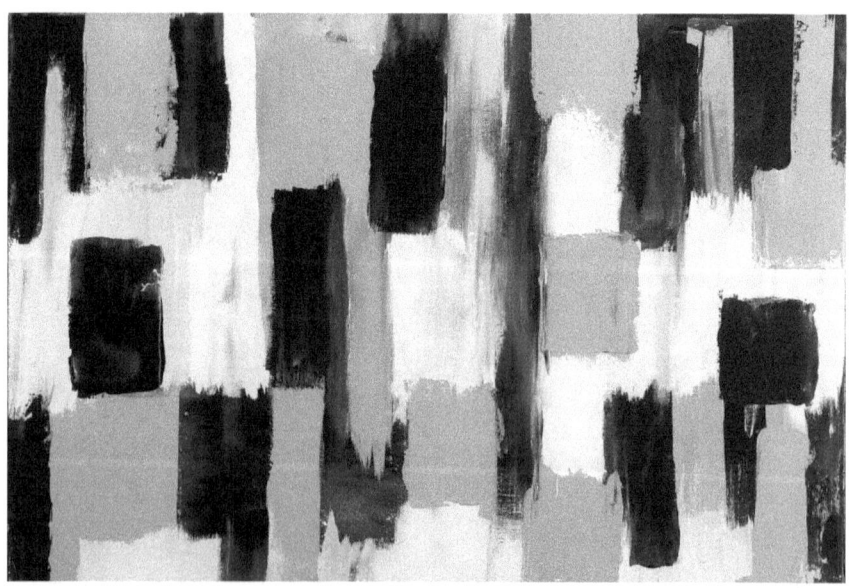

Norman Pirollo, "*Urban Brio*", 2015. Abstract Expressionist, gestural action painting, rectangular forms, palette knife, brushes.

In "*Urban Brio*", rectangular forms fill the composition. White space is limited to the light colored areas surrounding each of the colored rectangular forms. In this composition, a very limited selection of analogous and complementary colors was chosen for the palette. I wanted to transfer subconscious thought onto the canvas and not be overly concerned with choices of color. Instead, with a palette of essentially three colors, my focus could instead be on the action of applying the paint.

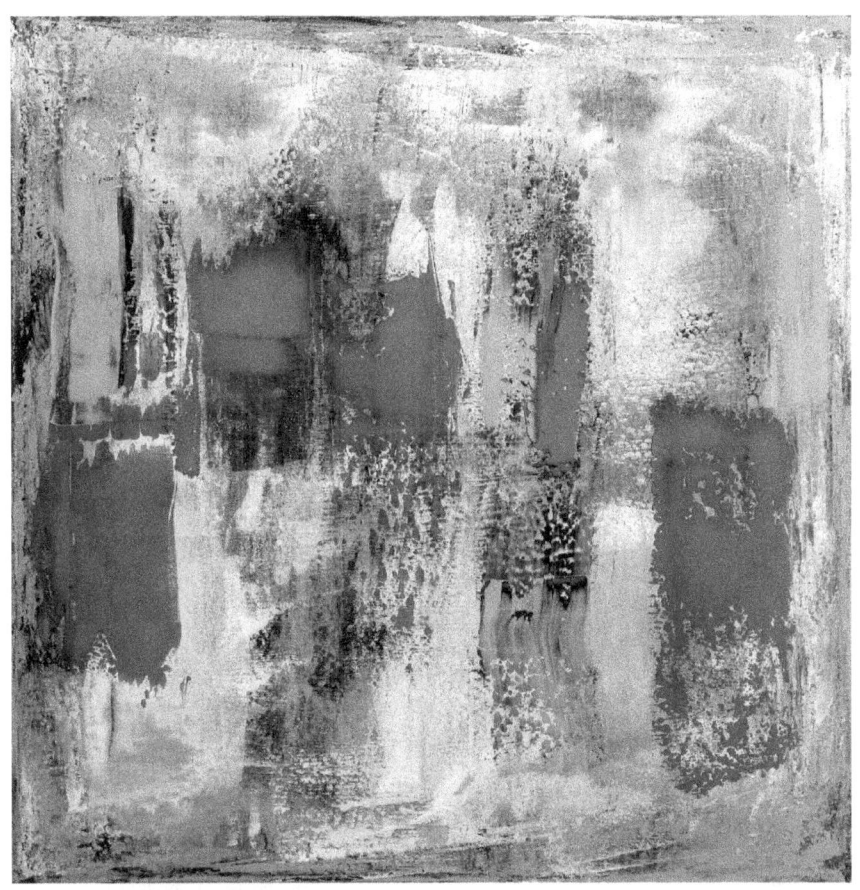

Norman Pirollo, "***Transpose 3***", 2015. Abstract Expressionist, gestural action painting, rectangular forms, palette knife, brushes.

In "***Transpose 3***", the composition consisted of a vertical array of colored forms adjacent to one another. The colored forms were randomly juxtaposed through the transference of emotion into colored areas. As in "***Urban Brio***", the color palette was purposely limited to two complementary colors. Instead, both a colored ground and underpainting were applied to the canvas. Mixing, scraping and scratching paints onto the canvas formed the underpainting. My goal was to have a more complex base over which to apply the colored forms. In contrast to "***Urban Brio***", the colored forms were also vertically separated, where the horizontal center of the canvas serves as a demarcation.

In *"Contra"*, rectangular forms serve as a component of the underpainting instead of being the main elements of the painting. I wanted to take the inclusion of rectangular forms to the next level and incorporate them as background elements of the painting. The color palette was once again purposely limited to a small selection of analogous and complementary colors.

Introduction of organically shaped elements to contrast with rectangular elements was the goal in this painting. Using layers of paint, these organic elements appear to be floating above the rectangular forms. Small, subtle touches of red paint were included to draw attention to areas of the painting. I have since successfully used this technique in other paintings. The underpainting was created with a brush, whereas the top layers were applied using a palette knife.

Norman Pirollo, *"Contra"*, 2015. Abstract Expressionist, gestural action painting, rectangular and organic forms, palette knife, brushes.

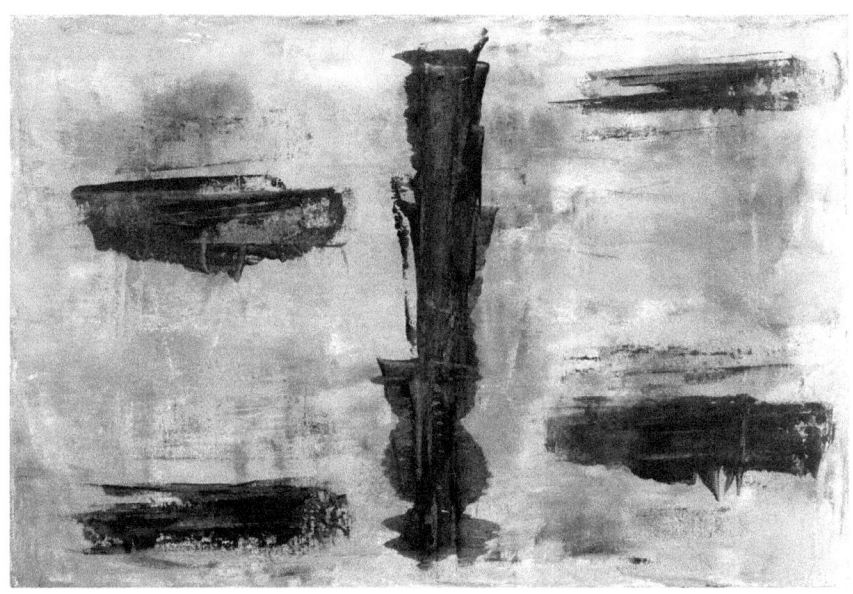

Norman Pirollo, "***Divergence***", 2015. Abstract Expressionist, gestural action painting, rectangular and organic forms, palette knife, brushes.

The feedback received from viewers of "***Transpose 3***" was overwhelmingly positive. The viewers of the art heaped praise on the composition, especially on the complex underpainting and colored ground. In "***Divergence***", I decided to use elements of "***Contra***" and apply them over a complex underpainting. The color palette was once again very limited. The dark, partially rectangular elements were scraped and scratched onto the underpainting in complete gestural action movements. Application of a third color to blend in with the dark forms was another exploratory addition. I was curious to how a contrasting light color blending with the dark color would lighten the forms in achieving a more luminous appearance.

"The creative process lies not in imitating, but in paralleling nature – translating the impulse received from nature into the medium of expression, thus vitalizing this medium. The picture should be alive, the statue should be alive, and every work of art should be alive." -- **Hans Hofmann,** his critical quote against imitation in modern art, since there is no life generated in imitating.

MULTIPLE STYLES, ONE GENRE

"What goes on in abstract art is the proclaiming of aesthetic principles...It is in or own time that we have become aware of pure aesthetic considerations. Art can never be imitation."

Hans Hofmann

AN ART STYLE IS how an artist expresses his or her vision and emotion through a paintbrush onto a canvas. Style is a combination of composition, form and color. It is composed of multiple elements including the medium, the canvas or substrate and the method through which an artist applies paint to the canvas. Some artists prefer to paint in a single style whereas other artists will paint in several styles. Whether the styles are all part of the same art genre is up to the artist. Artists have the freedom to explore new styles and genres of art. Many of the leading artists of past centuries have painted in multiple styles and genres. A few have also crossed disciplines into sculpture, ceramics and design. Reading about these artists was captivating as I also consider myself a multidisciplinary artist with work in sculpture, wood and on canvas.

In the past year, I have embraced Abstract Expressionism as a genre of art I wish to explore further. The (AbEx) Abstract Expressionist art movement is almost always associated with the post war period of the late 1940s through the late 1950s and early 1960s.

Each AbEx member conveyed their unique style and a few painted in multiple styles. The AbEx movement was considered groundbreaking by distancing itself from past art movements. The styles of art I currently paint in can be viewed in the spirit of Abstract Expressionism. AbEx art occurred during specific post-war years; therefore current art in this subgenre of abstract art can be better classified as **neo-AbEx** or a re-birth of AbEx art. Through my exploratory period, I have come to embrace multiple styles within this genre of art. As an artist, my work has evolved through an ever-increasing body of work created. However, my direction has remained constant. I was drawn to Abstract Expressionism and have been pursuing this genre of art ever since.

The evolution of an artist usually involves the embrace of more than one style and direction. A visual artist is characterized through the direction and styles pursued during their artistic career. Typically, an artist embraces a style and develops a body of work within the style parameters. The artist then evolves and optionally embraces another, different style or a variation of the style. It is perfectly fine as an artist, to work at multiple styles or to follow multiple directions, but focusing on one or two is a far better strategy for success.

The validity and prospects of an artist are reinforced through a narrow focus of styles. Not being a planner at heart, Abstract Expressionist art appealed to my character traits. Formal or objective art involves the tedious process of creating a painting based upon realism or an image. Spontaneous expression is the missing component in objective art. I enjoy the spontaneity of starting with a blank canvas and transferring my vision and emotion through a paintbrush or palette knife onto a canvas. The constants are the canvas, the brush and palette knife. The variables are the subconscious emotion, the colors and mood.

Over the course of a year, I explored the art and philosophy of various AbEx members. By studying the art of the AbEx members, an understanding of the politics and ideologies of the 1940-60 period was developed. The need to understand and appreciate this art movement in a more comprehensive manner was necessary before being immersed into it.

What drove these AbEx artists to repudiate their earlier work and embrace this new art movement? Was it the excitement of starting and establishing a new art movement? Was abstract, emotion driven art always on the AbEx artists mind but not widely accepted until the AbEx movement appeared? Was it the camaraderie of associating with fellow artists who pursued a similar vision of art? How much influence did the politics and ideology of the period influence the AbEx movement and the work of the individual artists?

One concern that surfaced was the fear that I would not be able to emulate the work of this period since the world has changed along with its politics and ideologies. Society has since evolved and issues of this earlier period are perhaps no longer relevant or important. I would need to work in the context of today's world and apply a vision to my work based on today's societal ills, politics and other current issues. My immersion into Abstract Expressionist art during the year 2014-15 was at times gratifying and at other times frustrating. In the short period of time I had been involved in the arts and specifically painting, understanding the AbEx movement was at times overwhelming. In previous studies of art history, I would immerse myself into the theoretical aspect of different art periods and movements. Instead, with the AbEx movement, I was not only enthusiastic in understanding its principles and philosophy, but keen on challenging myself to develop a style in this genre.

My already strong interest in art was further simulated through research into this groundbreaking, revolutionary art movement. The year 2014-15 had been a transitional period for me where painting as an art form was embraced. Only a few short years ago, it would be unheard of me to contemplate creating art through painting. I had already gained a reputation as a wood sculptor and wood artist. Establishing myself as a wood artist and working with wood as a medium occurred over a few years. Significant bodies of work in both sculptural work and wood art were created over this period and every opportunity was seized to show or exhibit my work. My vision of how to fit into the art world was however changing. Although still attached to wood art and sculpture, the appeal of painting as a method to express myself was growing.

The process of creating wood sculptures and wood art could be lengthy, with multiple steps involved from carving to finishing. Painting instead provided me more instantaneous satisfaction where a painting could be completed over a two to three day period. The painting could also be modified or painted over if I found it unsatisfactory or not appealing. This provided me the freedom to instead focus on my art and not so much the process of creating it. In the transition to painting it became important to learn color theory, how to work with substrates such as canvas, how to select and use paintbrushes and how to effectively use and manoeuvre a palette knife. Creating the composition was instead an acquired skill where emotion and subconscious thoughts were transferred to a canvas.

With wood art, a range of tools was available to work with wood as a medium. Chisels, scrapers and hand planes were all tools used to create sculptural work. Instead, with painting it was acrylic paint, brushes and palette knives that had now became the necessary tools used to create my art. Equipping myself with this new set of tools occurred over the span of a year from early 2014 into 2015. The canvasses I worked on began with small sizes and slowly progressed to larger sizes. It can be intimidating to work on a large canvas with so much expanse of cotton to cover; it was instead easier in the early stages to develop my art on smaller canvases.

Techniques were also developed and learned over this period. Should a blank canvas be tackled as a whole or in sections? I soon found that with abstract work, the spontaneous motion of applying paint should cover the complete canvas unless a form or color block was being applied to one area of the canvas. There should be a harmony of form and color in a composition to express emotion and mood. The early Expressionist painter **Wassily Kandinsky (1866 –1944)** refers to the "symbolism of color" where white is a silent color, equated to a transcendental state. The skill of understanding when to apply a new layer of paint over a previous layer also came up. Acrylic paints, although fast drying, still need a few minutes to skin over. This was to avoid dragging a previous layer of paint into the new layer. Occasionally, the mixing of layers was acceptable if this was the desired goal.

Another acquired skill gained over the year was when to stop painting the art. A painting can begin to appear overworked with too many brushstrokes or the application of too many layers of paint. The application of more paint begins to make less sense after a while. Why continue to obscure previous layers of paint? Is this the intention or is it to ultimately scrape the layers away?

Application of too many layers of paint would simply obscure the paint beneath. It was far better to have at most three layers of paint over a colored ground or an underpainting. The layers of paint could simply be swaths of paint that crossed each other in the composition. The amount of opacity in a painting would need to be factored in. I also invested time in learning about the elements of abstract expressionism, including color forms and blocks, expressive lines, geometric forms, organic forms, positive and negative space, hard and soft edges, and the best use of color.

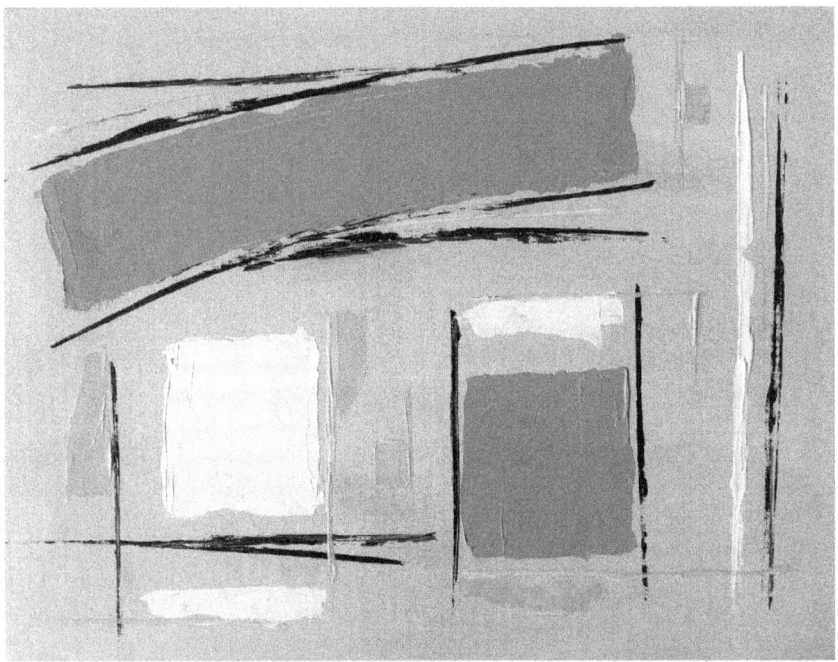

Norman Pirollo, "*Mélange 1*", 2015. Abstract Expressionist, gestural action painting, hard edges, rectangular color forms, lines, palette knife.

The early Expressionist work of Wassily Kandinsky (1866-1944) had a direct influence on my "*Mélange 1*" and "*Mélange 2*" series of art. In the mid 1920s, after the period in which he was primarily interested in the German Expressionist (1910-30) use of color and form, Kandinsky moved to a more formal theory of the elements of drawing in which line and point were the expressive elements. The symbolic language used was entrenched in his later works, without continuity between the feeling and the symbol, instead simply a correspondence. The subjective element was completely released.

"Of all the arts, abstract painting is the most difficult. It demands that you know how to draw well, that you have a heightened sensitivity for composition and for colours, and that you be a true poet. This last is essential." — **Wassily Kandinsky**

Norman Pirollo, "*Mélange 2*", 2015. Abstract Expressionist, gestural action painting, hard edges, rectangular color forms, lines, palette knife.

In the "*Mélange*" series, elements were included in the compositions that follow the philosophy of Wassily Kandinsky. The uses of lines and color forms are the expressive elements. The color forms are symbolic whereas the lines form a correspondence between the elements of the painting. The colors selected contrast sharply with the underlying colored ground.

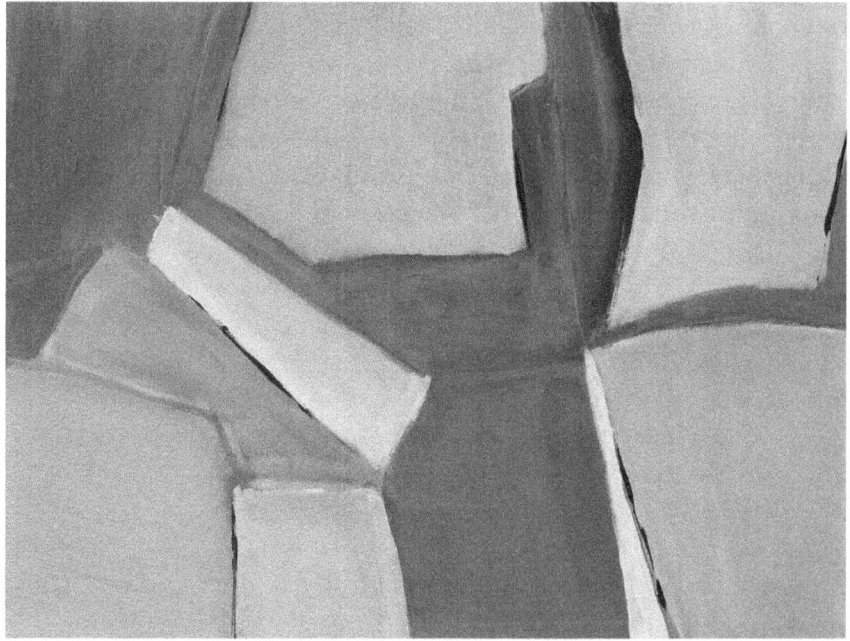

Norman Pirollo, "*Jumble*", 2015. Abstract Expressionist, expressive painting, irregular color forms, lines, juxtaposition, palette knife.

In "*Jumble*", the use of color, form and lines are combined in a more complex composition. The forms are of arbitrary shape, much like the pieces in a puzzle. I wanted to take this style of painting a step further than in the earlier "*Mélange 1 and 2*" series. The color palette is also softer in this painting. The irregular, geometric color forms are juxtaposed to create a more dynamic vision. The hard-edged linear divisions between colored forms are both subtle and enhanced. Enhanced lines delineate some forms whereas there is subtle blending between other, adjacent geometric forms. "*Jumble*" was an experiment in developing a new style.

"*Jumble*" was also a composition that included a simple arrangement of geometric color forms and lines. Each of the colors is symbolic in nature. Color balance and harmony were key components of the composition. Creating this art would help me to understand if this was the vision and direction I wished to pursue.

Jackson Pollock was an important figure in the Abstract Expressionist (AbEx) movement. It has been said that Pollock defined the movement. Much of the critical dialogue of the period revolved around his unconventional **action painting**. Instead of using an easel, Pollock would use everyday objects to lay paint down on an unstretched canvas on the floor. Jackson Pollock liked to express his feelings through paint rather than illustrate them. Jackson Pollock was characterized through the "drip and splatter" technique he developed. Even to this day, "action painting" is controversial. Unlike the contributions of other founding AbEx members, "action painting" was a complete break from conventional forms of art.

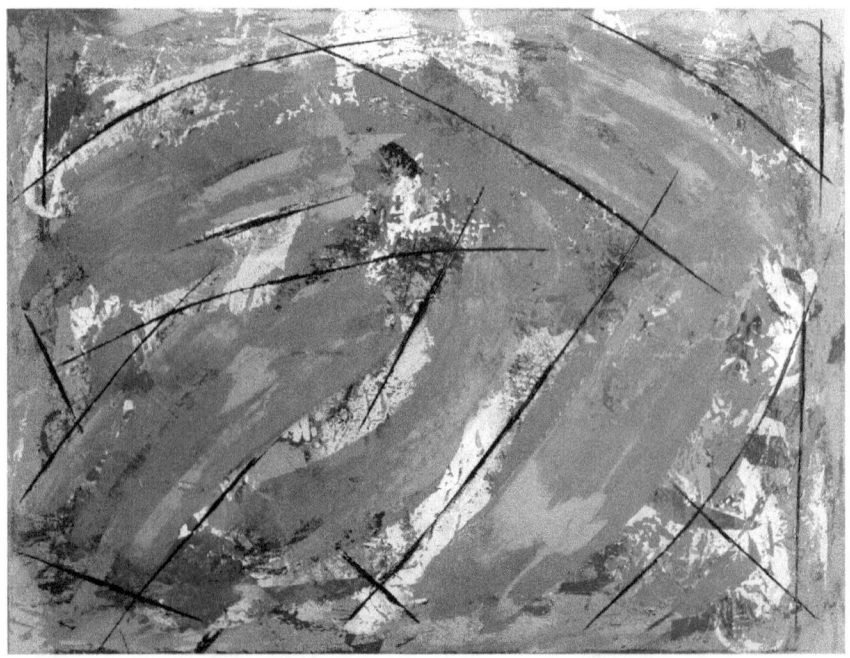

Norman Pirollo, *"Revolution"*, 2015. Abstract Expressionist, lines, action painting, layered colors, brushes, scraping, palette knife.

In the quest to develop my own identifying style, I realized that the "action" component was elusive in my work. Although my brush and palette knife strokes were expressive, the need was felt to demonstrate and accentuate an element of **action** in my work. "***Revolution***", a composition involving layers of vibrant paints in sweeping swaths, addressed this need. Complex layering of contrasting colors superimposed with wide red-orange swaths of paint were delineated by arching black lines. It received exceptional feedback from viewers when first shown. White was implemented as a transitional color.

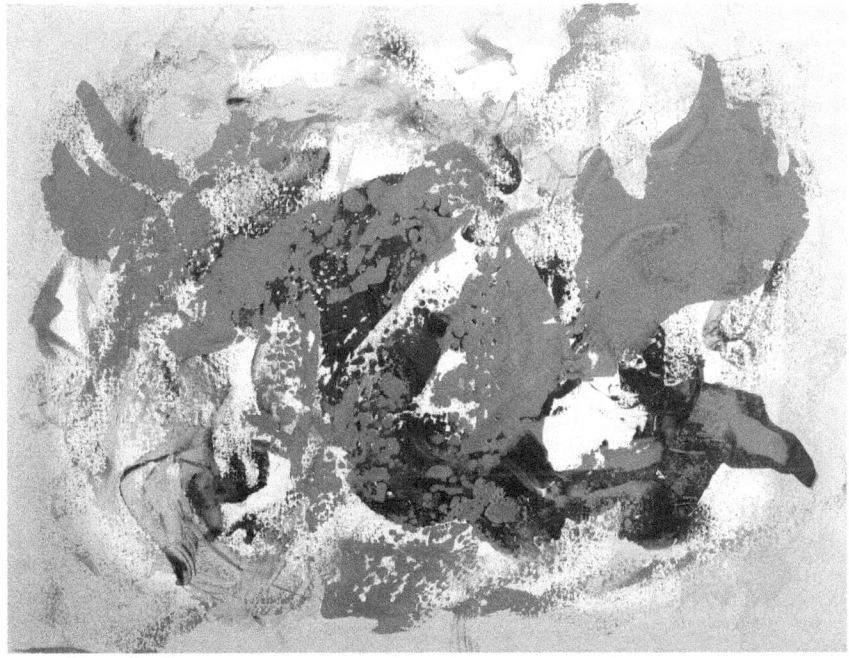

Norman Pirollo, "***Icarus***", 2015. Abstract Expressionist, expressive action painting, layered colors, brushes, scraping, palette knife

"***Icarus***" was another manifestation in the "action painting" continuum. A more complex color palette was used with the addition of the "drip and splatter" technique. The process of creating this art was thoroughly enjoyable. To create the composition, I worked exclusively with inner feelings and emotion. Very little conscious thought was placed into the art.

Working with a pre-selected palette of analogous and complementary colors, the art was created in layers with "white" as a silent, transitional color.

"Modern art to me is nothing more than the expression of contemporary aims of the age we're living in... All cultures have had means and techniques of expressing their immediate aims – the Chinese, the Renaissance, all cultures. The thing that interests me is that today painters do not have to go to a subject matter outside of themselves. Most modern painters work from a different source, they work from within" -- **Jackson Pollock**

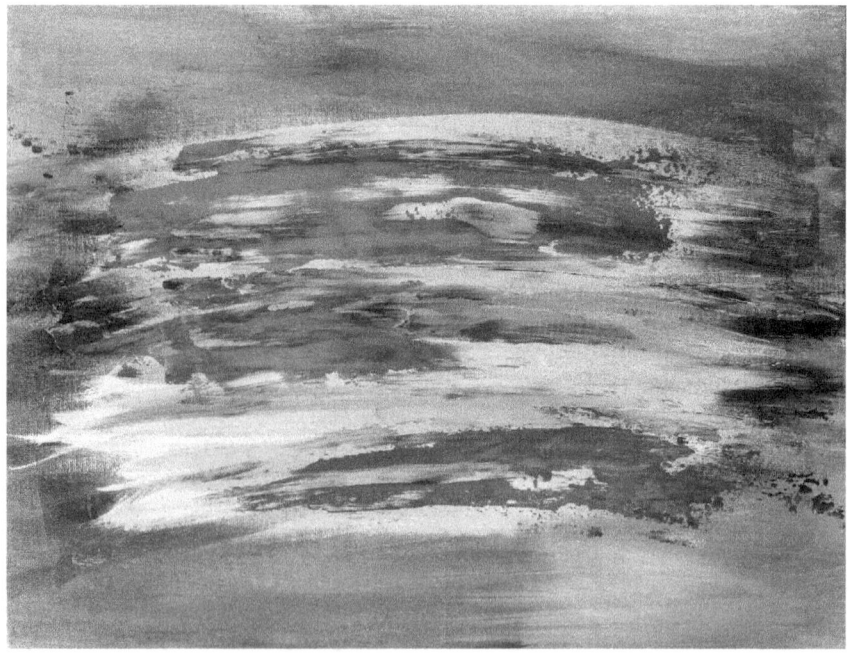

Norman Pirollo, *"Tempest"*, 2015. Abstract Expressionist, expressive action painting, layered colors, brushes, scraping, palette knife.

In *"Tempest"*, action painting was completely emphasized along with the element of movement. Working with a more complex underpainting, layers of complementary paints were applied in wide, horizontal swaths. The swaths were fairly solid in the middle layer whereas the final layer of red paint was broken up and fragmented.

The technique used to apply the final layer of paint involved a combination of palette knife and brush. To create the composition, I worked exclusively with inner feelings and emotion. Very little conscious thought was placed into the art.

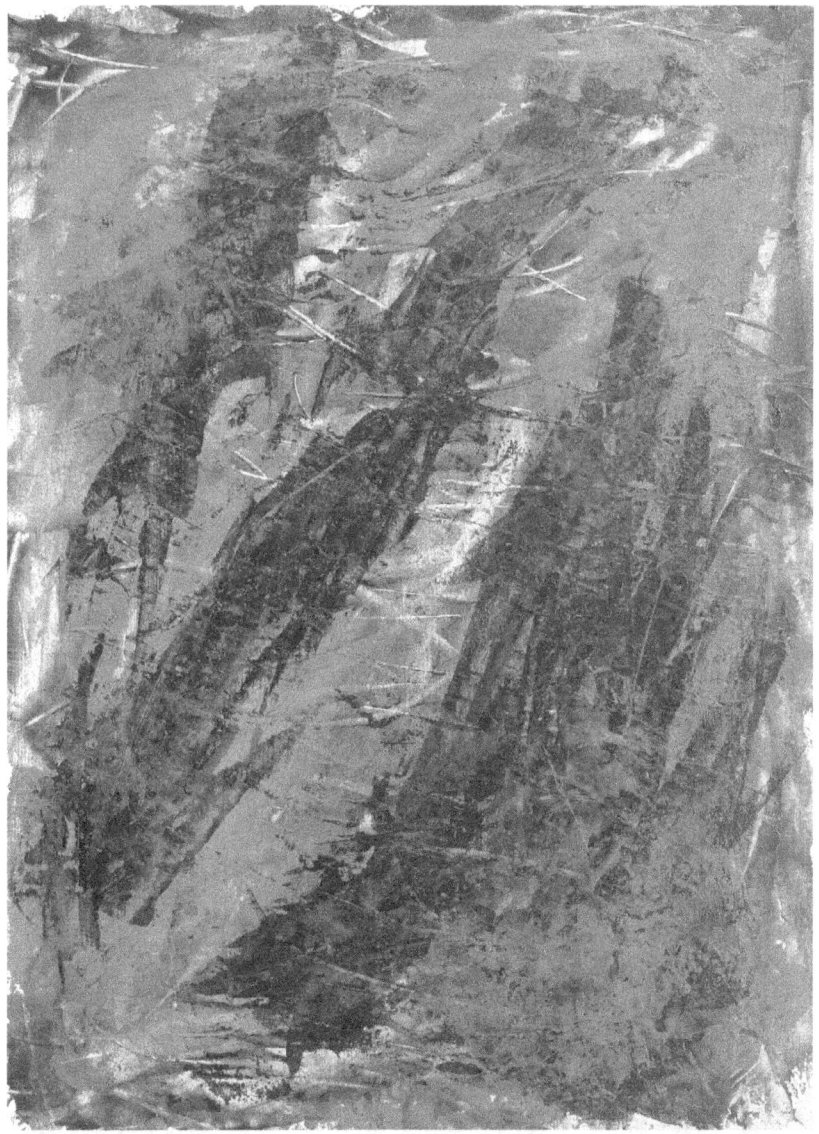

Norman Pirollo, "*Equinox*", 2014. Abstract Expressionist, expressive action painting, layered colors, brushes, scraping, palette knife.

"Equinox" was a complex composition with multiple layers of paint scraped away to reveal underlying layers. Light and dark effects were combined in a highly textured, expressive combination of elements to form an engaging composition.

Another renowned abstract artist, **Gerhard Richter (1932 -),** has had a considerable influence on my more recent work. Gerhard Richter began his art career as a representational painter and eventually transitioned to abstract work. His early work consisted of photo-realistic paintings to which he applied a "blur effect". Richter is better known for abstract work from the 1970s and on. In this genre of work, he paints layers of paint onto a canvas through the use of large brushes. The paintings evolve in stages and are based on his opinion of the direction of the painting. If the painting was progressing to his satisfaction, he would continue and complete the art. If not, he would paint over the complete canvas or large parts of it and start over. As part of the creation process, Gerhard Richter would walk away from a painting in progress and then return the following day. The time away would allow him to better reflect on the direction of the painting. In my own work, I often follow this approach. Walking away for a length of time and returning with an improved vision has positively impacted my art.

Gerhard Richter used blurring and scraping techniques to expose the underlying layers of paint. In his later work, he became innovative and made use of a squeegee to apply and to scrape wide swaths of paint to a canvas. The canvases he worked with were typically large and stretched against a wall. Gerhard Richter has often been referred to as the best artist alive. His recognition stems from the fact that he has created a resurgence of Abstract Expressionism. In the art market today, Gerhard Richter's paintings command very high prices. Gerhard Richter had a direct influence on the following art, *"**Brazen**"*. Some of the techniques I used had origins in Gerhard Richter's later work. This form of art was appealing to me and the process of creating it was both challenging and engaging. Scraping away layers of paint to reveal the paint underneath brought a new dimension to my creation of abstract art. The process involved both an **additive** phase and a subsequent **subtractive** phase.

In the "additive" phase, layers of paint were applied to the canvas. In the "subtractive" phase, the layers were judiciously scraped away to reveal a captivating, expressive composition. In the spirit of Gerhard Richter's style, "*Brazen"* is another departure into the uncharted expressionist genre of art. The action of scraping a bold, complimentary color horizontally across a complex underpainting revealed a fascinating, textured composition.

Norman Pirollo, "*Brazen*", 2015. Abstract Expressionist, expressive action painting, layered colors, brushes, scraping, palette knife.

The element of movement is clearly visible as are the interconnected forms. The prominent "red" color is separated from the "blue" underpainting through a complementary color. Abstract forms, expressive complementary colors, textures and a gestural process depict emotion in this abstract expressionist art. The "*Brazen"* composition was not planned beforehand but spontaneously painted through the subconscious. Through inspiration from Gerhard Richter's work, I enjoyed the process of injecting emotion into the development of this art piece.

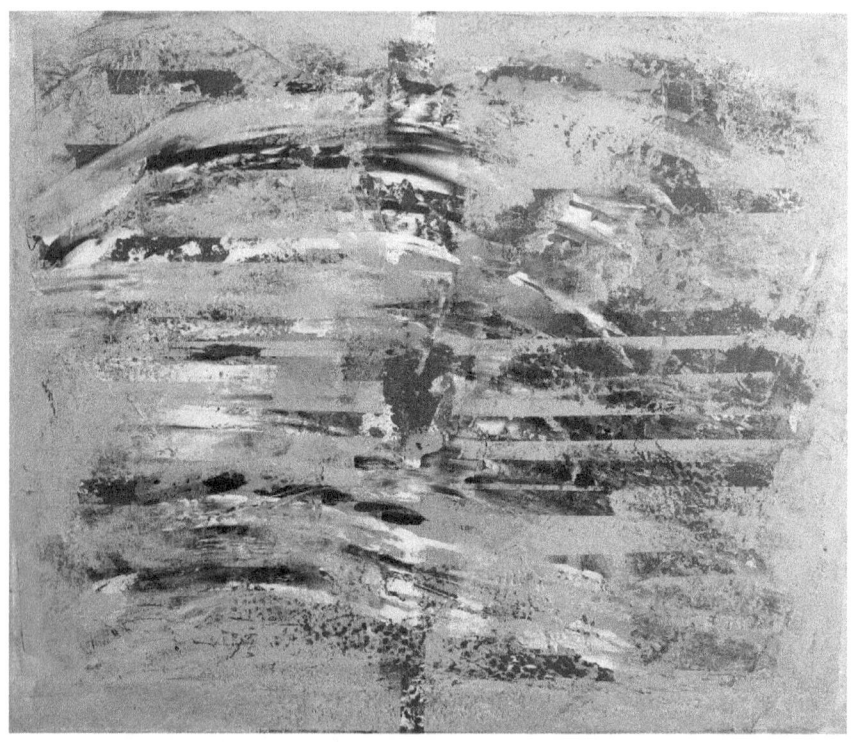

Norman Pirollo, "*Elan Vital*", 2015. Abstract Expressionist, expressive action painting, layered colors, brushes, scraping, palette knife.

In "*Elan Vital*", a different approach was followed in creating the composition. With the "additive" and "subtractive" process in mind, I contemplated updating an earlier painting that did not appeal to me. Rather than begin with a blank canvas, the original composition would instead serve as the underpainting with a single, complementary color applied over top. Using the "subtractive" technique, a judicious amount of the new layer of paint was then removed to reveal the original underpainting. A riveting composition was slowly revealed as the new, fresh layer of paint was intentionally scraped away. Applying this process to an existing painting was novel to me. Exposing the original painting in a partially obscured setting opened my eyes to the powerful effect of this process. From feedback received, the new painting garnered considerable attention and generated dialogue. This process was added to my repertoire of techniques.

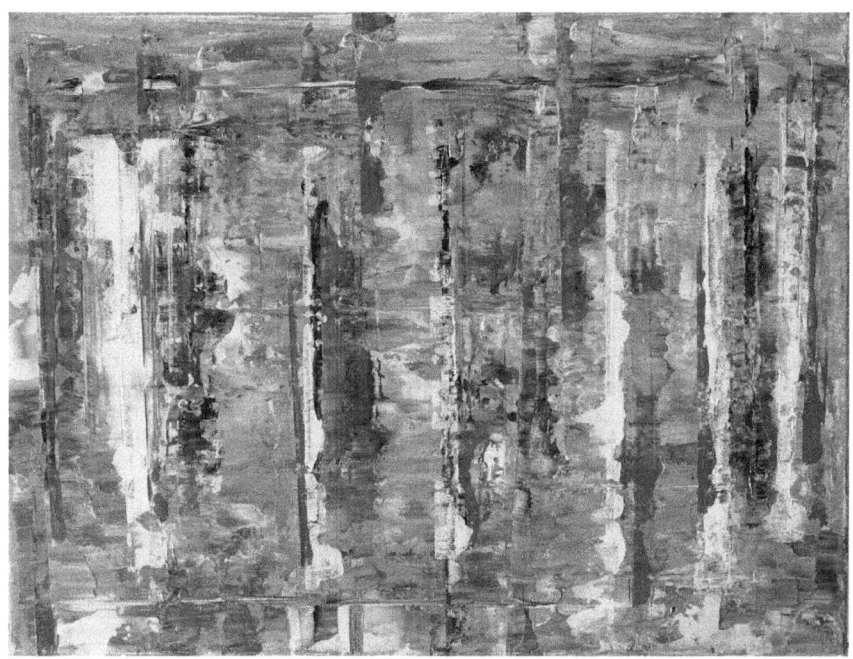

Norman Pirollo, "**Phantasm 1**", 2015. Abstract Expressionist, expressive action painting, layers, brushes, scraping, palette knife.

A later painting, "**Phantasm 1**", was as complex a painting that I had attempted to date. Multiple layers of both complementary and analogous colors were applied and then scraped away. The color palette included a mix of blue tints and shades, pure white, black and red. The blue shades were initially applied and slowly scraped away to create the unique composition. A layer of white paint was then applied and methodically scraped into the blue. Due to the heavy layering, I allowed a few minutes for the paint to skin over before continuing. The final layer of black and red were then applied in much smaller amounts, this served to add another dimension to the painting.

A new level of understanding of abstract expressionism was attained through this last series of paintings. No longer would I need to consciously think a painting through. Instead, a color palette was selected and prepared, my brushes and palette knives prepped, and subconscious thought transferred to the canvas. This was Abstract Expressionism!

THE ABSTRACT CONTINUUM

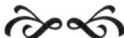

"I think we're much smarter than we were. Everybody knows that abstract art can be art, and most people know that they may not like it, even if they understand there's another purpose to it"

Roy Lichtenstein

THE PROGRESSION OF ART movements from the early to mid 20th century suggests abstract art is established and here to stay. The abstract art genre has been growing in appeal as the public embraces it as a unique and valid art form. The widely publicized debates of the Greenberg and Rosenberg era helped considerably in bringing abstract art to the forefront. These early debates involving opposing viewpoints were instrumental in creating a dialogue about the abstract art genre and the subgenre of Abstract Expressionism. The critical commentary fostered conversation about abstract art. Initial skepticism about this form of art slowly disappeared over the course of the mid-20th century.

Abstract art helped pave the way for successive Postmodern art movements such as Minimalism and Pop Art. As a reaction against the Minimalist art movement, a Neo-Expressionism movement was formed in the 1970s, influenced by the German Expressionism of the 1920s. In the later Postmodernist era of the 1980s and 1990s, earlier Postmodernist art movements such as Pop Art and Minimalism were similarly repudiated and replaced with new forms of representation.

Earlier research I had performed in the decorative arts refers to how throughout history, one movement often rejects or repudiates an earlier movement. Once an art movement has enjoyed widespread appeal and has become ubiquitous, it appears the public yearns for something different, a new art movement. The psychology behind the repudiation or rejection of a current visual or decorative art movement only to have it replaced with another often has merits. If this were not to occur, the gradual proliferation of a given art form would soon overwhelm society. Art has become commoditized through growth of the visual arts spectrum since the Renaissance era. When an art movement is superseded by another, this constitutes a cycle of change. A secondary effect of this phenomenon ensures that there will be a limited amount of art of the previous movement in circulation. Limiting the amount of art associated with an art movement is much like creating a limited series of prints. Once the world has experienced enough of an art movement, anticipation of the next movement develops and the cycle repeats.

With this in mind, repudiation does not necessarily infer that an art movement expired due to lack of appeal. It merely suggests that the movement has become omnipresent and the world is thirsty for change in the form of a new art movement. Typically, a new genre of art is developed with contrasting elements to the previous movement it supersedes. Occasionally, there is a resurgence of an earlier art movement where it is reintroduced, as in Neo-Expressionism. This phenomenon has occurred repeatedly throughout history.

Doubts about the Abstract Expressionist art movement began to emerge by the early 1960s. In the 1960s and 1970s, artists working in the new Postmodernist art movements of Minimalism and Pop Art, directly targeted Abstract Expressionism and vowed to replace it. Wild claims that AbEx art was somehow still associated with representational art were put forward. The basis for this argument was that many of the AbEx founding members had origins in representational art; therefore their abstract art was influenced or derivative of the former representational art genre.

In the mid to late 1960s, a completely new aesthetic in the contemporary art scene encompassing both Pop Art and Minimalism evolved, and began to supersede the Abstract Expressionist movement. While abstract expressionism was once considered an edgy form of art, had it lost its luster and appeal?

After all, by the early 1960s, it had become fairly mainstream. There is no doubt that artists working in competing, objective genres of art had a vested interest in the demise of Abstract Expressionism. Representational artists were striving for a resurgence of realism in art to replace the proliferation of Abstract Expressionist work over the twenty year period from 1942-62. As late as the early 1960s, two influential proponents of Abstract Expressionism, Clement Greenberg and Harold Greenberg, continued to advocate AbEx art as the definitive genre of art for the times. It was soon after; that the first Pop Art work of Andy Warhol appeared in 1962 and completely revolutionized the concept of modern, contemporary art. Even the stalwarts of Abstract Expressionism, Jasper Johns and Robert Rauschenberg capitulated and moved away from Abstract Expressionism to join the new, fledgling Pop Art movement.

In reaction to the subjectiveness of Abstract Expressionism, abstract art was steered to new directions in the late 1950s and early 1960s. Hard-edge painting and geometric abstraction began to appear in radical avant-garde art circles. New genres of contemporary art repudiated the emotion driven Abstract Expressionist art as well as rejecting the orthodox view of fine art viewed through modernism. Instead, new contemporary art drew its inspiration from "popular culture" icons and objects.

The cycle of a new art movement replacing a previous one was once again occurring. Abstract Expressionism began to fade away, replaced by modern movements that embraced illustration, advertising and objects as elements. Painting was no longer a primary art form in the Pop Art movement's new aesthetic. Minimalism, also a reaction against the expressive, emotional compositions of Abstract Expressionism, began to gain acceptance throughout the 1960s. The tenets of Minimalism included the removal of all visual references and were based on the complete work in itself.

Scaled down forms and structures along with repetition were elements of the Minimalist art movement. Although the Abstract Expressionism movement faded away by the mid 1960's, abstract art as a genre continued and grew over the next decades. Today, the abstract art genre is as large as the representational art genre. The public and society have come to accept this form of art. This acceptance can be attributed to the edgy, revolutionary abstract movements leading up to the complete abstraction of the AbEx movement. The trend towards separation of art from realism began with the Impressionism period of the late 1800s. The Impressionist era occurred approximately 300 years after the Renaissance period (1400-1600). In the intervening 300 years before Impressionism, it can be said that realism in both objective and figurative art had been perfected. The world's leading artists had over these years developed various new techniques to create photorealistic images on canvas. Developments such as perspective, improvements in oil-painting techniques, foreshortening, use of proportion, glazing techniques and chiaroscuro, all combined to provide a realistic representation of figures, objects and scenery.

In light of the exceptionally lengthy period of realistic art movements from the Renaissance period (1500s) into the late 1800s and beyond, succeeding Modernist periods were relatively short-lived in comparison. The abstract art genre has evolved to its present day state in a few short decades. If history is any indication, the abstract art genre will continue to grow and flourish for many decades and perhaps centuries. Unlike the pre-Impressionist era, there are vastly more choices of art in several genres available today. Objective, representational art is flourishing as much as abstract art is. The categories of modern art have also expanded to include mixed media and photographic art. The photographic art genre encompasses both realistic and abstract subgenres. Among artists, the abstract art genre has gained in popularity over the years. Arts communities as well as individual artists have embraced abstract art as a viable, mainstream art form. Large primary and secondary art markets have been created specifically for the exchange of abstract art. It is now common to find art galleries that cater specifically to the abstract art genre and its subgenre of Abstract Expressionism.

In contemporary art galleries, abstract art forms a large component of the available art. Today, many artists paint in both the abstract art and in the figurative or objective art genres. This flexibility provides them diversity, enjoyment, and access to a larger available art market for their work. Other artists have instead chosen abstract art as their sole genre and perhaps paint in a subgenre of this. It is reinforced in the art world for an artist to focus on a particular genre and style of art. This raises the profile of the artist to their followers and collectors. In the eyes of gallery owners or gallerists, an artist's appeal and validation are significantly raised if they paint in one genre and even more so in one style. Style in art is the arrangement of lines, forms and color in the composition. Style also includes technical execution in the creation of the art. By focusing on one genre and style, an artist has much more opportunity to develop the skills and techniques with which to master their chosen form of art.

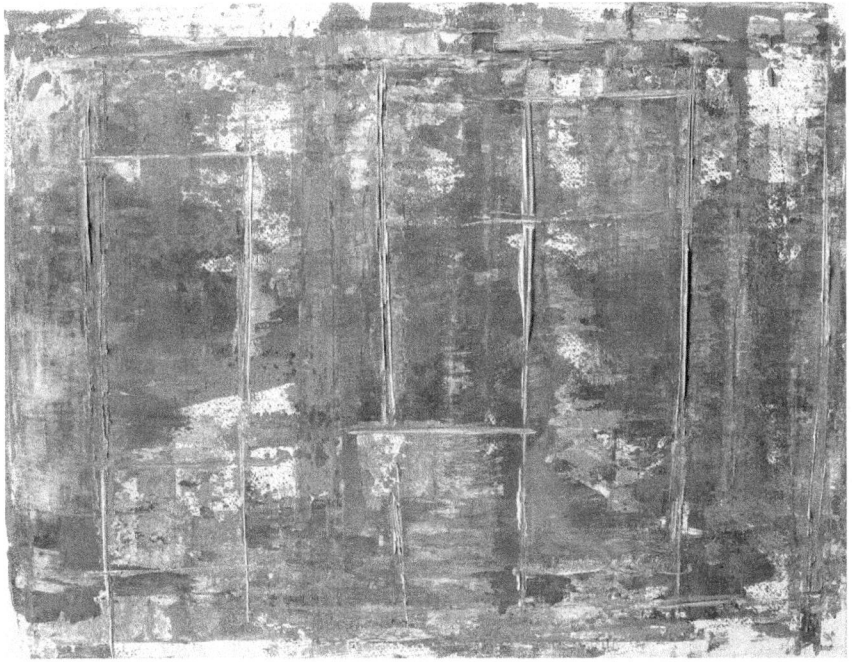

Norman Pirollo, "*Networking*", 2015. Abstract Expressionist, expressive action painting, layers, brushes, scraping, palette knife.

In the evolution of my art career, genres and styles have been in a transformative state. It was only within the year (2014-15) that my focus shifted to a single genre. Abstract art and the subgenre of Abstract Expressionism have become the focus of my recent art. Research into the work of AbEx artists and Gerhard Richter opened my eyes to the vast possibilities within the abstract art realm. Richter himself switched genres and styles multiple times over his career. The awareness of knowing that many, famous mid-20th century and contemporary artists had at some point in their careers moved from one genre of art to another was reassuring. In many cases, it is only in later life that an artist determines the style of art they are at peace with. When a paintbrush or palette knife becomes an extension of an artist's hand is when the artist can focus on their vision and not so much on the process of applying paint to a canvas.

In the early stages of an artist's exposure to a style of art, they sometimes imitate other artist's work in that genre and style. This can be viewed as part of the growth of an artist. Imitation allows the artist to gain confidence and move forward in establishing his or her own voice and style. The artist's own voice and style will eventually surface as their confidence and techniques improve. By following the progression in my work, it can be seen that in my later work, various elements and styles have coalesced into a defined style. Research into the Abstract Expressionist movement has informed the development of my own art style and voice within the realm of abstract expressionism. The exploratory process of developing a voice has helped me to grow as an artist. *"Networking"*, *"Wildwood"*, *"Phantasm 1"* and *"Phantasm 2"*, inspired by Gerhard Richter, were completed in the final months of the search for my own unique voice and style.

Since I did not carry the "baggage" of working in other genres of fine art, I felt liberated in my quest to seek my own voice and art style. At times, the sheer volume of research necessary to pursue this was overwhelming. It became critical to understand the origins and development of the Abstract Expressionist movement within the context of previous art movements to fully comprehend its impact on the art world.

My research timeline into art history was extended to previous periods of art to further understand the progression in the public's taste for art. It is obvious that the visual art field has significantly evolved only in the past century. Prior to the Impressionist period of art (1870-1890), change in the art world was gradual. Advances in painting techniques occurred primarily from the Renaissance period until the Impressionist period. Advances of realism in paintings were developed over this 300 year period. Impressionism was a game changer where realism was no longer the focal point of a painting. Although subject matter in the form of an image or figure was maintained, objectivity had slowly begun to be abstracted. A viewer of the art would need to make a conscious effort to visualize the image in the composition. Later art movements continued on the path to abstraction, culminating with Abstract Expressionism. The change in the public's perception of art over the recent ninety-year period (1870-1965) is what intrigued me.

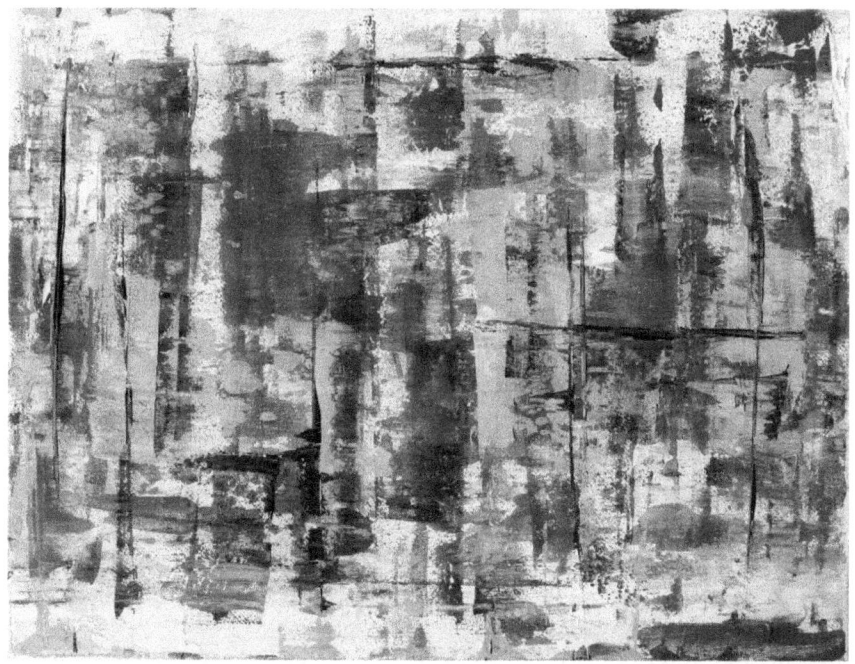

Norman Pirollo, "*Wildwood*", 2015. Abstract Expressionist, expressive action painting, layers, brushes, scraping, palette knife.

It is my opinion that one of the driving forces away from realism in art was that by 1870, realism had plateaued and that its enthusiasm and appeal were beginning to wane. I also believe the other driving force away from realism in painting has been the advent of photography. The concurrence of photography and abstraction in the late 19th century (1870-1890) cannot be dismissed. No longer was there a requirement and desire for realism in a painting. To understand the unequivocal desire for realistic paintings prior to the late 1800's, it becomes critical to place oneself in a world without photography. Since this time, the quality of photography has vastly improved and has supplanted realism in art. Today, the complementary genres of objective and non-objective art remain popular, as well as photography-based art and photorealism. The visual art world today has diversified with multiple genres of art available to the public.

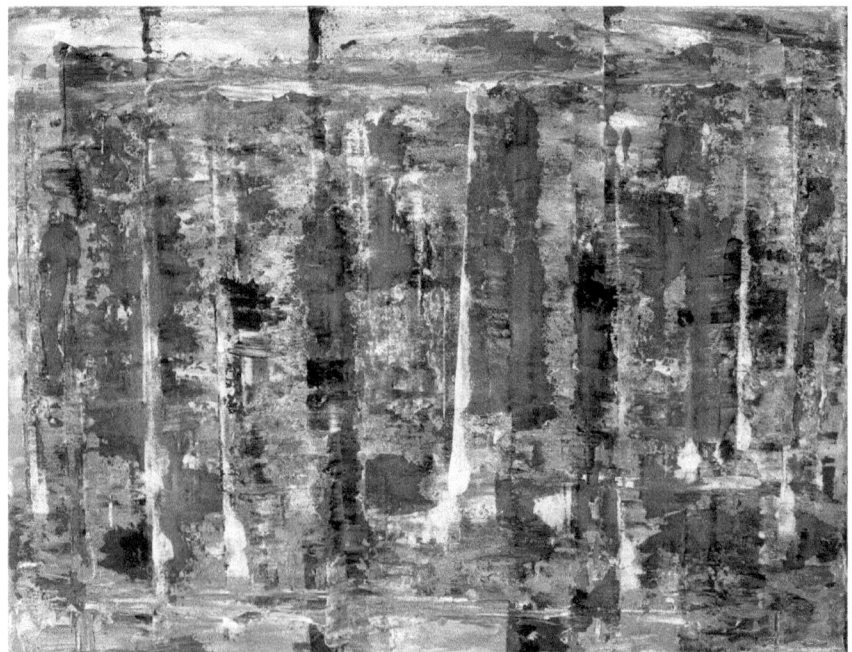

Norman Pirollo, "*Phantasm 2*", 2015. Abstract Expressionist, expressive action painting, layers, brushes, scraping, palette knife.

An understanding of abstract art involves both the imagination and an open mind. When a person first views abstract art, they ask "what is it about" or "what am I supposed to see" and these are fairly normal reactions. Aside from the formal elements of the artwork such as composition, colors, pattern and process; interpretation of the art is fundamental to understanding it. Several people can view an abstract art piece and arrive at different conclusions to what they see in the art.

There are typically no recognizable objects in abstract art, except for perhaps lines, forms or blocks of color. Interpreting the combination of visual elements in the art then becomes an exercise in subjectiveness. Emotion is also a component in understanding abstract art. The interaction of elements in an abstract painting can evoke certain emotions in a person. A narrative can also be articulated through a series of abstract paintings.

Through the development of abstract art over a period of decades in the 20th century (1920-1960), the public has finally come to embrace non-objective or abstract art as a viable and appealing art form. It is difficult to determine how much further abstract art can evolve. Every artist within the abstract art genre brings his or her own, unique style. The current, large availability of styles and the possibility of more styles in the future ensure that abstract art will continue to be an exciting and thriving genre of art.

Mediums used in the creation of abstract art are also evolving and growing. Advancements in paints have occurred over the past few years. Fluid paints are now available which can be poured onto a canvas to create random, flowing colors that combine to form fascinating organic compositions.

The art world is also moving away from paint as the sole medium in the creation of fine art. Mixed media forms of art have been developed where painting is combined with appliqués of common textiles or objects onto a canvas. In this form of art, it is common to see newspaper or magazine cutouts applied to a canvas as part of the composition. Mixed media lends itself well to the abstract art genre by increasing its appeal and demonstrating that abstract art embraces change and adapts itself to the contemporary art world.

Digital art is another growing medium in the abstract art world. Sophisticated computer software allows the artist to create unique and compelling abstract artwork without the use of conventional paints and brushes. Digital art or digital painting is slowly gaining acceptance as a valid art form. In digital painting, the compositions are created and rendered on a computer using digital paintbrushes. Digital painting programs emulate actual paint and paint brushes through electronic means. The brushes are digitally styled to represent traditional media such as oils, acrylics, pastels, charcoal and pen. Digital effects are also available to create realistic effects.

Technology today allows the final result to be printed on a canvas. The component that is lacking is the textural element of the print, although complex and stunning compositions easily make up for this. While there was an initial reluctance to accept digital art and digital painting as a form of art since conventional processes were not used in its creation; the trend is on the side of digital art.

Follow-on movements to abstract art were developed during the 1960s and 1970s. Through the natural evolution of art movements, Abstract Expressionism was beginning to be repudiated or rejected during this period (1962-1980). As referred to in earlier chapters, it is human nature to embrace change and this firmly applies to art.

With success in the art world comes monotony. The public seeks a new form of art typically after an art movement has peaked. Each successive art movement in modern art can be considered to be avant-garde. Modern art is considered to be the period from the 1940s onward. Postmodernism occurred in the 1960s. The Postmodern avant-garde movements of Minimalism and Pop Art succeeded Abstract Expressionism. Each of the new movements put forward a new philosophy and vision of what art should be. Novel ideas about art are included as elements of a new movement. The **Pop Art** movement of the early to late 1960s included illustrations, advertising posters and common household items as elements. The artists participating in each of the art movements closely followed each other and developed similar styles, therefore reinforcing the art movement. Often, there was an **art manifesto** associated with an art movement.

As an example, the Automatiste movement published an "art manifesto" to explain the meaning and understanding of the new form of art they were putting forward.

Art movement labels can themselves be interesting since they are not typically defined and labeled until the late stages of a movement. When a genre of art plateaus and the art form become ubiquitous, it is only then that art critics attach a label to the movement. This was the case with Abstract Expressionism, the label was only agreed upon in later years, when the art movement had become entrenched with the viewing public, gallerists and critics. Reasons for this are many, but a prominent one is to discern an art movement from a passing fad.

Another art movement **Minimalism** was formed in the latter years of the 1960s. Minimalism was formed in reaction to the flourishing Abstract Expressionism movement and its emotional expressiveness. Minimalism embraced the lack of reference; disassociating itself from any representation or objectivity. The elements of this form of art were sparse and typically consisted of simple geometric forms such as squares, rectangles, lines and triangles. Repetition was also part of this genre of art. The origins of "Minimalism" can be traced back to "The Bauhaus School" and the prominent painters associated with this school. Kazimir Malevich and Piet Mondrian of the **Die Stijl** movement, a forerunner to "Minimalism", are probably the most well-known artists to influence "Minimalism".

Minimalism was also directly influenced by the "color field" work of Abstract Expressionist artists Barnett Newman and Marc Rothko. A tenet of Minimalism was that the art was not based on self-expression as it was in AbEx work. Minimalism was not influenced by personal feelings; it was "objective" rather than "subjective". Minimalist art was characterized by the lack of expression and emotion. Another tenet of Minimalism was the complete disassociation from an artist's expression, where the materials and medium are prominent elements in the work.

Pop Art, another of the art movements to succeed Abstract Expressionism, had roots in illustration. Rather than expressing an artist's emotion and vision through painting, Pop Art instead created a new narrative utilizing elements of everyday living. Elements such as advertising, household items and mass culture were featured in its message. Andy Warhol is widely considered the founder of the "Pop Art" revolution. With a background in illustration, Warhol had a keen sense of what the public sought in art. Pop Art was also formed as a reaction to the then powerful and ubiquitous Abstract Expressionist art movement. The AbEx movement began its descent in the early 1960s and Pop Art along with Minimalism supplanted it. Pop Art was a return to a form of representational art where pop artists utilized found objects and household objects in creating their compositions. Advertising illustrations were also a component of the art. Use of these elements helped to make the art recognizable where the public could relate to what they saw.

With the advent of the "Pop Art" movement, art was no longer elitist. Pop Art had roots in the early 20th century Dada movement. The **Dada** movement and Pop Art both shared a similar philosophy although the Dada movement emphasized destruction and satire in it message. Pop Art instead presented more of a mass culture message. In the early 1960s, American advertising had begun to encroach on art by adopting elements of modern art. Artists of this period were challenged in developing a new art form that disassociated itself from pure advertising and illustration. Bold, aggressive work was created utilizing elements of the advertising world combined with illustration and vernacular subject matter people could relate to. Jasper Johns and Robert Rauschenberg pioneered the Pop Art movement where Andy Warhol embraced it. The Pop Art movement has often been characterized through Andy Warhol. Both the "Pop Art" and "Minimalism" art movements are an excellent testimonial to the evolution of art. Abstract Expressionism was tossed aside through the advent of these new art movements. Only in later years of the 20th century did Abstract Expressionism experience a renaissance and it is today firmly entrenched as a viable, successful genre of art!

CONCLUSION

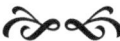

"To succeed, you need to find something to hold on to,
something to motivate you, something to inspire you"

Tony Dorsett

I HOPE YOU HAVE enjoyed this book and it has motivated and inspired you to move forward with your own journey. The best years of my life have been while self-employed in a creative environment and most recently as an abstract artist. Research into previous art periods and earlier artists has significantly informed my current work as well as motivating me to move forward with my art. Reading about the struggles and rewards these former artists experienced has provided me with an understanding of the challenges many artists experience during their art careers. The explorative phase into Abstract Expressionism provided me with a clearer and deeper understanding of both art and the art world. I was enlightened to how the former AbEx artists weaved their character traits and individuality into their personal lives. This understanding would push me through my own struggles in leading a career in the visual arts.

The author maintains a web site of his abstract art as well as chronicling news and updates from his art studio at:

http://www.normanpirollo.com

RESOURCES

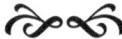

"Interpretation is the revenge of the intellectual upon art"

Susan Sontag

Pg. 84 Photos: © 2015 Marc Lavoie – Courtesy Marc Lavoie Photography

Pg. 113 Claude Monet, *"Régate à Argenteuil"*, 1872.
{{PD-1923}} The Yorck Project: *10.000 Meisterwerke der Malerei.*

Pg. 114 Paul Cézanne, *"Mont Sainte-Victoire"*, 1887. {{PD-1923}}
Wikimedia Commons File:Cezanne - Mont Sainte-Victoire, Courtauld.jpg

Pg. 115 Vincent Van Gogh, *"Starry Night"*, 1887. {{PD-1923}}
Wikimedia Commons File:Vincent van Gogh Starry Night.jpg

Pg. 117 Henri Matisse, *"La Coiffure"*, 1901. {{PD-1923}}
WikiPedia File:Henri Matisse, 1907, La coiffure.JPG

Pg. 118 Franz Marc, "Landschaft mit Haus, Hund und Rind", 1914.
Wikimedia Commons File: Marc - Landschaft mit Haus, Hund und Rind.jpeg
{{PD-1923}}

Pg. 119 Juan Gris, "Portrait of Pablo Picasso", 1912. {{PD-1923}}
Wikimedia Commons   File:Juan Gris - Portrait of Pablo Picasso - Google Art
Project.jpg

Pg. 120 Giacomo Balla, *"Landscape"*, 1913, © ESTATE OF GIACOMO BALLA /
SODRAC (2015) WikiArt - Giacomo Balla - Landscape

Pg. 121 Piet Mondrian, *"Tableau I"*, 1921 {{PD-1923}}
Wikimedia Commons   File:Tableau I, by Piet Mondrian.jpg

ABOUT THE AUTHOR

AS ABSTRACT ARTIST, Norman Pirollo discovered a passion for the arts at an early age. Following a career in the IT industry, he has since embraced his creative side and returned to his passion of creating unique contemporary abstract art.

Norman is self-taught in both the fine arts and decorative arts. He currently creates abstract art in the abstract expressionist genre. The compositions are painted to depict an abstract scene and include important elements such as form, analogous and complementary colors, light, lines and curves. Techniques used to create his art include brushing and scraping the acrylic medium onto canvasses to create a textured, organic experience to draw the viewer in. Rich vivid colors, curves and intriguing compositions are featured in his abstract work. Norman also enjoys working with microphotography techniques he developed to create new media art in unique, organic compositions.

"I am intrigued by the beauty of abstract expressionist art forms. My work is informed through that of the New York School of Abstract Expressionists (AbEx) as well as the Canadian artists of the Automatiste movement. This opens up a new genre of art to me. I seek out captivating and intriguing compositions to create. The abstract composition, vivid colors, tones and forms combine to create the final artwork." -- **Norman Pirollo,** professional artist. Ottawa, Ontario, Canada.

Norman's work has been featured in books such as "Studio Furniture: Today's Leading Woodworkers", "Wood Art Today 2", "500 Cabinets" "Rooted", "Ottawa Life", "Panoram Italia", as well as various international magazines. He is the recipient of numerous art awards. Norman has recently been selected as a finalist for the prestigious NICHE Awards as well as a finalist for the Art Trends Artist of the Year Award. He has recently authored and published two of his own books. As an award-winning artist, his abstract art can be viewed at **www.normanpirollo.com.** Norman currently resides and operates his art studio in Ottawa, Ontario, Canada.

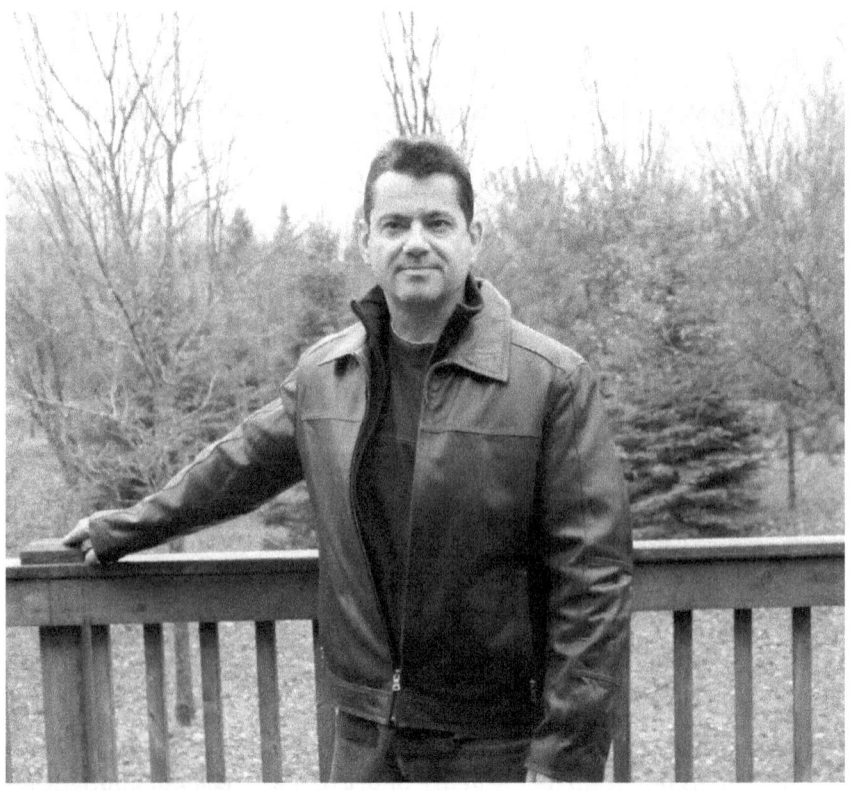

The artist and author, Norman Pirollo, outside his studio in Ottawa, Ontario, Canada

www.ingramcontent.com/pod-product-compliance
Lightning Source LLC
Chambersburg PA
CBHW060840170526
45158CB00001B/195